All In The Game

Martin Breheny

BLACKWATER PRESS

Editor
Susannah Gee

Design & Layout
Paula Byrne

Cover Design
Liz Murphy

Photos
Courtesy of Sportsfile

ISBN
0 86121 796 9

© 1996 Martin Breheny

Produced in Ireland by Blackwater Press
c/o Folens Publishers, 8 Broomhill Business Park
Tallaght, Dublin 24
British Library Cataloguing-in-Publication Data.
A catalogue record for this book is available from The British Library.
Breheny, Martin All In The Game

Contents

Acknowledgements

It's only when you start researching a book on the GAA that you come to realise and truly appreciate the deep and meaningful way in which hurling and football touch the lives of so many people. In most cases, it does more than that. It is a way of life for a sizeable cross-section of the community right across the country.

To those who feature in this book, I thank them for their contribution to enriching the lives of so many people. To those who don't figure, believe me, it's purely because space didn't allow. Another time, perhaps.

On a practical level, thanks to John O'Connor and his Blackwater Press team, particularly Susannah Gee, whose editing hand pulled all the strands together. Thanks too to Ray McManus and his Sportsfile team for providing the photographs.

Most especially, thanks to all my family, Rosemary, Alan and Linda for their patience and support at a time when the project took up more of my time than it should have.

Martin Breheny
November 1996

Chapter 1

❖ ❖ ❖

Great Breakthroughs

Without question, the most significant development in the GAA over the last twenty-five years has been the emergence, or in some cases the re-emergence, of so many counties to take their places at the top table in both hurling and football.

Up to then, there was an apparent inevitability about the senior championships. In hurling, the McCarthy Cup was being shared on an annual basis by the likes of Limerick and Wexford. In football, Kerry, Dublin and Galway were always likely All-Ireland winners, although Down broke the stranglehold with three wins in the 1960s.

Offaly footballers replaced them as the breakthrough kings of the 1970s, winning two-in-a-row. However, it was not until the 1980s that the order took a really dramatic turn.

In hurling, Galway's years of subservience out west gave way to a super-confident force which won their first All-Ireland final in 1980 after a fifty-seven year gap. Galway went on to be the dominant force in the 1980s, winning three titles. Offaly were only one behind, after making their dramatic breakthrough in 1981.

If the breakthrough pace quickened in the 1980s, it gathered speed in the 1990s when Donegal and Derry won all-Ireland football titles for the firt time while Clare hurlers bridged an eighty-one-year gap to take the McCarthy Cup in 1995. It was as if all the fresh growth in Gaelic games encouraged more. Clare footballers made the breakthrough in Munster in 1992, followed two years later by Leitrim in Connaght. In 1996 Wexford hurlers banished twenty-eight years of misery with a great All-Ireland campaign which ended with the McCarthy Cup heading to the south-east for the first time since 1968.

When Wexford won the All-Ireland final in 1968, the GAA's Central Council income was a little over one hundred thousand pounds. By 1996, it had soared to around seven million pounds. Despite the many pressures from other sports which are backed by the multi-million pound international television media, the GAA continues to gather momentum and increse its influence at many levels.

This book dips in and out of modern GAA life, chronicling the many facets which make hurling and football such great games. While there have been many exciting times in Gaelic Games over the past twenty years, not least the magnificent reign of Kerry footballers for much of the 1970s, nothing can stir emotions like the memory of the dramatic breakthroughs by the footballers of Donegal and Derry, and the hurlers of Galway, Offaly, Clare and Wexford.

Wexford 1996

('This is for the people of Wexford')

George O'Connor could feel the first swell of emotion. For the previous ten minutes he had been too busy to think of the finishing line. He could see it in the distance, a purple and gold oasis beckoning him on. He dared not think of reaching it, lest it turned out to be no more than a mirage. But now, as the Wexford fans whistled impatiently, willing the end of the game, O'Connor's heartbeat began to quicken. Could this be it?

He looked at the scoreboard as Limerick midfielder, Mike Houlihan prepared to take a free. The 1996 All-Ireland hurling final was into the third minute of injury time. Wexford 1–13 Limerick 0–14. It would take a Limerick goal to stop Wexford. Houlihan attempted to hoist the ball high into the Wexford goal in the hope that a Limerick hurley might make vital contact amid the thicket of swirling ash. However, in his anxiety to lob the ball as accurately as possible, he failed to get the right trajectory and, to the great delight of the Wexford fans, their man Larry O'Gorman was able to gather and prepare to clear.

George O'Connor looked towards the referee. Pat Horan was putting the whistle to his lips. Is this really it? The end of the misery? No more lonely walks down the Croke Park tunnel with nothing to break the awful silence but the mocking clank of studs on concrete. The final whistle sounded. O'Connor dropped to his knees, arms raised. For about three seconds, he was alone with his thoughts. Then the purple and gold stampede began as the Wexford fans galloped across Croke Park in a swaying mass of elation.

> This guy nearly broke my neck as he grabbed me. Then they were coming from all sides. It was an incredible feeling. We had done it. We were All-Ireland champions. Wexford, All-Ireland champions, the day I'd always waited for since I first hurled with the county. Now it was here and nobody could take it away from us.

The next thirty minutes saw some of the most incredible scenes ever witnessed in Croke Park as the Wexford supporters uncorked a generation's worth of delight. It was as if a giant fountain had opened in front of the Hogan Stand and every Wexford person was being hoisted higher and higher by its emotional charge.

Team captain, Martin Storey, who like George O'Connor had known misery and heartbreak for much of his career, encapsulated the moment in one line of his memorable victory speech: 'This is for the people of Wexford. We have been bridesmaids in the past but today we got married.' Life would never again be the same for the Wexford players or their manager, Liam Griffin.

It was all so very different to the Sunday evening just eighteen weeks earlier when the Wexford squad had trooped sadly out of the Limerick Gaelic Grounds after losing the National League semi-final to Galway by eight points. It wasn't so much losing a League semi-final that upset the Wexford fans. It was the nature of the defeat. Frankly, they had been taken apart and Liam Griffin was blamed.

By early September however, nobody in Wexford would admit to having abused Griffin after the League semi-final defeat. In September, Griffin was a hero. Just four months earlier he was depicted as being a failure, a manager without direction or plan.

The criticism hurt Griffin, not on a personal level but because he hated to see his players being portrayed as losers. The Wexford hurling public had another view. Those who weren't close to the scene thought that Griffin and his co-selectors, Rory Kinsella and Seamus Barron had contributed to Wexford's difficulties with their team selection. Ger Cush had lined out at centre-back in the League semi-final with Damien Fitzhenry on his left and Larry O'Gorman at left full-back. All three were uncomfortable in those positions, particularly Fitzhenry, who was wiped out by Galway's Joe Rabbitte, a giant of a man who preyed on his opponent's lack of height.

Liam Griffin never intended to leave Fitzhenry at wing-back. Fitzhenry would be best as goalkeeper but had outfield talents too and up until the joust with Rabbitte, he had coped well as a wing-back. Griffin's explanation for playing Fitzhenry at left half-back and Cush at centre-back during the League was quite simple, even if it didn't appease disgruntled Wexford fans, who thought they were heading into another summer of discontent. Griffin explained his decision:

> Damien got a whole new appreciation of how backs and forwards think by playing outfield. It was big help to him later on in the year. Ger Cush's positioning and mobility were improved by his stint at centre-back. Maybe people didn't believe us but we were working to a plan during the League. The Championship was everything as far as we were concerned and while we took some abuse after being beaten by Galway in the League semi-final, we knew deep down that we were a lot closer to the finished product than many people thought.

The weeks between the League semi-final and the first round of the championship against Kilkenny were significant. Wexford won a few tournament games and while it didn't make national headlines, the team felt good about itself as they headed for Croke Park to play Kilkenny on 2 June, even if they hadn't beaten their great rivals in the championship since 1988. They were certainly a lot more confident than twelve months earlier when they offered little more than token opposition to Kilkenny in the Leinster semi-final. There had been a controversy over the captaincy in the run-up to the game, with Liam Griffin taking a stand and removing the honour from Liam Dunne in a row over club v county loyalties. It didn't cost Wexford the game but it wasn't exactly the ideal way to go into battle against the All-Ireland champions.

While Griffin lost a match he had won a point. He was boss and would do things his way. If he was carrying the can he felt he was the only one entitled to put holes in it. By the start of the 1996 championship, Griffin's grip on the minds and spirits of the squad was much stronger than a year earlier.

Over the previous ten years, luck had never been much of a friend to Wexford. It was as if the fates took a delight in teasing Wexford into believing things were about to change, only to eventually come down on the side of the status quo. That was very much the case where Kilkenny were concerned. Kilkenny always seemed to reserve their most punishing routine for Wexford, quite often waiting until the closing minutes to snatch the victory. For whatever reason, luck nearly always sided with Kilkenny.

Not in 1996. Kilkenny had all sorts of problems going into the match with Wexford. D.J. Carey was injured; so too was Adrian Ronan while John Power had a bad dose of 'flu. Carey did line out but was way below his best and while Power came on as a sub, he was not at full throttle either. Wexford exploited the situation magnificently. They hurled with fire and passion to build up a five-point lead by half-time.

Liam Griffin warned his team to expect the typical Kilkenny revival. Despite his warnings, Wexford were unable to prevent the Kilkenny assault after half-time and when they cut the lead to a single point, 0–9 to 0–8, after 47 minutes, it looked liked the classic Kilkenny–Wexford scenario, with Kilkenny eventually coming out as the winner.

This time it was different. Wexford dug deep into their resources and were four points ahead by the time Billy Byrne, who had come on as sub, scored a goal in the 59th minute. The minutes prior to the goal were to become one of the defining periods in Wexford's whole season.

After the Kilkenny game I had a good feeling about things, not just because we had won but because we had shown such passion and character when they came back at us after half-time. I felt that if we could do that against Kilkenny, we would do it against anybody,' said Liam Griffin. While Wexford celebrated a 1–14 to 0–14 win, Offaly remained firm favourites to retain the Leinster title.

Nonetheless, the season was opening out in front of Wexford. The draw had lined them up against Dublin in the Leinster semi-final, while Offaly played Laois in the other semi-final. It suited Wexford perfectly. They knew that they were better than Dublin but they now had to prove that they could handle a situation where they went into a game as favourites.

They managed it but with no great conviction. Early on they looked likely to demolish Dublin. They led by 2–8 to 1–3 at half-time but lost their way in the third quarter and led by just four points with eleven minutes remaining. They then to win by 2–12 to 1–9. Liam Griffin recalls:

> I wouldn't say I was completely happy with the Dublin game but it did send out the right signals as far as we were concerned. Deep down, we knew we were a lot better than we looked but we also knew that everybody in hurling would fancy Offaly in the final. It wasn't a bad position to be in.

In the week before the Leinster final, Griffin described hurling as the 'Riverdance of Sport'. He gave interviews to everybody who asked for them. He talked of pride and passion and of how his Wexford team would die rather than lose to Offaly. It made impressive listening. Although nobody could have known it at the time, Griffin was speaking from a feeling of destiny. It was as if he had been told by some supernatural power that nothing could possibly go wrong. There was an almost eerie confidence about everything he said. Not brash or arrogant, just the honest assessment of a man who believed passionately that Wexford's nineteen-year wait for a Leinster title was about to end.

It did. Sunday, 15 July 1996 has gone down in history as one of the most historic days in Wexford hurling, the day when they beat Offaly by 2–23 to 2–15 to win the Leinster title for the first time since 1977. It was a truly magnificent game laced with quality and endeavour which made Griffin's glowing description of hurling look extremely apt.

Griffin's belief that the steely resistance in the face of a spirited Kilkenny revival in the first round had made the Wexford team, was again underlined. This time Wexford had to come from behind, after falling four points behind in the opening eighteen minutes. In previous seasons that might have been the signal for a Wexford collapse. Not this time. Their sense of unity was far more finely tuned. They were no longer a collection of good individuals, all working hard but not in unison. Now they were playing as a team which would refuse to take no for an answer.

By half-time Wexford had taken a narrow lead, 1–10 to 1–9. They had pulled three points clear with fifteen minutes remaining. A Tom Dempsey goal was cancelled out within a minute by a Michael Duignan goal for Offaly and when Offaly cut the lead to two points with thirteen minutes left, the odds seem to favour the defending champions, who hadn't lost to Wexford in the championship since 1979. Not for the first time though in a remarkable season, Wexford refused to read the script.

Quite the opposite, in fact. Over the final twelve minutes, they out-scored Offaly by 0–7 to 0–1. It was a truly memorable scoring burst, one which left Offaly demoralised and beaten while Wexford spun into celebrational orbit.

Griffin identified three key elements in Wexford's win: passion, desire and resilience. Offaly captain, Shane McGuckin concurred and also talked of Wexford's refined style. 'In other years the man with the ball would go for a score. Now they'll give it off. They certainly do seem to have a new style of play and they also seem to have full trust and respect for their manager,' he said.

That was an understatement. Liam Griffin was the new hero, the Wexford Messiah. Wexford had put in 152 training sessions right through the season and at long last they had been rewarded. There was more to follow. Three nights after the Leinster final win, Liam Griffin had his squad back in training. By now, the county was involved in an orgy of celebration. Sports shops were sold out of Wexford jerseys within days as Storey, Dempsey, O'Gorman, McCarthy and Co. replaced international soccer stars as the youngsters' idols.

It would have been easy for the Wexford squad to turn off the ambition switch after the Leinster final win and join in the fun. Irrespective of what happened in the All-Ireland semi-final, the season would have been a success. Liam Griffin put them to the test on their first night back in training.

> It's been some few days hasn't it. I hope everybody is enjoying it.
> That's what it's there for. But have we enough? Do we want more?
> Do we want to really crown the season by winning the All-Ireland.
> It's there, lads, if you want it. Are we on for it?

He was delighted by the response. Naturally, all the players said they wanted to press on but he knew that it was more than mere words. 'I could sense it in them. I was a happy man going home from training that night. I knew that their appetites still hadn't been satisfied. It was a lovely feeling.'

Most Wexford people regretted the fact that the All-Ireland semi-final draw pitted their side against Galway. The general view was that Wexford needed an easier semi-final after all the Leinster final euphoria and that a clash with Antrim would have been much more appropriate. Griffin viewed it differently. If Wexford were to win the All-Ireland final, then he wanted to beat all the major powers. They had already beaten Offaly and Kilkenny in Leinster. Next, he wanted Galway, followed by the Munster champions.

Wexford were very relaxed going into the game with Galway. The season had already been crowned a success, now it was a question of building on that. They did it most efficiently. Galway contributed greatly to their own demise, notably through missed frees, but once again Wexford's doggedness under pressure was crucial.

They led by a point at half-time but really dug in as Galway came at them in the third quarter. It was by means a classic encounter but Wexford proved that they could cope with a dour, tense struggle as effectively as a high-speed, flowing game like the Leinster final. The maturing process was going well. They eventually won by 2–13 to 3–7 to qualify for their first All-Ireland final since 1977.

The hype in Wexford prior to the All-Ireland final was unbelievable. It lived up to its reputation as a hurling county waiting to explode. The scenes on the night the players met the press in Wexford Park were remarkable. A huge crowd turned out, pressing their faces against the wire fence, begging their heroes to come over and sign autographs.

Liam Griffin stood in the middle of it all, grinning. 'Whatever happens against Limerick, Wexford hurling is back. We'll have to work on it, of course, but look around you. Look at the enthusiasm. This is a great county.'

The All-Ireland final was always going to be a wide open affair. Limerick had come though a tough Munster campaign but had wobbled ominously against Antrim in the All-Ireland semi-final. They still went into the final as favourites, mainly on the basis that they had been there before in 1994 and the experience would stand to them. It was a pretty spurious theory, one which Wexford never took to heart, even when they fell 0–5 to 0–1 behind after fourteen minutes.

Their revival qualities were well documented by now and it really was no surprise that they made a complete recovery. Tom Dempsey's goal was the defining moment in that fight back. Eamonn Scallan's dismissal for a wild pull on Stephen McDonagh a minute before half-time steeled Wexford even further and they coped superbly in the second half. With Dempsey and Gary Laffan playing brilliantly in a two-man full-forward line, Wexford prospered and were four points clear with ten minutes remaining. Limerick's desperate finale produced two points but they could never break through for the vital goal. Wexford eventually won by 1–13 to 0–14 to take the McCarthy Cup for the first time since 1968.

The story of Wexford's amazing season was perfectly illustrated by George O'Connor and Billy Byrne, two veterans with a vision of success, even when it seemed as if time had run out and left them. Every spring for the previous seventeen years, O'Connor had set out on a voyage which never got past July. More often than not it ended with defeat by Kilkenny or Offaly. Yet, he kept coming back, year after year. Hurling was his drug and he needed the annual fix. It was the same for Billy Byrne. By the start of the 1996 campaign, he knew that his role would be as a sub but even then he was happy just to be there. He ended the season with an All-Ireland medal, having scored vital goals against both Kilkenny and Galway. His contribution was as great as many of those who played all through.

O'Connor would have retired two years earlier, were it not for Liam Griffin's persuasive powers. Griffin convinced him that he would change the team's style so that combination play would replace individualism, the curse of many previous Wexford teams. Griffin was as good as his word and there really was little comparison in terms of style between Wexford 1996 and the Wexford teams of previous years.

When George sustained a hand injury right in the middle of the championship it seemed as if his role would be purely as a motivator. But having had every finger broken in a long career, he was determined not to be forced off the most exciting train he had ever boarded.

By an amazing irony, it was injuries to others which allowed him back into the first class department. He came on as a sub for his brother, John, in the All-Ireland semi-final against Galway, and was first choice to step into a re-shuffled side when Seanie Flood was forced to miss the All-Ireland final through injury.

Dubbed 'the uncrowned king of Wexford hurling' by Liam Griffin, O'Connor's presence on All-Ireland day epitomised the spirit of Wexford through bad times and good, a spirit which was never more obvious than in the amazing summer of 1996.

WEXFORD: (All-Ireland final 1996): Damien Fitzhenry; Colm Kehoe, Ger Cush, John O'Connor; Rod Guiney, Liam Dunne, Larry O'Gorman; Adrian Fenlon, George O'Connor; Rory McCarthy, Martin Storey (captain), Larry Murphy; Tom Dempsey, Gary Laffan, Eamonn Scallan.

Subs: Billy Byrne for Murphy, Paul Finn for Guiney, Paul Codd for Laffan.

(Note: Seanie Flood played against Kilkenny, Dublin, Offaly and Galway. Dave Guiney came on as a sub against Dublin).

Clare 1995

(*'We're in the promised land at last.'*)

The dimly-lit tunnel which leads to the dressing-rooms in Semple Stadium, Thurles seemed the perfect setting for a litany of well-worn excuses. It was the evening of 7 May 1995 and Clare hurlers were once again assessing the damage after another horrific crash with reality. Heads bowed, hurleys held limply by their sides, they trooped by, lost in the lonely world occupied by beaten teams.

Down the corridor, Kilkenny players were in an indulgent mood. Team captain Bill Hennessy strolled in, clutching the National League trophy. His colleagues showed no great urgency to get their hands on it. Full-back, Pat Dwyer explained to journalists how he wasn't at all happy with his own performance. This, despite the fact that his direct opponent, Eamonn Taaffe had scored just one point. D.J. Carey, always the master of diplomacy, remarked that Clare were a lot better than they had looked.

They needed to be. They had lost the League final by 2–12 to 0–9 after leading by four points early on. It was the classic Clare flop. A good start was seen as no more than a baiting exercise for Kilkenny who quickly gathered momentum before chewing up Clare's weakening challenge. It was all so typical of Kilkenny. Sadly, it was also typical of Clare, who had gone into that final with a dreadful big day record, having lost twelve, drawn one and won two of their fifteen previous finals.

Team manager, Ger Loughnane had been personally involved in many of those heart-breaking days both as a player and, in latter times, as a selector, under coach, Len Gaynor. Now the full managerial responsibility rested on his shoulders and a sympathetic media awaited his explanation of Clare's latest flop.

Loughnane's opening remarks were predictable. He conceded that it wasn't just the two goals which beat Clare. Kilkenny had more craft, he said. Besides, Clare's hurling wasn't fast enough. Journalists had heard it all before and were about to move off when Loughnane delivered a defiant finale: 'Still, we'll win the Munster championship. There's no team in Munster as good as Clare'. At the time, Loughnane's comments seemed like an exercise in self-delusion. Convince yourself that the rest are no better and guess what — it might turn out that way.

Loughnane had more immediate concerns. The Munster semi-final against Cork or Kerry was only four weeks away, instead of five, as the GAA fixtures list stated. It had been brought forward at Cork's request and the prospect did not please Loughnane as some of his players had exam commitments in early June. Suddenly, all the hard work of the previous eight months appeared to be yielding nothing. On the evening of the League final, Loughnane met former Galway manager, Cyril Farrell in Hayes' Hotel. More than anybody, Farrell understood how Loughnane and his players felt. Galway hadn't just been down this road before; they knew every turn. But, through sheer perseverance, they had gradually widened it before eventually creating a super highway, which enabled them to return home in triumph. Farrell confirmed Loughnane's initial impressions. Yes, Clare had been well beaten but Kilkenny looked to be a long way ahead of anything Clare would encounter down south. And, since it was sixty-three years since Clare had won a Munster title, it represented a sufficiently lofty goal to keep Clare's ambitions alive.

The Clare squad were anxious to take a short break following the League final. They felt that after working incredibly hard since the previous September, they needed a rest to re-charge their batteries for the championship. Loughnane and his co-selectors, Michael McNamara and Tony Considine disagreed. For better or worse, training would continue.

A fiercely rigorous training regime had been at the heart of Clare's campaign. Ollie Baker, who wasn't on the League final team, talked later in the season of his first night training with the senior squad in the previous October. As Michael McNamara drove the players up to, and through, the pain barrier, he kept telling them that they were training for next September. Baker wasn't the only player who thought McNamara was, to put it mildly, viewing affairs from an optimistic viewpoint.

Clare's concentration on the 1994/95 League was no accident. Loughnane reckoned that after losing two successive Munster finals, the team badly needed to maintain momentum. Inwardly, the squad was beginning to doubt itself after losing by eighteen points to Tipperary in 1993 and by nine points to Limerick a year later. To add to Clare's sense of disappointment, neither Tipperary nor Limerick went on to win the All-Ireland final so Clare could not even claim to have been beaten by the best teams in the country in those years.

In the circumstances, it would have been easy to lose direction in the 1994/95 League. Loughnane's promotion to the manager's chair, which was vacated by Len Gaynor after the 1994 championship, ensured that this would not happen. Loughnane decided to make a real push for the League, operating on the basis that winning it could work wonders. He set a series of targets for his team. Beat Kilkenny in the first game and it would launch the season nicely. The players obliged, winning by 0–14 to 0–9. Go to Athenry and beat Galway on home ground, which is never easy. Again, the team responded, winning by 3–12 to 1–10.

A five-point win over Antrim next time out set Clare up for an end-of-season shoot-out with Limerick, who had beaten them so comprehensively in the Munster final. Clare won this time, by 2–8 to 1–9. In the space of six weeks they had progressed from a team with a Munster final hangover to Division One table toppers. Things were taking shape.

They were back on the training ground in early January. Loughnane & Co. were adamant that it was vital to press along at pace during the spring section of the League. Laois folded easily in the first game in February, setting Clare up for another important test against Tipperary. By now confidence was brimming in Clare and it was no surprise when they won by 2–9 to 0–10, thereby guaranteeing themselves of a place in the League semi-final. Clare still had one Division One game to play, against Cork in Pairc Ui Rinn. Having already qualified for the semi-finals, Clare's focus was not as sharp as usual. Neither was their shooting, as they shot sixteen wides before going down by 1–9 to 0–10. It was a big disappointment for Clare, not in League terms, but because Cork had derived a psychological edge for their likely championship encounter in June.

Meanwhile, the improving Waterford team had emerged from Division Two of the League to beat lifeless Galway (they failed to score in the first half) convincingly in the quarter-final. Clare were pleased by that, for while they realised that Waterford were on a roll, they reckoned that Galway would have been tougher semi-final opponents. They were right. Waterford hurled poorly and were well beaten, 2–14 to 0–8. Clare were back in their first League final since 1987.

In retrospect, Clare's championship ambitions were probably helped by the big defeat by Kilkenny in the League final. A win, or even a narrow defeat, would have suggested that all was well with the squad which, as subsequent events proved, was not the case. Having lost so heavily to Kilkenny, the selectors decided that major adjustments would have to be made in the midfield–forward areas.

By the time Clare's first championship game with Cork came around, on 4 June, much had changed in those departments. Midfielder, Ken Morrissey and corner-forwards, Jim McInerney and Ger 'Sparrow' O'Loughlin were not included on the team, replaced by Fergus Tuohy, Fergal Hegarty and Stephen McNamara. As it happened, O'Loughlin started against Cork, coming in as a replacement for the injured Eamonn Taaffe. O'Loughlin's career always had been based on a series of ups and downs. A wonderfully gifted player, he had a tendency to combine the good with the bad in a very infuriating mix. More often than not, his best displays came when he was brought in as a substitute.

Although he played the full game against Cork, he was only in because of Taaffe's injury so, in a sense, he was still acting out the super-sub role. He did it magnificently, scoring 1–3 on a day which buried one myth about Clare. Conventional wisdom decreed that Clare could never win in a tight finish against Cork. Laden down by memories of the past, Clare were supposed to melt when subjected to the intense heat generated by the likes of Cork in championship games.

That theory seemed to be holding solidly when Kevin Murray scored a Cork goal in the 69th minute to put his side two points ahead. Clare, who had clawed their way back from an interval deficit of 2–4 to 0–7, looked beaten. Once again, it seemed as if Cork's cuteness had enabled them to get their noses in front just on the finish line.

This time, though, things were different. Clare won a line ball which Fergus Tuohy cut into the Cork square in an inviting arc. Ollie Baker, who had come on as a sub for Stephen Sheedy in the first half, rose highest of all and batted the ball to the net for what proved to be the winning goal. One of the amazing features of that game was that Clare survived despite shooting twenty wides while also having to finish the game with fourteen fit players. Centre-back, Seanie McMahon switched to corner-forward for the final quarter after injuring his shoulder. Clare had used the last of their three subs in the 47th minute. McMahon really should have gone off but, showing the spirit which typified Clare's efforts all season, he stayed on so as not to hand Cork the psychological edge of playing with an extra man.

Clare finally held on for a 2–13 to 3–9 win, their second championship success over Cork in three seasons. Despite the dramatic conclusion, there was nothing to suggest that Clare were about to embark on a record-breaking season. Writing in the following day's *The Irish Times*, Jimmy Barry Murphy observed: 'I said at one stage that I wouldn't like to see either team play Tipperary. It's hard to see Clare winning anything when they're hitting nineteen or twenty wides in a match.'

Two weeks later, Tipperary were out of the championship, beaten by a point by Limerick. A second consecutive Clare–Limerick Munster final did not excite hurling fans in the same way as a Cork–Tipperary decider would have done. Clare's collapse against Limerick in 1994, followed by their cave-in against Kilkenny in the League final, had raised so many questions about their big-day resolve that the quest for Munster final tickets was not as frantic as usual, certainly not in Clare.

Although it is now virtually impossible to find a Clare person who admits to not having been in Thurles for the Munster final, the truth is that Limerick fans far out-numbered them in the 46,361 crowd. Despite the confident predictions by Ger Loughnane and his closest allies, there was no great faith in the Clare team going into the final. The pessimists seemed justified in their view when Limerick pulled three points clear after twenty-two minutes. Not they had been playing very well but they were still good enough to keep the Clare attack in control.

Clare's first big break came in the 26th minute when Conor Clancy was fouled in the Limerick square. Goalie, David Fitzgerald, galloped the full length of the pitch to blast the semi-penalty to the net. Suddenly hope wrapped its comforting arms around Clare. The second half was one of the most joyous occasions ever experienced by Clare. With Jamesie O'Connor in total control in the midfield-half-forward area, Clare outscored Limerick by 1–12 to 0–4. It was amazing really. After so many years of misery and heartbreak Clare were winning a Munster final in a landslide, eventually taking the title by 1–17 to 0–11.

The scenes at the final whistle were incredible. It was as if the lid which had been pressing down on Clare was blown off, allowing the county to breathe again. Munster Council chairman, Noel Walsh, who is also a Clare man, could scarcely contain himself as he prepared to present the cup to captain, Anthony Daly. The fans, heaving and swaying in a jubilant mass, demanded an early hand-over. And then the presentation. The Munster trophy was in a Clare captain's hands for the first time in sixty-three years.

Many of the Galway players, who were to meet Clare in the All-Ireland semi-final, were among the crowd that day. And, as Anthony Daly invited Clare to the mother of all parties that night, they felt that they were watching a county which had reached the promised land. They would have no further ambitions left for 1995! The fact that Clare did not regard the Munster final win as an end in itself for 1995 illustrates the maturity and intensity of the squad's character.

Details of their early morning training sessions were, by now, well documented. Loughnane had changed the training routine, mixing the traditional evening sessions with 7 a.m. starts. It wasn't so much a question of doing anything revolutionary in the dawn air; more a matter of testing the attitude of players who were asked to leave their beds at six in the morning. Their willingness to do that convinced Loughnane that he was dealing with a special group.

Clare had four weeks to prepare for the All-Ireland semi-final against Galway. It was long enough to allow some time for celebration followed by a period of concentrated planning for the new challenge. Despite their poor performance against Waterford in the League quarter-final, Galway were a side to be feared. Their record in All-Ireland semi-finals was enough to convince Clare that, whatever their shortcomings on other days, Galway were expert at getting it right on the first Sunday in August.

Clare had an ace in their sideline pack for the game against Galway. Physiotherapaist, Colum Flynn, had spent several seasons with Galway and knew most of the players as well as the Galway team management did. Flynn's contribution to the preparations for the Galway game was extremely important. Clare were heading into new territory but were doing so with the comforting knowledge that they had an experienced campaigner in their ranks. Not only that, but Flynn had been at the heart of Galway's action for many years, including the glory period in 1987–88.

Galway hurled poorly in the All-Ireland semi-final, allowing Clare to win a the game without every really being asked serious questions. Once again, Galway's inability to manufacture goals costly them dearly and Clare won by 3–12 to 1–13. It was not the sort of performance which encouraged people to put much money on Clare to win the final but it scarcely mattered — they were back in an All-Ireland final.

Offaly were backed down to the tightest of odds to retain the All-Ireland crown. The popular view was that despite Clare's carefully charted course to the final, they would be seriously deficient in big-day experience. Besides, Offaly's demolition of Kilkenny in the Leinster final had been by far the best performance of the season so far. Offaly's right to be favourites could not be challenged, even if there was a nagging doubt in some people's minds about whether or not the team actually deserved to win two-in-a-row. It takes a really great team to retain the title and Offaly hadn't proved that they were that good. Nevertheless, they looked certainties to make it two-in-a-row when they led by 1–6 to 0–5 after thirty-four minutes. The fact that the goal had come through the most fortuitous of circumstances when Clare goalkeeper, David Fitzgerald, failed to control Michael Duignan's shot, which spun agonisingly over the goal line, did not seem unduly important at the time. All the signs were that Offaly would win.

In 1981, Galway scored just two points as Offaly staged a memorable comeback to win the All-Ireland title. In 1995, Offaly scored just 1–2 (both points were from frees) as Clare slowly built up a winning platform. Yes, history does tend to repeat itself. Johnny Pilkington's goal in the 54th minute put Offaly three points ahead but some terrible shooting prevented them from exploiting their position. Meanwhile Clare, using the hard-work ethos which had stood to them all season, dug deep into their personal reserves of courage. Eamonn Taaffe, who had been out injured all summer, made a dramatic appearance and put Clare ahead with a quick reaction goal after Anthony Daly's free had thudded off the woodwork. Job done, Taaffe retreated to the subs' bench.

Johnny Dooley levelled it for Offaly before Daly, underlining the value of a truly inspirational captain, took responsibility from a '65' which he drove over the bar in the 69th minute. Jamesie O'Connor 's pointed free, awarded rather harshly after Kevin Kinahan was adjudged to have fouled in his desperate effort to clear the ball, in injury time sealed the greatest day in Clare's hurling history. Clare 1–13 Offaly 2–8.

From the steps on the Hogan Stand, Anthony Daly wondered why it had taken so long for Clare to win an All-Ireland final. He told the thronging masses that better Clare teams had failed to make the breakthrough and he wanted to dedicate this success to them. It was a lovely touch by a really great captain. 'There has been a missing person in Clare for eighty-one years. Today that person has been found. His name is Liam McCarthy,' said Daly.

His comment that better Clare teams had failed to win an All-Ireland final may well be true. The difference in 1995 was that all the strands came together at the same time; pulled, tweaked and mended, as the occasion demanded, by Ger Loughnane. 'We're in the promised land at last,' said a delighted Loughnane from the steps of the Hogan Stand. No county deserved it more.

CLARE (All-Ireland final 1995): David Fitzgerald, Michael O'Halloran, Brian Lohan, Frank Lohan; Liam Doyle, Sean McMahon, Anthony Daly; Jamesie O'Connor , Ollie Baker; Fergus Tuohy, P.J. O'Connell, Fergal Hegarty; Stephen McNamara, Conor Clancy , Ger O'Loughlin.

Subs: Eamonn Taaffe for McNamara, Cyril Lyons for Clancy, Alan Neville for Taaffe.

Leitrim 1994

(No Longer The West's Poor Relations)

It was the sporting picture of 1994; 95 year-old Tom Gannon standing on the rostrum at Dr Hyde Park, Roscommon proudly raising the trophy with team captain Declan Darcy, to the tumultous approval of all of county Leitrim. Tom had been Leitrim captain when Leitrim had last won the Connacht football final in 1927 — now he was sharing in the limitless joy of a county which had experienced over two generations of persistent failure.

Perhaps that is an exaggeration. A county which continues to battle with such pride, commitment and spirit against so many odds is never a failure. But, in a harsh sporting world where success is measured essentially in honours and trophies, Leitrim were deemed to be, to put it diplomatically, non-achievers. Not only that but they were patronised by the bigger counties who liked to toss complimentary words their way before squelching their ambitions.

There were so many times down the years when Leitrim might have made the Connacht championship breakthrough. In the 1950s, for instance, they reached four consecutive finals, losing them all to Galway. The 1958 final was especially disappointing for a Packy McGarty-inspired Leitrim. Galway were well in control at half-time but Leitrim roared back into contention in the second half and drew level. Galway's experience (they had won the All-Ireland title in 1956) told in the end and they won by 2–9 to 1–10. Leitrim's flirtations with Connacht finals in the 1960s were far more uncomfortable. Galway hammered them by fourteen points in 1963 while Mayo had twenty to spare in the 1967 decider. Amazingly, Leitrim were not to reach another Connacht senior final until 1994.

If football required titles to survive in Leitrim — or indeed a great many other counties — then it would long since have died. It doesn't, of course, simply because of the dedication of so many people for whom playing the sport is the first and only essential. Success is a welcome by-product but is not an imperative. Such is the essence of real sport.

Leitrim's gradual climb to its present status can be traced back to 1975 when they won the Fr Manning U-16 competition. Two years later, Leitrim won the Connacht U-21 title, before losing to Kerry in the All-Ireland semi-final. In 1983, Mickey Quinn inspired Leitrim to heights which should have beaten Galway in the Connacht semi-final but, as so often happened when confronted by the maroon-and-white, Leitrim lost their resolve in the closing minutes, allowing Galway to sneak through for a victory they did not deserve.

Somewhat surprisingly, Leitrim ran out of momentum in the late 1980s, losing heavily to Mayo in the 1988 championship and going down to Sligo the following year. A disastrous start to the 1989/90 League prompted Leitrim to look outside for a manager and they settled on Cavan's P.J. Carroll, a man whose optimism was — and indeed still is — boundless. Within a year, Leitrim had won promotion to Division Three of the National League and had also captured the All-Ireland 'B' championship, which was introduced as a sort of consolation competition for teams which lost in the first round of the championship proper. That was an important breakthrough for while it lacked the glamour and glitz of the 'real' championship, it gave Leitrim a winning feeling. It had exactly the same effect on Clare, who also used it as a springboard to launch themselves in the early 1990s.

Leitrim's steady progress up the League rankings brought them to within a game of Division One in the spring of 1991. In fact, they had two chances to make it but failed in both, first losing to Tyrone by three points in a game which Leitrim blew in the first half. That setback left them facing a play-off with Kildare for a place in the quarter-finals and promotion to Division One.

Leitrim had beaten Kildare in the League some months previously but Kildare had now established an impressive momentum under Mick O'Dwyer and although Leitrim led by four points at half-time in the play-off in Navan, they lost their way in the second half and were eventually beaten by 3–11 to 2–8. Leitrim were bitterly disappointed at having missed promotion but, on the positive side, they were learning all the time through getting regular games against top opposition. The actual benefits of such exposure would take a few seasons to come to fruition.

If Galway had been Leitrim's long-time bogey team, they were very definitely replaced by Roscommon in the early 1990s. Roscommon beat Leitrim in four consecutive championships in 1990–91–92–93. The 1993 defeat in Carrick-on-Shannon was especially sickening for Leitrim who felt that they didn't at all do themselves justice when going down by 1–12 to 1–10 in the Connacht semi-final. By then, John O'Mahoney, who had guided Mayo to the All-Ireland final in 1989 had taken over as manager, and had presided over Leitrim's first real championship breakthrough, a win over Galway in Tuam.

It came on 30 May 1993 and while it was a major triumph for Leitrim, it got little attention in the national media as it coincided with Derry's eleven-point demolition of Down in the Ulster championship. Despite Galway's problems, few thought that Leitrim would beat them in Tuam Stadium, a venue which usually held all sorts of terror for other Connacht teams. Besides, Leitrim had not beaten Galway in the championship for forty-four years. That statistic counted for little as Leitrim played superbly in a very close game which was eventually decided by Aidan Rooney's last-second point.

Luck might have cast an admiring, if deserved, glance Leitrim's way that day but it was very definitely absent from their corner when the draw for the 1994 championship was made. It left them with the very daunting task of having to beat Galway, Roscommon and Mayo to win the Connacht final. What's more, they would have to travel to Dr Hyde Park for their first-round game.

They had beaten Roscommon in a crucial League game some months earlier, which was important from a psychological viewpoint. At last, the Roscommon hoodoo had been laid and it counted for nothing in the championship as team captain, Declan Darcy showed when he calmly slotted over the winning point from a '45' to set up a semi-final clash with Galway in Carrick-on-Shannon. In truth, this was a quite awful game. No score at all for fifteen minutes...0–3 to 0–2 (Leitrim led) at half-time... and a final score of 1–6 to 0–9. Conor McGauran's goal just after half-time seemed to swing the agenda Galway's way but Leitrim battled on and earned a replay with another long range point from a free by Declan Darcy. The only saving grace of a dreadful game was the fact that both sides were given a chance to prove that they could do better.

The replay in Tuam a week later was better. Significantly so for Leitrim who recovered from a two-point deficit with fifteen minutes remaining to squeeze home by a point, 0–11 to 0–10. Padraig Kenny slotted over the winner in the 68th minute. Two hurdles had been cleared but there was still one to go in the form of a Mayo team which had won the 1993 Connacht final. Mayo, who had been hammered by Cork in the '93 All-Ireland semi-final, had undergone some radical changes under Jack O'Shea but were still quite confident of taming Leitrim.

When Pat Fallon's speculative lob was fumbled into their own net by a hesitant Leitrim defence after just eighteen seconds of the start, Mayo looked to be on their way. It was a disastrous start for Leitrim, particularly for young full-back, Seamus Quinn, who was very definitely helping with enquiries as to how the ball ended up in the net.

Quinn's response typified Leitrim's new-found confidence. Instead of allowing it to upset him, he dug in and gave a fine performance. Mayo's attacking limitations were repeatedly exposed and they failed to score again in the first half at the end of which Leitrim led by 0–6 to 1–0. Mickey Quinn and Pat Donohue were in control at midfield and Leitrim were 8 points clear with fifteen minutes left. Kevin O'Neill's goal revived Mayo, who pressed on with great urgency in the closing minutes but Leitrim's earlier dominance left them with a comfortable cushion and they eventually won by 0–12 to 2–4. Glory at last!

It was ironic that Leitrim should have beaten a Jack O'Shea-coached Mayo side in the final. Only two years earlier, Jacko had been at the receiving end of another famous breakthrough when Clare beat Kerry in the Munster final, a game which signalled the end of his magnificent playing career.

The scenes in Hyde Park as Declan Darcy hoisted the trophy will never be forgotten by those who were lucky enough to witness such a historic day. It was as if all of Leitrim had packed into the ground in anticipation of a unique occasion. They were not disappointed.

The sheer euphoria generated by the Leitrim supporters is something which other counties could not comprehend. For while the Connacht title may have become a de-valued currency in national terms in previous years, it was the Holy Grail to Leitrim, who had endured so much heartbreak down the years. Veteran midfielder, Mickey Quinn epitomised the spirit of the occasion better than anybody. For years, he had been one of Leitrim's anchor men, striving against the odds, losing many of the close calls but never doubting that one day it would all come right. It did. Normal routines were ditched as the whole of Leitrim embarked on an orgy of celebration which didn't reach its official conclusion until around 4 a.m. on Tuesday morning when the team bus, having gone on a triumphant tour of the county, finally reached Ballinamore. The heavy rain did its best to dampen spirits but was fighting a losing battle against a people who felt that a great weight had been lifted off their shoulders. Leitrim were no longer the poor relations of Connacht football.

Even as the celebrations continued, manager, John O'Mahoney, and his co-selectors, Ollie Honeyman and Joe Reynolds were beginning to look ahead to the All-Ireland semi-final. Leitrim were due to face the Leinster champions and although the final had not been played, it was pretty clear that either Dublin or Meath would provide very tough opposition. In the event, it was Dublin who qualified. That was somewhat unfortunate for Leitrim for while there was very little to choose between Meath and Dublin, the latter tended to be more ruthless at exploiting weaknessess in opposition. Meath, even in their great days in the 1986–91 period, had never been especially good at putting teams away. Instead, they tended to scrape through most games.

The All-Ireland semi-final turned out to be more of an occasion than a match. With their vast experience and their greater depth, Dublin had all the aces and eventually won by 3–15 to 1–9. It would be wrong, however, to dismiss the game in purely scoring terms. Leitrim made a huge contribution in terms of atmosphere and colour. Their support had swollen considerably since the Connacht final as Leitrim people returned from all over the world to be in Croke Park for the semi-final.

Leitrim led by two points after nine minutes but were rocked back by a Charlie Redmond-goal seven minutes later. Still, Leitrim were hanging on grimly — with Seamus Quinn particularly outstanding at full-back — when Dublin struck for the killer goal two minutes into injury time. Mick Galvin applied the finishing touch to leave Dublin leading by 2–7 to 0–5 at half-time. Colin McGlynn scored Leitrim's goal nineteen minutes into the second half but Dessie Farrell hit Dublin's third some minutes later to put lots of daylight between the sides.

The semi-final defeat in no way deflated Leitrim. After all, Mayo, who had far more experience in Croke Park, were beaten by a bigger margin by Cork a year earlier. Besides, the 1994 season was all about winning Connacht, as far as Leitrim was concerned and while they would have dearly loved to have put up a better show in the All-Ireland semi-final, the odds were piled high against them. Leitrim fans remain convinced that it would have been all so different had their side managed to retain the Connacht crown in 1995. They lost the semi-final by a point to Galway after looking certain winners and then watched Galway replace them as Connacht champions, before running Tyrone close in the All-Ireland semi-final.

LEITRIM (Connacht final 1994): Martin McHugh; Joe Honeyman, Seamus Quinn, Fergal Reynolds; Noel Moran, Declan Darcy, Gerry Flanagan; Mickey Quinn, Pat Donohue; Aidan Rooney, George Dugdale, Paul Kieran; Colin McGlynn, Padraig Kenny, Liam Conlon. Subs: Jason Ward for Dugdale, Brian Breen for Conlon.

Derry 1993

(Sweet Melody In The Derry Air)

When Eamonn Coleman took over as Derry manager early in 1991, he peered up from the basement area of Division Two and felt the weight of twelve teams perched above him in the National League standings. Derry were joint sixth with Antrim in Division Two and slipping. Two years and seven months later, Derry had won an All-Ireland, a National League and an Ulster title.

The precise extent to which Coleman was responsible for Derry's remarkable turnaround is impossible to quantify. Suffice to say that his reign coincided with the best period in the history of Derry football. Not that his successful reign counted for much in 1994 when he was sensationally dropped as manager by the Derry County Board, two months after the county had been beaten by Down in the Ulster championship. The decision unleased a tornado of ill-feeling in Derry, climaxing in a threat by the players to boycott the county team. The County Board refused to relent, however, and gradually the players reluctantly returned to duty, following calls from Coleman to put Derry football ahead of personal considerations.

Coleman's dismissal as manager disappointed a great many people who felt that Derry's rise from also-rans to winners had been charted mainly by the man from Ballymaguigan. Coleman's fans alleged that he had been betrayed by people whom he thought were his friends. They also claimed that if Derry could sack a manager who had presided over such a glorious run, they scarcely deserved any success in the first place.

It was a great pity that the Coleman era should have ended in such controversial circumstances, as unquestionably it had brought a whole new sense of well-being to a county which had lived with so many disappointments down through the years. Coleman's reign began on a grey February day in 1991 when he took charge of the Derry team, for the first time in a League match against Tyrone in Celtic Park. In a scrappy, niggly game, Derry won by a point to begin a run which took them to new, uncharted heights over the next few years. Wins over Leitrim, who were also beginning their upward surge at the time, and Longford followed but Derry still finished outside the promotion zone that spring.

Nevertheless, it was clear that things were beginning to come together. The speed with which that was happening became apparent in the 1991 championship when Derry beat Tyrone and Monaghan and drew with Down before losing the replay. Later that year, Derry would have the satisfaction of realising that they came closer than any other team to beating All-Ireland champions, Down. By the spring of 1992, Derry's standing had improved further. They had remained unbeaten right through the League, over-powering such ambitious forces as Down, Meath (twice) Kerry and Kildare to reach the final against Tyrone. It was a match which Tyrone looked like winning most of the way until Plunkett Donaghy misjudged a relatively easy catch on his goal line and the ball spun into the net for the goal which turned the game. Derry 1–10 Tyrone 1–8. The Derry revival was now complete — they had won the League title for the first time since 1947.

There are many who feel that Derry were the best team in the 1992 Ulster championship. They repeated their League final success over Tyrone, hammered Monaghan in a replay after being caught in the closing stages of the drawn game, and then dethroned champions, Down, in a tough, tense semi-final. When they led early in the second half of the final against Donegal, who were down to fourteen men, it looked odds-on a Derry win but Donegal dug incredibly deep to summon enough courage and tenacity to come back and win. Derry were initially devastated, convincing themselves that this was a game which they had thrown away. Once again, though, Derry had the consolation of watching their conquerors go on to win the All-Ireland final. Besides, they had the League title so the season was a very definite success.

Progress through the Divisional stages of the 1992/93 League was equally comfortable, spoiled only by a surprise defeat by Galway at home. However, when Derry finally got their chance to avenge the 1992 Ulster final defeat by Donegal they failed, losing 0–10 to 2–3 in the League quarter-final. At face value, it was a bad result for Derry, who led by 2–2 to 0-4 just before half-time. Derry had the wind in the second half but made no use of it whatsoever. In fact, they scored just one point in that period and, to add to their misery, they had Kieran McKeever sent off.

Many people misread the signs from that match. Derry's heart was set on the championship and, having won the League a year earlier, they weren't over-enthused about expending much energy to retain it. All-Ireland champions, Donegal, who had never won the League, were very keen to complete the double and seemed far more fired up for action than Derry. While the nature of their defeat disappointed Derry, they felt it was not as serious as it might have looked. A get-together on the following night, which involved some very straight talking, quickly restored the focus and Derry got down to work for their championship opener against Down.

Donegal had a more leisurely introduction to the championship, having drawn Antrim in the first round in Ballybofey on June 6. That gave them the option of having a real shot at the National League title, without in any way impacting on their championship preparations. It was different for Derry who were drawn against Down in Newry in the first round on May 30. Despite having beaten Down in the 1992 Ulster semi-final, Derry were very much the outsiders. Conventional wisdom had it that 1992 had been no more than a blip on Down's championship screen. They had adjusted their sets for 1993 and were confident that normal service would be resumed.

The Derry players and management were surprised to read so many experts predicting that not only would Down beat them, they would go on to regain the All-Ireland trophy. Down pinned their faith on the 1991 All-Ireland winning team — thirteen of them lined out against Derry — but while they were present in body, their spirit was elsewhere. Playing in Newry was supposed to be a help to Down. It wasn't. In fact, nothing could save them as Derry thundered into the game on full throttle. Down's stomach for battle was very questionable. It was as if they expected Derry to reach a certain level but instead found them operating at a much higher pitch.

Goals tend to be extremely important in championship games, mainly because they are so hard to come by but also because of the psychological damage they inflict on the opposition. Dermot Heaney's first-half goal set Derry on their way and midway through the second half, Down were like lost little boys waiting for the game to end. Derry rattled in two more goals through Richard Ferris and Eamonn Burns to round off a most comprehensive win. Derry 3–11 Down 0–9.

Eamonn Coleman let fly at the assembled media afterwards. With mischief gleaming in his eyes, he told the journalists that he didn't have to motivate his team at all. No, that had been done for him by all the tipsters who predicted a Down win. 'Do youse boys know anything about football at all', he asked?

Despite their emphatic win, there were still question marks against Derry. Down had been simply awful, something which was freely admitted by their manager, Peter McGrath afterwards. He described it as a 'complete shambles' and said that the Down fans were owed an apology from all concerned with the team. McGrath's honesty did not endear him to his players but, in truth, he was right.

Derry clinched a place in the Ulster final a few weeks later with an 0–19 to 0-11 win over Monaghan. It was a functional, rather than brilliant performance. Monaghan stayed with Derry until the 50th minute but were run out of it from there on and were well beaten in the end. As expected Donegal had come through on the other side, after surviving a real scare against Armagh in the semi-final. It took all of Donegal's survival skills to earn a replay but once they did, they made no mistake second time round.

And so to Clones for the final on July 18. The game should never have been played after one of the worst deluges for years had dumped inches on water on the freshly laid pitch. The problem was that while there had been a lot of overnight rain, the main downpour didn't take place until lunchtime, by which time the 25,000 crowd were converging on St Tiernach's Park. Ulster Council officials decided that they couldn't possibly cancel the game at such a late stage. Given their predicament, they might have shown a little more imagination and at least cancelled the minor final but no, it was allowed to go ahead with several inches of water on the surface.

It was a great pity that the elements intervened so spitefully to ruin the day. Derry v Donegal was to have been one of the highlights of the year but instead it turned into a lottery. Derry eventually won by 0-8 to 0-6, with Anthony Tohill giving a superb exhibition, especially in the crucial period immediately after half-time when Derry scored four quick points which effectively won the match. There were suggestions afterwards that the heavy conditions suited Derry better than Donegal, something which infuriated Coleman and his team. They contended that far from helping them, the weather had seriously restricted their play and that they would have won more easily on a dry day. Although they could never prove that, they derived considerable satisfaction from a League win over Donegal in Casement Park the following October. Played on a lovely October day, Derry destroyed Donegal and a beaming Coleman remarked afterwards: 'See, we can beat them on a dry day too,'

Having carefully picked their way through the Ulster maze, Derry headed for Croke Park and an All-Ireland semi-final clash with Dublin. As in 1992 when Dublin were fancied to beat Donegal, they were also installed as favourites to beat Derry. That suited Derry, who felt that if Donegal could handle Dublin, so could they. Derry started out as if they would eat Dublin alive. They scored three quick points and missed a few others before Dublin slotted their own jigsaw pieces together and began the recovery. Gradually Derry wilted and by half-time they were trailing by 0–9 to 0-4. There seemed no way back.

Derry started the second half in a more upbeat mood with points from Tohill and captain, Henry Downey but they were still three points behind with fourteen minutes left, 0–13 to 0–10. Then came a Derry surge which will never be forgotten in the county. They kicked three points in six glorious minutes to take the lead. Charlie Redmond equalised from a free on sixty-five minutes but it was Derry who dug deepest in those final, hectic minutes. The winning point came in the 68th minute when John McGurk collected a Dermot McNicholl pass on the right and angled it beautifully over the Dublin crossbar. Derry were in the All-Ireland final for the first time since 1958.

The fact that Down and Donegal had won the previous two finals was a major psychological plus for Derry. Ulster football was now feeling comfortable about itself and while Derry recognised that Cork had looked very impressive *en route* to the final, they reckoned that the quality of opposition had been nowhere as good as that which they had to contend with.

Cork had hammered Mayo by twenty points in the semi-final. The obvious conclusions to be drawn were that either Cork were brilliant or Mayo were terrible. After six minutes of the All-Ireland final, the 'Cork were brilliant' option looked the more likely as they galloped into a 1–2 to 0–0 lead. Derry needed a score badly and it came in the 7th minute from John McGurk. It had an immediate effect on Derry who settled into a rhythm and routine which quickly overwhelmed Cork. By the 15th minute Derry were 1–4 to 1–2 clear, the goal coming from Seamus Downey who punched a dropping ball to the net past a static Cork defence. By half-time it was 1–9 to 1–6 for Derry. To add to Cork's problems, they were down to fourteen men, having had Tony Davis sent off after charging into Dermot Heaney. Earlier, Niall Cahalane was lucky not to have been sent off after a foul on Enda Gormley. Cahalane had merely been booked but it was subsequently felt that Davis had paid for his colleague's 'sin' a few minutes later.

Despite their apparently comfortable half-time position, Derry knew the dangers which lay ahead. History is littered with examples of teams which have won games with fourteen players and Derry feared that Cork's plight might prod them into producing a fiery second half. For a time that seemed certain. Ten minutes into the half, John O'Driscoll fired in Cork's second goal to put his side ahead, 2–8 to 1–10. Amazingly, that was to be Cork's final score. The next ten minutes were scoreless before Derry drew level. From there on the outcome was never in doubt as Derry tightened their control to add three more points. Derry 1–14 Cork 2–8.

The unthinkable had happened. After so many years of failure, Derry had made the breakthrough. Not only that but they had done it in style beating all the top teams. Eamonn Coleman returned to the theme he had launched in Newry in May after the win over Down. 'I told youse we were the best team in the country. Maybe youse will believe me now,' he said, amid the chaos and mayhem of a winning dressing-room. By then, there was no doubt about that.

DERRY (All-Ireland final 1993): Damien McCusker; Kieran McKeever, Tony Scullion, Fergal McCusker; Johnny McGurk, Henry Downey, Gary Coleman; Brian McGilligan, Anthony Tohill; Dermot Heaney, Damien Barton, Damien Cassidy; Joe Brolly, Seamus Downey, Enda Gormley.

Subs: Dermot McNicholl for Cassidy, Eamonn Burns for Seamus Downey.

Donegal 1992

(Goodbye Frustration, Hello Success)

Within days of losing the 1992 All-Ireland football semi-final to Donegal, the Mayo squad revolted. The target for their mutinous behaviour was team manager, Brian McDonald. In an unprecedented move, a lengthy statement, which was signed by most of the panel, was circulated to national and local media, outlining the players' grievances.

Basically, the squad were unhappy with McDonald's management techniques and made it clear that they would not play for Mayo again while he was in charge. It was a sensational development in Gaelic Games, opening up all sorts of possibilities for future relationships between managers and players. The players' move split the GAA population in

Mayo. Some felt that they had a solid case while others accused them of trying to off-load responsibility onto McDonald when, in fact, they should have been looking to themselves for an explanation of why they had lost to Donegal.

Eventually, McDonald resigned, thereby sparing the Mayo County Board a huge embarrassment as they would have had to make a choice between the team manager whom they had appointed or the players who were threatening a boycott. The Mayo episode was a national talking point for weeks as GAA fans discussed the implications of player-power. Amid all the controversy one point was overlooked. It centred on the real reason why the Mayo players chose to take such drastic action. Quite simply, they could not accept losing to Donegal, who had never before reached an All-Ireland final.

Mayo fancied themselves as a being a notch or two above Donegal. They had contested the 1989 All-Ireland final, after beating Tyrone in the semi-final and while they failed to win the Connacht title in either 1990 or 1991, they were extremely confident in 1992 after surviving four games to regain the No.1 spot in the west. Losing to Donegal was a sickener. Although Down had won the previous year's All-Ireland final, Ulster football was not regarded as being in any way superior to the rest of the country, including Connacht. In fact, Connacht–Ulster semi-finals had usually ended in western triumphs.

So when Donegal won the 1992 semi-final by 0–13 to 0–9, the Mayo players couldn't cope with it and launched into their September revolution. Had they taken their time and waited to see how Donegal fared in the All-Ireland final, they might have been far less confrontational. The truth was Donegal had been knocking loudly on the All-Ireland door for the previous two seasons. In 1990, they had won the Ulster title and given Meath, who were then the dominant force in Leinster, a real fright in the All-Ireland semi-final. A scoreline of 3–9 to 1–7 gives a totally wrong impression of that game. Donegal dominated for long stretches but failed to reflect their superiority on the scoreboard and eventually fell apart in the closing ten minutes.

Meath midfielder, Liam Hayes said that Donegal were far too reliant on Martin McHugh around then. If McHugh functioned, Donegal functioned. If he didn't, they didn't. Meath designated Kevin Foley as McHugh's marker and he did a very good job, restricting Quigley McHugh to just a few chances. In 1991, Donegal were beaten 1–15 to 0–10 by

Down in the Ulster final. Again, it looked like a Donegal wipe-out but it wasn't. Down had opened up a seven-point lead by half-time but Donegal pared it back to 4 and then had a great chance to cut it to one but Neil Collins made a fine save from Barry McGowan when a goal looked certain. The ball was swept upfield and Barry Breen pointed to put Down five points clear when they might well have been just one in front. While Donegal were extremely disappointed by that defeat, Down's subsequent All-Ireland win went some way towards consoling them. At least they had been beaten by the All-Ireland champions.

Donegal manager, Brian McEniff thought long and hard about his set-up after the 1991 campaign. Donegal weren't that far off the pace but somehow always managed to press the self-destruct button under sustained pressure. It was very, very frustrating. Donegal's tendency to inflict damage on themselves continued into early 1992. They qualified comfortably for the League quarter-finals and looked certain of a semi-final place when they led Dublin by 1–10 to 1–6 with just two minutes to go in Breffni Park, Cavan. Then, in a blue bolt, Dublin struck with goals from Paul Clarke and Vinny Murphy, both of whom had come on as subs. Dublin 3–6 Donegal 1–10. Same old story for Donegal.

Losing matches which they might have won had become a Donegal trademark. Back as far as 1983, they had dominated Galway for most of the way in the All-Ireland semi-final and yet somehow contrived to blow it in the final minutes, eventually losing by a point. Almost ten years on and little had changed apparently. Meanwhile a new force had emerged in Ulster. Derry won the 1992 League final and built on their achievement with a smashing three-point win over All-Ireland champions, Down in the Ulster semi-final. They had earlier confirmed their League final win over Tyrone with a three-point victory in the Ulster quarter-final. They were very definite favourites to win the final.

Donegal's progress to the Ulster final was far less impressive. They drew with Cavan in the first round (1–15 each) in Breffni Park, which was scarcely the type of result required to send Donegal supporters dashing to the bookmakers to back their team for an All-Ireland win. Donegal won the replay easily (0–20 to 1–6) and then hammered Fermanagh by 2–17 to 0–7 in the semi-final. Despite the high scoring average (twenty points per game), there was no great optimism in Donegal, certainly not among the fans anyway, going into the Ulster final. Derry were firm favourites.

That rating looked entirely appropriate when the sides went in level (0–5 each) at half-time. Donegal had played with the wind in the first half but had made little productive use of it. Also, they were now down to fourteen men, having had right full-back, John Cunningham, sent off just before half-time. Disaster all round, or so it seemed.

The second half of that final was the making of Donegal. Deep in their hearts, the team knew that most people expected them to collapse. Even their most avid supporters were prepared for the worst. For apart from being a man short, they had also lost full-forward, Tony Boyle, injured in a collision with Anthony Tohill. Significantly, Tohill had to retire at half-time, providing Derry with a headache for which they hadn't bargained. Still, when Seamus Downey scored the only goal of the game thirteen minutes into the second half, to put Derry a point ahead, it looked ominous for depleted Donegal. This time though, they weren't going to take no for an answer. They appealed to their emotions and got a brilliant response. As so often happens with a fourteen-man team, every player went in search of extra responsibility. In contrast, Derry's sense of responsibility became diluted. Donegal improved with each passing minute and eventually won by 0–14 to 1–9.

It would be wholly dishonest to say that Donegal's All-Ireland semi-final against Mayo was a high-quality affair. In fact, it was an awful game. Both sides wasted several great chances but when Mayo led by 0-8 to 0-6 in the second half, it looked as if they might at least have the chance to get back to the practice ground and prepare for the final.

But then Donegal played their master card by bringing in Manus Boyle who scored three points in a revival which eventually ended in an 0–13 to 0–9 win. An unusual feature of that game was that Padraig Brogan came on as a sub for Mayo, having played for Donegal in the League quarter-final just four months earlier. It was alleged afterwards that the sight of Brogan in a Mayo jersey had been a big motivating point for the Donegal players, who were annoyed by his switch of allegiance between League and Championship.

As in the Ulster final, Donegal were outsiders for the All-Ireland final. Only more so. For while Dublin had not appeared in an All-Ireland final since 1985, their rating as one of the top teams in the country had been consistent right through the late eighties and into the nineties. Now it was delivery time, the day when Dublin would take over from Down as the country's No.1 team. Brian McEniff had other plans. Donegal's League quarter-final performance against Dublin had convinced him that there was very little between the teams. He reckoned too that Dublin's rating as favourites had been earned purely on the basis of their tradition. After all, Dublin had won twenty-one All-Ireland titles while Donegal were appearing in their very first final.

On closer examination, Donegal could find optimistic signs. For while they had not played particularly well against Mayo, their win over Derry had to be regarded as superior to anything produced by Dublin in their run to the final. Dublin had beaten Wexford, Louth, Offaly, Kildare and Clare, none of whom had the experience or all-round depth which Donegal possessed. Dublin's hype machine cranked into full working order in the days before the final. They would later insist that they were not over-confident but few accepted that. Deep down, they believed that Donegal would push them pretty hard but, in the end, Dublin would win, probably by four or five points.

All-Ireland day started badly for Donegal. Veteran defender, Martin Shovlin had to withdraw from the team hours before the game, due to a neck injury which he sustained during the previous week. It was a heartbreaking decision for Shovlin but, after going through a fitness test, he knew he wouldn't be up to the demanding rigours of an All-Ireland final. John Joe Doherty was drafted in to replace him. Donegal were extremely keen to make a good start and might have had a goal in the 7th minute but James McHugh's shot crashed back off the Dublin crossbar. Two minutes later, Donegal (trailing by 0–2 to 0–1) were facing the first crisis of the day when Dublin were awarded a penalty. A Dublin goal at that stage would have been a disaster for a Donegal team struggling to adapt to their new surroundings but they were let off the hook as Redmond shot wide. It was neither the first nor the last time that Dublin's inability to capitalise on penalties cost them dearly.

Vinny Murphy hoisted Dublin's third point shortly afterwards but from there on Donegal grew in confidence. They were level in nineteen minutes, ahead in twenty-three minutes and led at half-time by 0–10 to 0–7. The general belief among neutral observers was that Dublin would improve in the second half and eventually overtake Donegal. Instead, Donegal went on to win the second half by 0–8 to 0–7, having led by six points at one stage.

Donegal's only problem period was when Dublin kicked three points between the 60th and 62nd minutes. Then Manus Boyle, who scored nine points altogether, pointed a free in the 64th minute to steady the Donegal ship as it sailed into the home waters. Donegal eventually won by 0–18 to 0–14.

It was a remarkable triumph really as they had failed to score a single goal in the Ulster final, the All-Ireland semi-final or final. But it didn't matter to the thousands of Donegal supporters at home and abroad who united in celebration of possibly the most memorable day in the county's history. For sheer emotion, it would be difficult to rival Donegal's homecoming on the Monday night after the All-Ireland final. Hundreds of fans gathered in Connolly Station, Dublin, to see their heroes board the train to Sligo, where 10,000 people turned out to greet the team. Then it was onto the team coach for the journey home. Brian McEniff and team captain, Anthony Molloy got off the coach at the Donegal border and carried the Sam Maguire trophy into their beloved homeland. From there, it was an endless procession as the whole of Donegal congregated to be part of the great night. Things would never be the same in Tir Conaill.

DONEGAL (All-Ireland final 1992): Gary Walsh; Barry McGowan, Matt Gallagher, Noel Hegarty; Donal Reid, Martin Gavigan, John Joe Doherty; Anthony Molloy, Brian Murray; James McHugh, Martin McHugh, Joyce McMullan; Declan Bonner, Tony Boyle, Manus Boyle. Sub: Barry Cunningham for Murray.

Offaly 1981

(Refusing To Take 'No' for an Answer)

In the week before the 1981 All-Ireland hurling final a forecast card in a pub in Tullamore showed the prediction rate running at 2/1 in Galway's favour. Almost all of those who fancied Galway had Offaly addresses, proving that however much their hearts supported their own county, their heads said a pound on Galway made better business sense.

At half-time in the All-Ireland final, their judgement seemed to have been well vindicated when Galway led by 0–13 to 1–4. Indeed, ten minutes from the end, the smart money remained on Galway, for while Offaly had built up an impressive momentum, they were still four points adrift. What happened in the closing stages has gone down in history as the spell which shaped the impressive course of modern Offaly hurling history. But while those sensational minutes were unquestionably crucial, it would be inaccurate to characterise them as the sole turning point in Offaly hurling. No, that had happened more than twelve months earlier.

When Offaly reached their first Leinster final in eleven years in 1980, neither friend nor foe believed in them. It was claimed that they only got there because the open draw had thrown the 'big two', Kilkenny and Wexford on the same side. Offaly played Dublin in the other semi-final and while they won by 0–18 to 0–10, there was nothing in their performance to hint at the great days ahead.

Only 9,500 turned up for the Leinster final clash with Kilkenny, who were then the reigning All-Ireland champions. Estimates put the Offaly contingent at no more than 3,000. It was the lowest Leinster final attendance since the 1940s.

It was also one of the best finals. In fact, it was an amazing game which produced thirty-five scores, including eight goals. Had hurling fans been told in advance that Kilkenny would have scored 5–10 and still lost, they would have assumed that it was some sort of joke. It wasn't. Offaly scored 3–17 to scrape home by a single point. There was nothing fluky about their win. They had hurled superbly against a Kilkenny team which was oozing confidence, experience and class. This time though, they met their match. Gone were the days when Offaly would cope with Kilkenny for three-quarters of the way before running out of ideas in the closing stages.

Even after beating Kilkenny, Offaly failed to win over the sceptics and so they went into the All-Ireland semi-final against Galway as outsiders too. They played accordingly for a long time and trailed by nine points after fifty-seven minutes. But goals by Brendan Bermingham and Mark Corrigan ignited the comeback fuse and, in the end, Galway were hanging on, winning by just two points, 4–9 to 3–10. Offaly fans complained, with a degree of justification it must be said, that a minute or two more should have been played because of earlier stoppages.

At the time, Galway attached no great significance to the searing power of Offaly's revival. Galway argued that they had contributed to their own problems with a series of giveaway scores. Nevertheless, it left Offaly with the firm impression that, even when they had a big lead, Galway were vulnerable, something which was of enormous help to Offaly going into the 1981 All-Ireland final.

So what had happened to bring about the change in Offaly hurling? Basically, it was down to a lot of hard work at local level but the County Board also made a very wise decision to draft in Kilkennyman, Dermot

Healy to coach the side. Galway had tried the 'outsider' policy to no great effect in the late 1970s but it was different in Offaly. For a start, Healy was with the players right through the year, rather than coming in merely for the summer campaign. Also, he didn't have as high a profile as 'Babs' Keating, who was with Galway in 1977 and 1979, so the media spotlight didn't beam in as much on his activities. That left him free to work quietly and effectively.

Healy had enjoyed considerable success as a coach with Kilkenny minor and college teams and saw the Offaly job as the sort of challenge he wanted. Had he aspired to, and got the job as Kilkenny senior coach, the sense of personal satisfaction would not have been as great, as Kilkenny fans viewed All-Ireland titles as a right rather than an aspiration. It was very different in Offaly. Healy worked hard on refining Offaly's skills. He had willing players to work on while men like Andy Gallagher and Paudge Mulhaire provided a shrewd and enthusiastic back-up for him. All in all, the package worked.

Offaly found themselves in an unusual position at the start of the 1980–81 League. They had to play all of their group games away from home, as punishment for an incident which marred their game with Clare in Tulla late in 1979. The same fate befell Clare. Offaly coped brilliantly with their 'away' campaign. They beat Galway by 2–12 to 3–7 in the champions' very first League game in Pearse Stadium and while Galway did not regard it as important at the time, it put down a little marker in Offaly minds. Offaly made it all the way to the final in the following May and while they lost to Cork in Thurles, there were enough encouraging signs in the performance to nourish them as they looked ahead to the championship.

Offaly won the toss but decided to play against a very strong wind. It was a mistake. Cork were handed the initiative and they made maximum use of it, scoring 2–3 without reply in the opening ten minutes. Offaly steadied the ship from there on but had left themselves with far too much to do. They eventually lost by 3–11 to 2–8. When hurling fans reflect back on the 1981 campaign, Offaly's brilliant comeback against Galway is their abiding memory. While that is understandable, it is also important to remember how close Offaly came to defeat in the Leinster semi-final against Laois. Offaly have always found Laois to be difficult opponents and 1981 was certainly no exception. Laois had run Offaly to a single point in the League semi-final in April (2–13 to 4–6) and when Laois led them by two points with four minutes to go in the Leinster semi-final, Offaly's case looked well and truly tried. Typically, they had one last piece of evidence to throw into the argument. In a dramatic finish, they drew level and then Paddy Kirwan shot the winner from a long range free. Offaly 3–20 Laois 6–10.

Wexford had beaten Kilkenny in the other semi-final and were extremely confident of taking their first Leinster title since 1977. But, in a pattern which was to haunt them many times subsequently, Wexford left their best form behind them in the semi-final. At one stage, they trailed by eight points, and had also lost ace goal-getter, Tony Doran through injury. This time, it was Wexford's turn to launch a comeback. While they did it with great courage and tenacity they fell just short, losing by 3–12 to 2–13. Offaly were back in the All-Ireland final.

It can be reasonably argued that their opponents should have been Limerick. Although reduced to fourteen men when Sean Foley was sent off in the first half of the All-Ireland semi-final against Galway, they held on to draw. The gods deserted Limerick completely for the replay. Foley was out through suspension; Dom Punch and Pat Herbert were out injured; they missed a penalty when leading 0–5 to 0–1 and they lost Leonard Enright and Michael Grimes through injury in the course of the game. Galway eventually won by 4–16 to 2–17.

Galway's attacking problems in the drawn game had prompted them to coax John Connolly out of retirement for the replay and, quite naturally, he was the first choice full-forward for the final. Galway had two changes from the 1980 team — Iggy Clarke (injured in 1980) in for Conor Hayes (injured) in a re-shuffled defence and Finbar Gantley in for Frank Burke in attack.

Having survived the dual fright against Limerick, Galway were favourites to retain the title. They played accordingly in the first half, shooting a string of magnificent points. A goal by the late Pat Carroll kept Offaly's hopes afloat but they were still well off the pace when they trailed by 0–13 to 1–4 at half-time. It wasn't just the size of the lead, it was more the way it had been established. There was a swagger about everything Galway did while Offaly looked hesitant and uncomfortable.

When Joe Connolly extended Galway's lead just after half-time, neutrals feared the worst. This would be a one-sided second half, perhaps even a rout.

Amazingly, Galway scored just one more point (Noel Lane) for the remainder of the half while Offaly went on to notch 1–8, enough to win the game by three points. Unlike Offaly's late blitz against Limerick in the

1994 final, this was far more structured. The comeback began slowly. Increased pressure, more confidence, a point here and there. Psychologically those points were very important as Offaly began to spot a chink of hope: 'Hey, this lot are getting rattled. If we keep at them, they will crack.'

Wing-back, Aidan Fogarty switched positions with centre-half, Pat Delaney, which proved a double bonus. Fogarty was a more solid stopper while Delaney thrived in the freedom of the wing, bursting upfield in inspirational drives on several occasions. It was only when Offaly had cut the lead to three points that Galway seemed to wake up to the fact that they were in trouble. A good move gave Noel Lane a goal chance and while his shot was powerfully struck, Damien Martin made a smashing save, deflecting the ball out for a '70', which Iggy Clarke hoisted wide.

A Johnny Flaherty point cut the lead to two points with five minutes left. Two minutes later, Offaly struck for the tie-breaker. Delaney started the move with another upfield run, passed to Brendan Bermingham who drew the Galway cover before passing to Flaherty. Galway goalie, Mike Conneely tried to close him down but Flaherty flicked the ball over his shoulder and into the net. Offaly 2–10 Galway 0–15. Having built an unstoppable momentum, Offaly kept up the pressure and Danny Owens and Padraig Horan shot two more points to seal a splendid victory.

As Galway fans looked for excuses, all sorts of rumours hit the hurling circuit, the most popular being that there had been a row in the dressing-room at half-time. Utter nonsense, of course, but a losing county can be amazingly fertile when it comes to producing fairy tales.

The truth was that Offaly had shown greater application and toughness. They were a very strong team in a mental sense. They were also physically powerful right up the middle where Damien Martin, Eugene Coughlan, Pat Delaney, Joachim Kelly, the under-rated Brendan Bermingham and team captain, Padraig Horan all had strength and character to burn.

In the end, it was those two attributes, liberally sprinkled with some delightful skills, which won the 1981 All-Ireland title for Offaly. Galway had both in glorious abundance in 1980 and while they might well have won the 1981 final too, subsequent events suggested that the team no longer possessed the obsession for success, which saw them through the previous year's campaign. Offaly were hungrier for the title and ultimately that enabled them to overcome all other problems to carve their own special place in the county's sporting history.

OFFALY (All-Ireland final 1981): Damien Martin; Tom Donoghue, Eugene Coughlan, Pat Fleury; Aidan Fogarty, Pat Delaney, Ger Coughlan; Joachim Kelly, Liam Currams; Paddy Kirwan, Brendan Bermingham, Mark Corrigan; Pat Carroll, Padraig Horan, Johnny Flaherty.
Subs: Brendan Keeshan for Donoghue, Danny Owens for Kirwan.

Galway 1980

(Awaking The West After 57 Years)

Eyre Square had never seen anything like it. It was as if the whole of Co. Galway had slammed their doors behind them and headed for the city, eager to be part of one of the greatest nights in the county's sporting history.

While it was impossible to put a precise figure on the number of people who turned out to welcome home the Galway team after winning the 1980 All-Ireland hurling final, informed estimates placed it at somewhere over the 30,000 mark. It was 2 a.m. on the Tuesday morning, several hours behind schedule, when the coach carrying the triumphant squad eventually arrived in Galway city. It was that sort of occasion.

From the moment the team crossed the bridge of Athlone, it was as if the entire county had been raised on a platform and was now staring down at the rest of the hurling world. At last Galway hurling was on top... ahead of the Corks, Kilkennys, Tipperarys and the Limericks. Yes, Limerick. Nobody in a thronged Eyre Square thought very much about Limerick that night. A subdued Limerick had returned home earlier, trapped in a curious twilight zone. For while they were bitterly disappointed at having lost an All-Ireland final, they derived some consolation from the thought that, if they had to lose, better that it should happen against a county like Galway, which had been in isolation for so long. Fifty-seven years, to be exact.

Not only that, but Galway had endured some awful times in those lean, lonely years. Like the 1960s, for instance, when Galway made the fatal mistake of competing in the Munster championship where they lost eleven of twelve games, many of them by huge margins. They started the decade with a 7–11 to 0–8 defeat by Waterford and finished it with a 3–15 to 1–10 hammering by Cork. Eleven years later, they had the McCarthy Cup in their grasp. The re-birth of Galway hurling was complete.

Galway's 1980 success was the product of patience, courage, commitment and effort over several years. Yes, and planning too.

Essentially, it began in the 1960s at a time when the senior team was making no progress in Munster. It was decided that the only viable way forward was to start with juvenile players and build up slowly and carefully. A great many dedicated people put a huge amount of work into it and gradually, the rewards began to emerge.

An All-Ireland U-21 title in 1972 and a very close call for the minors (they lost by a point to Kilkenny) in the 1973 final was followed by a National League final win by the seniors in 1975 and an All-Ireland final appearance later that year where they lost to Kilkenny. The 1975 League win was a watershed for Galway hurling. Masterminded by the late M.J. 'Inky' Flaherty, it was their first League success since 1951 and had been achieved off a triple win against hurling's super powers, Cork, Kilkenny and Tipperary in the quarter-final, semi-final and final. Galway followed up with another win over Cork in the All-Ireland semi-final but were well beaten by Kilkenny in the final.

Nevertheless, the script was going very much to plan for Galway as they headed into the second half of the 1970s. Expectations had been raised and the county began to believe that an All-Ireland senior title was a real probability before the end of the decade. Then, for some strange reason, Galway hit the 'wall.' They lost three consecutive All-Ireland semi-finals in 1976–77–78 to Wexford, Cork and Kilkenny. Depression was setting in, especially after Galway were wiped out by Tipperary in the 1979 League final.

As Galway trooped out of Limerick that evening after losing by 3–15 to 0-8 it was impossible to locate any hopeful signs for the championship, particularly when All-Ireland three-in-a-row champions, Cork retained the Munster title. But, as Galway would prove over and over again in the 1980s, the element of surprise was a formidable weapon in their kit bag. Cork, the reddest of red-hot favourites to beat Galway in the 1979 semi-final, were stunned by a brilliant display and eventually lost by four points.

If the 1980 final has gone down in Galway history as a match to remember, the 1979 final was very definitely one to forget. Pumped high by the adrenalin of expectation, Galway forgot to hurl and virtually handed crafty Kilkenny the title. It was by no means a great Kilkenny performance — it didn't have to be. Galway led by 1–8 to 1–6 thirteen minutes into the second half but failed to score for the remainder of the game. They even missed a penalty as their game plan completely fell asunder. Meanwhile, Kilkenny scored another 1–6 to win by 2–12 to 1–8.

Babs' Keating was Galway coach that year. It was his second term with Galway, having also been there in 1977. Joe McGrath had been drafted in to coach the team in 1978. This 'foreign' policy looked good in theory but in practice it simply didn't work. There was a significant development later on in 1979 when Galway won the U-21 title, beating Tipperary in a replay. Cyril Farrell, who had been senior trainer, was coach/trainer to the U-21 side and it was decided to appoint him as senior manager for 1980. 'Inky' Flaherty and Bernie O'Connor were appointed co-selectors.

Farrell's appointment did not please the more senior players. Farrell had never played at inter-county level other than in a few challenge games. Galway's experienced players, who had operated at the highest level for the five previous seasons, felt he lacked the expertise necessary to manage a senior team. Farrell knew their feelings but decided to ignore them.

> The fact was that they had failed. I didn't give a damn what they thought of me. I knew as much about winning as they did. I made up my mind that, whatever happened, I would do things my way. The only opinions I listened to were Bernie's and Inky's because they were the only ones who counted. Galway had looked over the wall for outside help in previous years. Now it was my turn and I was going to give it my best shot, irrespective of what the older players thought. If they wanted to be part of the squad, fine, but they would be there on my terms, not theirs.

His new regime was tough. Some of the panel thought he was plain mad when he had them hurling as early as 6 January on cold, wet, miserable days and nights. Farrell himself had a plan. 'Without actually saying anything about it, I decided that we should make a push for the Railway Cup. Connacht hadn't won it since 1947 so it was well worth pursuing,' said Farrell. His plan worked and Galway (Connacht) beat both Leinster and Munster. So far, so good.

Over the years, Kilkenny had been a real bogey team for Galway. So when Offaly chose 1980 to make the breakthrough and win their first ever Leinster title by beating Kilkenny, it was seen a major plus for Galway. For while Offaly were undoubtedly a good team, they held no psychological edge over Galway.

Galway beat Offaly in the All-Ireland semi-final but not without all sorts of trouble. Galway were nine points clear with thirteen minutes left but leaked goals at an alarming rate and just held on for a 4–9 to 3–10 win. Frankly, it was not an All-Ireland winning performance. Galway had shot several woeful wides; goalie Mike Connolly had played poorly; Sylvie Linnane had been sent off and Iggy Clarke had wrecked his shoulder, an injury which would keep him out of the final. Is it any wonder that Limerick, who had dethroned Cork in Munster, were installed as 4/6 favourites to win the final?

With doubts about Linnane's availability for the final, Galway sent an SOS to Conor Hayes, who was working in Holland for the summer. Hayes, a star of the previous year's U-21 team, had been ruled out earlier in the season due to a thumb injury and had decided to take a summer job in Holland. Suddenly, he had Farrell on the phone, pleading with him to come home and train for the final. Farrell had a plan in mind. With Clarke out, he wanted Seamus Coen, who had been at corner-back against Offaly, to switch to left half-back, with Hayes coming in at No.2.

The tension in Galway in the run-up to the final was incredible. For while the side had not played well against Offaly, there was a sense of destiny around the county. Surely, at last, Galway would get it right on the big day. They did. Inside ten minutes, Galway were 2–1 to 0–0 ahead, thanks to goals by Bernie Forde and P.J. Molloy and a pointed free by captain, Joe Connolly. Galway were far sharper than in the semi-final with corner-forwards, Bernie Forde and Noel Lane especially lively.

One of Galway's biggest fears going into the final centred on the Limerick full-forward line of Ollie O'Connor, Joe McKenna and Eamonn Cregan. McKenna was very much the goal-scoring king around then, while Cregan was the supreme opportunist in the corner, as he showed when he rose to flick the ball to the Galway net. Galway led by 2–7 to 1–5 at half-time and still had five points to spare with ten minutes to go. Then Cregan blasted a penalty to the net to set up a storming finish. This time, Galway held their nerve. Conor Hayes made a magnificent interception from a Cregan pass to McKenna, saving a certain goal. Earlier, Mike Conneely, who gave a superb performance, made a stunning stop from McKenna.

John Ryan, who had come as a Galway sub, put Galway four points clear late on but Limerick had one final chance when they were awarded another penalty. Cregan's drive for goal was powerfully struck but was deflected over the bar by a desperate Galway stick. Galway 2–15 Limerick 3–9. Champions at last!

Cyril Farrell recalls the scenes which followed as being among the most emotional ever witnessed in Croke Park. 'It was as if a giant gusher had opened in front of the Hogan Stand and we were being hoisted higher and higher by its magical force. We had finally made it. The years of frustration counted for nothing now. That's the great thing about sport. It doesn't matter how much disappointment you endure — it can all be wiped away with one big win,' said Farrell.

It was altogether fitting that Galway had a Connolly as captain. Joe, the youngest of the three brothers on the team, had been chosen by the team management the previous autumn because he represented neither the old guard nor the new set. Farrell knew him well from his UCG days and calculated that he would be a unifying force. He also believed that, far from affecting his own game, the captaincy would bring the best out of Joe. He was right on both counts. Joe's older brother, John was at full-forward while Michael lined out at midfield, making it a special family day for Galway's most popular hurling family.

Joe's 'People of Galway' speech from the presentation podium on the Hogan Stand brought tears to the eyes of Galway people at home and abroad. Current GAA President-Elect, Joe McDonagh, who had been a sub after captaining the team in the 1979 final, followed up with a lovely rendition of *The West's Awake*. The beautiful song had a special significance on that particular September afternoon. Truly, the west was awake.

GALWAY: (All-Ireland hurling final 1980): Michael Conneely; Conor Hayes, Niall McInerney, Jimmy Cooney; Sylvie Linnane, Sean Silke, Seamus Coen; Steve Mahon, Michael Connolly; Frank Burke, Joe Connolly, P.J.Molloy; Bernie Forde, John Connolly, Noel Lane.

Subs: John Ryan for Molloy, Finbar Gantley for Michael Connolly.

Chapter 2

✢ ✢ ✢

Memorable Comebacks

In 1990, Cork hurlers peered up the intimidating slopes of an All-Ireland final and saw Galway preparing to place the maroon and white flag on the summit. From somewhere inside their spirit, Cork found the strength to go in pursuit. They did it with a relentless streak of determination and self-belief which eventually enabled them to out-pace Galway and reach the top first. It was an amazing final. Galway had scored 2–21 and still lost while Cork had survived a second-quarter blitz which would have buried most teams.

Ten months later, the same Cork team looked back down from another mountain and saw Tipperary gathering pace back in the foothills of a Munster final replay. Of all teams, Cork might be expected to know how to cope. But no, they too got lost in the high altitude fog while Tipperary charted a rapid climb which brought them to the peak ahead of a bewildered Cork.

Great comebacks are an exciting and integral part of Gaelic Games. While analysts attempt to attach rational explanations to them, usually based on tactical and managerial considerations, the truth is that nobody can explain precisely how a team which is facing a big lead can turn a game around, often amazingly quickly.

The Offaly hurlers' dramatic revival in the 1994 All-Ireland final was a typical example. Five points down to Limerick after sixty-five minutes, they scored 2–5 in five incredible minutes to win by six points. Limerick, who had played so well for so long, were rooted to the ground as Offaly ran them off the pitch in an incredible final drive.

Meath footballers always had a reputation for putting together great rescue packages in difficult situations. Never was that quality more obvious that in the third replay of the record-breaking Leinster championship saga against Dublin in 1991. Six points down after playing poorly, Meath made one final appeal to their instincts and were rewarded with a sensational surge which earned them a one-point win. In 1996 they produced two more amazing comebacks, twice coming from behind against Mayo in the drawn and replayed All-Ireland finals.

While Meath's heart for battle, irrespective of the odds, is legendary, Kildare footballers have acquired something of an opposite reputation, regularly collapsing in games which seem to be going their way. However, Kildare too joined the great comeback club with one marvellous recovery. It came in the 1993 Leinster championship when they staged a storming second-half revival to beat Wicklow in Croke Park. Just two weeks earlier, Armagh had pulled off an even more dramatic comeback against Fermanagh in the Ulster championship. Armagh were trailing by eight points in the 67th minute but hit Fermanagh with three stunning goals to win the game by a point.

Great comebacks are an essential part of GAA life since they provide precious hope for players when things are going wrong. This chapter is a celebration of seven of the more dramatic revival stories of the 1990s.

Five Minutes Which Ruined Limerick

Offaly 3–16 Limerick 2–13
(All-Ireland Hurling Final 1994).

All his life Gary Kirby had dreamed about the moment. Now it was about to happen. Just another five minutes and he would be heading for the steps of the Hogan Stand to receive the McCarthy Cup. He could see it now, an ocean of green and white below him as Limerick fans celebrated the county's first All-Ireland senior hurling title since 1973. Five more minutes....

Brian Whelehan, who had switched to centre-back to mark Kirby, had virtually conceded to the inevitable. Standing alongside each other, Kirby understood Whelehan's frustration as Offaly shot another wide. Kirby had known disappointing times too. The clock ticked on. Offaly captain, Martin Hanamy had made a mental note of the time the second half had started and as he stared up at the Croke Park clock, it confirmed the worst.

Time was running out on Offaly. Rapidly. Five minutes to go, plus a little bit of injury time. Limerick 2–13 Offaly 1–11. No way back.

Offaly were looking like a beaten team. Heads had dropped and one or two of the forwards, in particular, were not showing any great eagerness to get into the action. Runs were being made but with no apparent conviction. Avoiding the ball meant avoiding responsibility. The spirit was almost broken. Hill 16, which had been almost an exclusive Offaly reserve, was silent and sad. The exits were beginning to do good business as dejected Offaly fans made an early departure.

They would take bitter memories with them. Offaly had rarely functioned to the levels which saw them comprehensively out-play Kilkenny, Wexford and Galway *en route* to the final. Joe Dooley's third-minute goal should have been the fuse to light Offaly's fire but Limerick corner-forward, Damien Quigley had cancelled it out by the fifth minute. Things were pretty even for the next fifteen minutes, even if there were some ominous signs for Offaly. Quigley had the beating of Shane McGuckian down the left hand side; Gary Kirby was getting the better of Offaly centre-back, Hubert Rigney while Ger Hegarty was a commanding figure at No.6 for Limerick.

All season, Offaly had led from the start, never allowing Kilkenny, Wexford or Galway to settle into any rhythm. Now, for the first time, Offaly were facing a whole new examination. How would they cope when they fell behind? The final fifteen minutes of the first half were a nightmare for Offaly.

Limerick's all-round dominance had to be reflected on the scoreboard. In fact, they scored 1–4, the second goal coming in the 28th minute when Quigley doubled on Ciaran Carey's centre and whipped the ball past Jim Troy. Johnny Dooley 's pointed free for Offaly in injury-time broke the spell but by half-time, Limerick were in a very comfortable position when they led by 2–8 to 1–5. The fact that they had shot twelve wides did not seem especially significant at that stage because there was no sign that Offaly would be good enough to launch the sort of comeback which might actually win the game.

Conscious of Quigley's capacity to ruin them (he scored 2–2 from play in the first half), Offaly brought in Joe Errity for the luckless McGuckian in the 30th minute. Errity fared little better and it wasn't until captain, Martin Hanamy switched over to mark Quigley that Offaly sorted out that particular problem. Indeed, had Offaly lost the game the team management would have had a lot of explaining to do as to why they didn't switch Hanamy over on Quigley earlier.

Limerick were prepared for an Offaly blitz early in the second half and it duly came. They scored four points in the opening ten minutes to cut the lead to (2–8 to 1–9) but significantly, there were no signs of panic in the Limerick ranks. It was as if they were on a damage limitation exercise, convinced that they could eventually quell the Offaly rebellion, step up a gear and win the match. They succeeded in the first two objectives. Kirby's pointed free in the 48th minute was the start of a ten-minute period of high Limerick productivity. They scored four points and had the very distinct look of All-Ireland champions when they led by 2–12 to 1–9 as the game reached the hour mark. Michael Duignan, who was doing extremely well since coming on as a sub for Daithi Regan, and Johnny Dooley, knocked over two Offaly points. As Gary Kirby faced up to a free in the 65th minute, he assumed that if he pointed it, there would be no way back for Offaly. Limerick were lucky to have been awarded the free as Limerick pair, Ger Hegarty and T.J. Ryan actually collided with each other. Neither was fouled but the free still went Limerick's way. 'Not my problem', Kirby thought to himself as he slotted the ball over the bar. Limerick 2–13 Offaly 1–11. Time elapsed: 64 minutes.

Offaly goalie, Jim Troy hoisted the puck-out into Limerick territory. Johnny Dooley gathered and lobbed it towards his brother, Billy, who was fouled. Limerick lined up six defenders in the goal but Johnny Dooley managed to squeeze the free between Dave Clarke and Ciaran Carey for a goal. Limerick 2–13 Offaly 2–11.

Limerick goalie, Joe Quaid took the puck-out very quickly. He was later criticised for this on the basis that he should have taken his time and allowed his colleagues to settle outfield. Limerick's Ger Hegarty won possession but lost the ball and Johnny Pilkington fired in a high, hopeful lob towards goal. The Limerick full-back line was caught flat-footed and Offaly sub, Pat O'Connor galloped in and whipped the ball to the net. Offaly 3–11 Limerick 2–13.

Once again, Limerick won possession from the puck-out but carelessly lost it and the ball was whipped down into their half. Dave Clarke got it but was dispossessed by Billy Dooley. Brendan Kelly picked up the loose ball, flicked it out to the unmarked Johnny Dooley who scored a point. Offaly 3–12 Limerick 2–13.

Yet again, Limerick lost possession from the puck-out. The ball was transferred from Hubert Rigney to Johnny Pilkington who fed John Troy. Another point. Offaly 3–13 Limerick 2–13.

Limerick were now in chaos. They won possession from the puck-out but Ger Hegarty's shot was blocked and cleared by Joe Errity. Billy Dooley picked up and hit another point. Offaly 3–14 Limerick 2–13.

Johnny Pilkington took the puck-out but knocked his shot over the sideline. Joe O'Connor's cut was missed by Mike Houlihan. John Troy collected, fed Billy Dooley, who scored another point. Offaly 3–15 Limerick 2–13.

Brendan Kelly continued the Limerick misery by winning the puck-out. He passed to Billy Dooley , who scored his third consecutive point. Offaly 3–16 Limerick 2–13.

Offaly's amazing 2–5 blitz had been scored in just four mins fifty-two seconds. During that time, Offaly players either had the ball or made a clean strike on twenty-nine occasions, compared with thirteen for Limerick. That statistic goes some way to explaining *how* it all went so horribly wrong for Limerick. However, it does not explain *why* it went so wrong. Nothing ever will.

The scenes at the finish were unbelievable. Some Offaly fans, who had left the ground before their side started the comeback surge, galloped back to watch Martin Hanamy being presented with the McCarthy Cup. Even the Offaly players looked mesmerised. Most of them admitted that they thought their chance was gone, once Limerick went five points clear with five minutes to go. There was a curious atmosphere in the Limerick dressing-room afterwards. It was as if they were in a state of shock and could not come to terms with what had happened. Close your eyes and you see the McCarthy Cup in front of you. Open them and it's gone. Limerick's return home on the Monday night was one of the most emotional every witnessed. Players cried openly as they faced the mass of fans who had turned out to greet them. They felt that they had let themselves, their supporters and their county down. Untrue, of course, but try telling that to any player who has lost an All-Ireland final in such amazing circumstances.

As the days passed, the inevitable search for scapegoats began. The losing team manager is always an easy target for disappointed supporters so Tom Ryan's role came under intense scrutiny. It was alleged that he was out-thought by another Limerick man, rival manager, Eamonn Cregan. The basis for that assessment was downright spurious. Ryan's tactics had worked well enough for sixty-five minutes so how could he possibly have realised that the roof would cave in the final minutes?

Besides if Limerick had won Cregan would have been blamed for taking so long to sort out the Damien Quigley problem? The reality of modern management is that winners are always deemed to have got it right while losers get it wrong. That may be straight from the kindergarten school of analysis but it's part of present-day GAA life.

What happened in the closing minutes of the 1994 All-Ireland final had nothing to do with the respective managements. Quite simply, Offaly scored two goals, both of which could be put down to defensive errors. Certainly, the alignment of the Limerick defence for Johnny Dooley goal's was suspect while the full-back line was woefully lax for Pat O'Connor's goal. Limerick's big-time inexperience told after that. O'Connor's goal put Offaly a point ahead but instead of holding their shape and their concentration, Limerick panicked.

Forwards tried to rescue the match on their own, rather than maintaining the systematic approach which had served them well earlier on while defenders became so desperate to clear the ball that they forgot about basic marking duties. That combination of errors was critical.

OFFALY: Jim Troy; Shane McGuckian, Kevin Kinahan, Martin Hanamy; Brian Whelehan, Hubert Rigney, Kevin Martin; Johnny Pilkington (0–2), Daithi Regan; Johnny Dooley (1–5), John Troy (0–1), Joe Dooley (1–2); Billy Dooley (0–5), Brendan Kelly, Declan Pilkington (0–1).
Subs: Michael Duignan for Regan, Pat O'Connor (1–0) for Joe Dooley.

LIMERICK: Joe Quaid; Seamus McDonagh, Mike Nash, Joe O'Connor; David Clarke, Ger Hegarty, Declan Nash; Ciaran Carey (0–2), Mike Houlihan (0–1); Frankie Carroll, Gary Kirby (0–6), Mike Galligan; T.J. Ryan, Pat Heffernan, Damien Quigley (2–3).
Sub: Leo O'Connor (0–1) for Galligan.

Winners, All White

Kildare 2–13 Wicklow 2–11 (Leinster Football Championship 1993)

Kildare footballers and great comebacks are not instantly recognisable companions. Not in latter times anyway. Quite the opposite, in fact.

Mention Kildare to your average football supporter and the response will run like this: 'always promising, never delivering; lack heart on the big day; too much flash, not enough dash; forwards who cannot shoot straight; made a big mistake to let two of their best players, Larry Tompkins and Shea Fahy switch to Cork; thought Mick O'Dwyer could solve all their problems just by joining them.'

So why then can a county which hasn't won a Leinster senior title since 1956 continue to create a sense of excitement every time they string a few decent results together? How come that virtually every year some expert or other will predict the end of Kildare's barren run in Leinster?

Tradition plays its part. For while Kildare haven't sat at football's élite table for a long time, the fact is that they still rest 9th in the All-Ireland seniors honours list with four titles. Granted, they were achieved way back in the 1920s but nevertheless they provide a foundation for every optimist and dreamer in the county.

When Mick O'Dwyer took over as Kildare manager in September 1990 in the highest-profile coaching appointment in GAA history, the optimists and dreamers couldn't believe their luck. For years they had argued that an injection of expertise was the only requirement to plot Kildare's way to the top.

O'Dwyer took over in Kildare on a bandwagon of goodwill. Those who queried why there was such excitement over the appointment of a man who couldn't even play for the county, two weeks before two genuine Kildare men, Larry Tompkins and Shea Fahy, were due to line out for Cork in the All-Ireland final were told to be quiet. This was a new era for Kildare football. Larry and Shea who?

O'Dwyer did make an impact in Kildare. Nobody can dispute that. In his first season in charge, they negotiated a tricky path through Division Two, eventually winning promotion before embarking on a solo run which ignited the county. First Kerry in the League quarter-final, then Donegal in the semi-final.

It was too good to be true. Not only were Kildare in the League final, but O'Dwyer had presided over them as they beat his beloved Kerry *en route* to the decider.

Kildare lost the final to Dublin by two points, a margin which was very definitely respectable enough to convince people that the glory days were ahead. In hindsight, that League final probably represented Kildare's best chance of winning a title under O'Dwyer. Even O'Dwyer was surprised by

Kildare's apparent rate of progress. What was all this about Kildare lacking heart and conviction? At the start of the '91 championship campaign, the signs were that all had changed under O'Dwyer.

It hadn't. Kildare fell at the first hurdle, having failed to get high enough against a Louth team which derived much of its motivation from O'Dwyer's highly publicised presence in the Kildare dug-out. Yet again, Kildare had not delivered on the big day. Kildare enjoyed a better campaign in 1992. Admittedly, they were on the easier side of the Leinster draw (Meath, Dublin, Laois and Louth were all on the other side) but showed positive signs when beating Wicklow by 1–20 to 1–6 in the quarter-final before beating Westmeath by 4–11 to 2–5 in the semi-final. Once again though, they failed against Dublin in the final, 1–13 to 0–10.

Kildare still believed they were making progress. Although there were ever-increasing signs that the bad habits of old were still nagging away, O'Dwyer's positive outlook kept the county buzzing. What the Kildare fans — and indeed the team — needed was a definite sign that something fundamental had changed. For instance, could Kildare cope with a situation where they faced a big lead? Did they have the heart for a fight?

The answer to that came in Croke Park on 6 June 1993 when Wicklow presented Kildare with the sort of target which would have sent them galloping out the gate in previous times. After beating Wicklow by fourteen points in the 1992 championship, Kildare quite understandably believed that, while it might not be as easy this time, they would still have more than enough ammunition to shoot down their neighbours. Nothing happened in the first twenty-five minutes to suggest any deviation from the script. Wicklow, with the wind behind them, were leading by 0–5 to 0–3 and while they were also in command territorially, there was a general feeling about that once Kildare settled into their routine in the second half they would quickly take control.

Two minutes later, Wicklow launched the blitz which was to set the scene for a remarkable second half. Terry Allen climbed highest to flick a Raymond Danne free to the net. Niall Buckley's point provided a brief respite for Kildare but Conan Daye and Robert McHugh shot two more Wicklow points before Daye pounced after sloppy defensive work to shoot a second goal. Half-time: Wicklow 2–7 Kildare 0–4.

The Kildare team sprinted to the dressing-room like demented rabbits. Whether their urgency was due to embarrassment or a wish to get the quietest corner before O'Dwyer arrived in is open to question. Suffice to say, O'Dwyer delivered a pretty straight forward analysis of Kildare's first-half 'efforts'. He told them that they had a choice. Either watch three years' work go down the drain or go out and win the match. Given Kildare's history, nobody could be quite sure which option they would choose.

This time, they went for the positive one. In fact, Kildare took just eleven minutes to wipe out Wicklow's nine-point lead. By any standards, it was an amazing comeback. Kildare scored 1–6 without reply in a great salvo, the goal coming from Martin Lynch. With the sides level and twenty-four minutes to go, suddenly the betting had changed. Now it was odds-on an easy Kildare win. With most other top counties it would have been but no sooner had Kildare struggled out of one hole but they fell into another.

Fergus Daly regained control around midfield and, once again, Wicklow began to assert themselves. In fact, they had pulled three points clear by the 65th minute. Could Kildare recover a second time? They could. Kildare needed a goal to survive and they managed to engineer it. Martin Lynch twisted and turned as he tried to wriggle through the Wicklow defence and while there may have been legitimate question marks about whether or not he over-carried the ball, he kept going and rifled in the equalising goal. This time, Kildare were not going to discard the fruits of their second revival and in the closing seconds, sub Dermot Doyle and Paul McLoughlin added two points to win the game, 2–13 to 2–11.

Many people thought that game would be a watershed in Kildare's development. Having recovered from what looked an impossible position, they would surely have a lot more confidence in themselves from then on. It didn't work out that way. Kildare lost the Leinster final to Dublin by 0–11 to 0–7 in a game where they were caught in a tactical bind. They did well in a containing role in the first half and looked to be in a great position when they trailed by just one point (0–3 to 0–2) at half-time. However, once the pattern of play opened up in the second half, it was Dublin who prospered. Their score-to-chance ratio was much better than Kildare's and they won pretty comfortably in the end.

A year later, the Leinster draw took a less kind look on Kildare, matching them with Dublin in the very first round. Of all their championship clashes with Dublin, this was one they definitely should have won but, in the end, they were betrayed by insecurity. Dublin, despite playing poorly, grabbed a draw before going on to win the replay comfortably, 1–14 to 1–9.

KILDARE (v Wicklow 1993): Kieran Moran; Denis Dalton, John Crofton, Seamus Dowling; Ken Doyle, Denis O'Connell, Glen Ryan; David Malone, Sean McGovern; Anthony Rainbow (0-1), Martin Lynch (2–0), Niall Buckley (0–6); Liam Miley, Paul McLoughlin (0–3), Johnny McDonald (0–2).

Subs: Tom Harris for Malone, Dermot Doyle (0–1) for McGovern, Brian Nolan for Harris.

WICKLOW: John Walsh; Donal Lenehan, Hugh Kenny, Brendan Brady; Billy Kenny, Raymond Danne, Michael Murtagh; Fergus Daly (0–1) Pat O'Byrne; Ken Cunningham (0–1), Kevin O'Brien, Terry Allen (1–0); Conan Daye (1–6), Ronan Coffey, Robert McHugh (0–3).

Subs: Ashley O'Sullivan for Lenehan, T. Doyle for Cunningham.

Hollywood Glitz, Armagh Blitz

Armagh 4–8 Fermanagh 1–16
(Ulster Football Championship 1993)

Seldom in their history have Fermanagh footballers scored seventeen times in an Ulster championship game. On only a few occasions have they led a championship game by eight points with less than three minutes of normal time remaining. Put the two together and you have the sort of blissful occasion which should forever remain etched on the memories of Fermanagh supporters.

Let's take it a step further. Give Fermanagh an extra man as well. Throw in the fact that the opposition have missed a penalty and are looking totally washed up and you can have only one result — an easy Fermanagh win. Not when the game in question is a first round Ulster championship replay against Armagh in the Athletic Grounds on 23 May 1993.

Many of the crowd left the ground early that day, convinced that Fermanagh had pulled off a famous win on 'enemy' territory. They sat into their cars, switched on the radios to pick up other results from around the country and could scarcely believe their ears. By some outrageous fluke Armagh had come back to win.

Impossible! Weren't Fermanagh leading by 1–15 to 1–7 as the game ticked toward the 68th minute. Surely an Armagh attack which had scored just two goals up to then in the two games against Fermanagh couldn't score three in two minutes. They could and they did. Events in the Athletic Grounds on that May Sunday will never be forgotten, especially by Fermanagh fans who stood in silent horror as yet another season blew apart, having been detonated by their own team.

Fermanagh went into that championship with very high hopes. The experimental League system, which had been in operation in the previous winter/spring, had shown Fermanagh in a very positive light. Operating in Section C, together with Kerry, Mayo, Armagh, Tyrone, Wicklow, Laois and Kilkenny, they had made a magnificent start, reeling off four straight wins in the pre-Christmas games.

Three of their victims were Tyrone, Laois and Wicklow, teams whose ambition would normally be pitched far higher than a win over Fermanagh. However, all three found Fermanagh far from willing victims this time and, when the League broke for Christmas, Fermanagh were sharing the top spot with Kerry and Mayo, who were also unbeaten. Fermanagh's profile had been raised dramatically. They became the centre of media attention as journalists zoomed in on their progress, dissecting and analysing it from every angle. Fermanagh glowed under the spotlight. For once, things were going their way.

Admittedly, Fermanagh's toughest matches were to come in the spring but the early power surge had generated so much optimism in Fermanagh that they were extremely hopeful of winning at least one more game. If other results went their way, two more League points might just be enough to take them into Division One of the League for the following season.

First up in 1993 was a game against Mayo in Lisnaskea, which drew a huge crowd. Fermanagh had prepared very well for the resumption of the League but, unfortunately for them, they seemed to tense up against Mayo and lost by 0–13 to 1–6 in a rather poor game. Mayo led by three points just after half-time and while a Mark Gallagher goal raised Fermanagh hopes, they ran out of momentum. All round it was a depressing day. The team felt that they had let a lot of people down while the management began to wonder if the side was capable of coping with pressure.

Two weeks later, Fermanagh lost to Armagh by 1–8 to 0–9 in Lurgan. More disappointment but this time there were some encouraging signs. Fermanagh started sluggishly and were six points behind at half-time but made a very definite statement of intent in the second half, which they won by 0–8 to 0–4. The comeback wasn't enough to save the day but it at least showed that the team had the resolve to battle on when things went against them. Although Fermanagh also lost the final game to Kerry, they were reasonably happy with their overall League effort as it guaranteed them a place in Division Two for the following season, while Armagh and Tyrone were both in Division Three. It was against this background that Fermanagh manager, Hugh McCabe took his team into the first round Ulster championship game against Armagh.

A crowd of 8,000, the vast majority of whom were from Fermanagh, squeezed into Irvinestown, for the preliminary round clash. Early on, it looked as if the occasion would again overwhelm Fermanagh, who were four points down in eleven minutes. In fact, Armagh dominated most of the first half and a Ger Houlahan goal just before the half-time looked as if it might be the tie-breaker, especially when Armagh again stretched their lead to four points shortly after the re-start.

There was a time when such a perilous situation might have been followed by a Fermanagh collapse but the confidence and match-hardiness, which had been acquired during the previous League campaign, came to the side's rescue. A Colm McCreesh goal launched the Fermanagh surge and they led by a point as the game drifted towards the 70th minute. But just when it looked as if they would make it to the quarter-finals Armagh captain, John Rafferty, intervened to shoot the equalising point. An incident which resulted in Fermanagh's John Rehill and Armagh's John Toner being sent to the line nine minutes from the end may have cost Fermanagh dearly as Rehill's absence from the midfield area was especially noticed in the closing minutes.

The replay in the Athletic Grounds a week later was only two minutes old when Armagh were reduced to fourteen men, having had full-back Dominic Clarke sent off for an off-the-ball foul. Even allowing for the historical trend of teams tending to play better with fourteen men, it was still asking an awful lot of Armagh to hold out for sixty-eight minutes with fourteen players. Fermanagh had most of the possession right through the first half but wasted much of it and were just one point clear (0–7 to 1–3) at the break. Armagh levelled just after half-time, which looked ominous for the visitors, but suddenly Fermanagh clicked into overdrive and scored an amazing 1–8 without reply. Armagh even missed a penalty. It was one of the most productive periods Fermanagh had enjoyed for years in the championship. Young Raymond Gallagher, who had scored 1–8 for the minors a week earlier, was a revelation in attack and his 57th minute goal looked certain to be the match-winner.

Armagh, desperate to re-establish some attacking focus after a long scoreless spell, replaced Ollie Reel with championship debutant, Denis Hollywood in the 54th minute. Hollywood, a member of the St Michael's, Newtownhamilton club, had been voted Division Three player-of-the-year in Armagh a year earlier, but would not have been regarded as the sort who turned round lost causes, especially at this level. When he scored his first goal in the 68th minute, it seemed no more than a consolation effort by a well beaten team. Fermanagh countered straight away with a Mark Gallagher point to lead by 1–16 to 2–7. The game had ticked into injury time when Hollywood kicked a point, followed by another goal to take his personal tally to 2–1 and the score to 1–16 to 3–8. Fermanagh were now in total chaos. Armagh pressed forward once more, sensing that a sensational win was possible. Ciaran McGurk hoisted a high lob into the Fermanagh goal area; Ger Houlahan knocked it down and John Grimley drove it into the net for the winning goal. Unbelievable. Armagh 4–8 Fermanagh 1–16. Final whistle.

Fermanagh manager, Hugh McCabe, made an astonishingly honest admission afterwards, blaming himself for the defeat on the basis that he had brought on a sub which changed the balance and gave Armagh the vital initiative. McCabe was being excessively harsh on himself. Clearly, the responsibility rested with his team, which failed to defend a big lead against fourteen men in the final minutes. By any standards, it was one of the most amazing comebacks in Ulster championship history. It was also one of the luckiest. For while Armagh celebrated their great escape, they knew deep down that this was a game Fermanagh had handed to them. Armagh were greatly encouraged by that win and went on to beat Tyrone (in another replay) in the quarter-final. Yet again, Armagh had to show their survival qualities, coming from behind in both games. Now on a roll, Armagh came within seconds of beating defending All-Ireland champions, Donegal in the semi-final but a late point by John Duffy earned Donegal a replay, which they won comfortably.

Despite losing to Donegal, it had been a most exciting championship for Armagh, who managed to squeeze in six games (two wins, three draws and a defeat). Bemused Fermanagh watched from a distance, still trying to figure out how it all went so wrong for them and wondering what might have happened had they held their nerve in the last five minutes of that remarkable replay against Armagh.

ARMAGH: Brendan Tierney, Colm Hanratty, Dominic Clarke, Mark McNeill, Martin McQuillan, John Grimley (1–0), John Rafferty, Jarlath Burns, Neil Smyth (0–1); Shane McConville, Ger Houlahan (1–0), Barry O'Hagan (0–4); Ollie Reel (0–2), Ciaran McGurk, Damien Horisk.
Subs: Paul McGrane for Burns, Cathal O'Rourke for McConville, Denis Hollywood (2–1) for Reel.

FERMANAGH: Cormac McAdam, Raymond Curran (0–1), Michael O'Brien, Bart O'Brien, Tommy Callaghan, Paddy McGuinness, Tony Collins, Paul Brewster, Brian Carty (0–1), Malachy O'Rourke (0–2), Colie Curran (0–1), Raymond Gallagher (1–6), Mark Gallagher (0–3), Colm McCreesh, Greg McGovern.
Subs: Simon Bradley (0–1) for Callaghan, Paul Coyle for McCreesh, Michael McCaffrey for R.Curran.

Dublin Fall By Royal Command

Meath 2–10 Dublin 0–15
(Third Replay — Leinster Football Championship 1991)

Fourteen minutes into the second half of the third Dublin–Meath replay, Dublin captain, Tommy Carr went off injured. By now, the epic saga had lasted five hours and eighteen minutes and there were still twenty-two minutes to go. High up in the RTE television box on the Hogan Stand, Mick O'Dwyer, who was analysing the game alongside commentator, Ger Canning, remarked: 'Dublin are playing so well at the moment, that I don't think it will make any difference.' O'Dwyer's comments seemed perfectly justified for while Carr had been an inspiring figure in the Dublin defence, events further afield were proving even more influential.

Dublin were leading by 0–11 to 0–6 at the time. Even more importantly, they were playing like a team which had finally solved the Meath puzzle once and for all. Meath, so often the comeback kings, looked remote and switched off. It was as if the great adventure they had embarked upon with Dublin a full five weeks earlier had drained them, physically and psychologically.

Bernie Flynn, the master score-getter, had limped off with a leg injury, sustained in a sprint for possession. The sight of Flynn pulling up in obvious pain while Mick Deegan darted forward to launch yet another

Dublin attack seemed destined to encapsulate the day. Earlier on, Meath had lost Padraig Lyons with a hamstring injury. But at least Lyons had been able to sample the action, unlike Terry Ferguson, who had pulled a muscle in his back while togging out.

Ferguson had come through three of the toughest games in championship history. Now, by some outrageous freak, he had injured his back in the dressing-room while getting ready for the fourth game. Earlier, Sean Kelly had failed a late fitness test on the pitch. Within minutes of the start, Colm O'Rourke took a terrible wallop, which might have forced some other players out of the action. O'Rourke continued but was groggy for some time. Shortly afterwards, Padraig Lyons, who had replaced Ferguson, had to go off. Omens? Yes, and not of the variety which pleased Meath.

As their fans stared wistfully at the scoreboard midway through the second half on that scorching July Saturday, most felt that the gods had finally lost interest in their team. Meath had recovered from a five-point deficit to force a draw in the second replay but it was different this time. There was something horribly flat about the team. 'Dublin are looking very good — they're winning all over the pitch.' Mick O'Dwyer told TV viewers. The margin was now six points.

Meath players admitted afterwards that it was the only time in the four-match series that they began to doubt themselves. Winning the game no longer looked a possibility. Damage limitation was the top priority now. Having played such a huge part in the most dramatic first round championship game in history, the thought of losing the third replay by a big margin was hard to take. As Dublin grew ever more self-assured, it appeared a very likely scenario. But, just when all seemed lost, something stirred deep in Meath's consciousness. Damn it, we cannot let Dublin destroy us now. Not in front of 61,543 spectators in Croke Park and millions of others both at home and abroad (the match was being shown 'live' on RTE television and in selected venues all over the world). The thought of losing to Dublin sickened that particular Meath team. Their immediate predecessors had lived under Dublin's imposing thumb for years. This Meath team had turned things around in 1986 and, apart from 1989, had enjoyed the upperhand against Dublin. Now it seemed they were about to be thrashed by a team that they were very close to hating.

Meath had always flourished when confronted by the prospect of others ridiculing them. For whatever reason, the Meath team of 1986–92 had wrapped itself in paranoia at birth and carried it right through life until

Laois finally administered the last rites in Navan in the 1992 championship. Leinster, All-Ireland and National League titles had all been won but nothing changed. The Meath squad felt that the entire sporting world was against them. They rarely stopped to analyse if that were actually true. Far better to believe the worst and use it as a motivating force.

So as the Meath team faced up to a 0–12 to 0–6 scoreline shortly after 5 p.m. on Saturday, 6 July 1991, they were confronted with a choice. Battle on and hope to get close enough to Dublin to justify the day or fade quietly away as Dublin themselves had done against Meath in the second half of the 1988 National League final replay. The first option was the only viable one, even if Meath were playing poorly. Surely, they could summon some reserve strength for one last fling. After all, it wasn't as if Dublin were supermen. Brian Stafford started the revival with a pointed free. It didn't make much impression on critical eyes in the stand. 'Meath badly need a goal — Dublin are going a lot better at the moment,' remarked Mick O'Dwyer. The badly-needed goal he referred to came in the 54th minute when O'Rourke placed Stafford who drove the ball past John O'Leary.

In the previous three games, that would have the signal for a Meath take-off. Not this time. The goal seemed to fire Dublin more than Meath and they retaliated quickly with points from Mick Galvin and Niall Guiden. Mattie McCabe's point from Meath looked no more than a token gesture of defiance when Dublin broke upfield and a foul on Declan Sheehan earned them a penalty.

Keith Barr was entrusted with the spot-kick and, quite rightly, opted to go for goal. It was argued afterwards that he should have been instructed to kick a point, thereby putting Dublin four points clear. Surely that would have been a sign of weakness, something which Meath would instantly have seized upon, even in their rather unsettled mode. Barr's kick was low and hard to Michael McQuillan's right. It was so close to the upright that commentator, Ger Canning initially called it a goal. Barr's drive had flattened the umpire's flag but, sadly for Dublin, was just outside the post. The kick should have been re-taken as Meath full-back, Mick Lyons was virtually alongside Barr in his run-up.

Not that it seemed to matter a whole lot when Guiden kicked another point to put Dublin four clear. It was the perfect response to Barr's miss and frankly, there seemed no way back for Meath, even when Stafford cut the gap to a goal with a pointed free. When Dublin stormed forward again, it looked all over for Meath. A flowing Dublin move left sub Vinny Murphy with a chance to kick the insurance point but instead he tried to pass the ball to Declan Sheehan. It was knocked away from Sheehan and as Martin O'Connell picked up the ball one foot was actually behind his own goal line. Eleven passes later, Kevin Foley found himself facing an open Dublin goal and he gleefully booted the ball to the net. Meath 2-9 Dublin 0-15. Unbelievable.

The build-up to the goal was a classic mixture of Meath defiance and Dublin innocence. O'Connell found Lyons who poked the ball forward to McCabe. On to Harnan who booted it downfield to O'Rourke. He was fouled by Mick Kennedy as he got possession, took a quick free to his left and found Beggy. One hop, one solo and Beggy despatched it to Foley, who was virtually standing still when he received possession. On to Gillic who flicked it to Dowd. It was at this point that real pace and conviction was injected into the move for the first time. Dowd took the ball at speed about thirty-five yards from the Dublin goal, galloped forward and passed to O'Rourke. Dowd kept on running and took the return pass from O'Rourke. At this stage the goal chance was on for Dowd himself but involved some risk. He glanced across the goal and spotted Foley (of all people) 110 yards from his wing-back berth, waiting unmarked about eight yards out. A quick pass and Foley had the entire goal to aim at before driving the ball to the net.

Dublin's failure to respond to the attack as it developed was beyond comprehension. Kennedy's foul on O'Rourke was the most sensible option as it delayed the Meath approach but from there on the defence was static. The Dublin backs were out of position and with their concentration gone (presumably they thought the game was won), Dowd's injection of pace completely destroyed them.

While Foley's goal will never be forgotten in either Meath or Dublin, it was not the score which won the game. It merely levelled it. From the kick-out, Mattie McCabe fed the captain, Liam Hayes, who galloped up the Hogan Stand side. 'I looked up and decided to have a go for a point. Then I spotted P.J. Gillic in a better position to shoot. I kicked a cross-field pass, which I suppose was risky enough because had it been intercepted Dublin would have been up and running on a counter attack. Thankfully, it found Gillic who passed it on to Beggy and he did the rest,' recalled Hayes. Meath 2–10 Dublin 0–15.

Dublin had one final chance to level the match but Jack Sheedy's long-range free-kick drifted wide on the left. Some Dublin fans were critical of

Sheedy afterwards, claiming that he should have dropped the ball in front of the Meath goal, in the hope that (a) a forward would win possession and score or (b) that Dublin might earn a free-in. After all, there was a draw culture about the game by now and the benefit of the doubt would probably have gone to the attack. Sheedy saw it differently. He reckoned he would get the distance and felt he had to go for a point. Dropping it short would have left him open to accusations of lacking courage.

At last the great saga was over after 340 minutes. That it should end in such amazing circumstances added enormously to the memory of a four-game contest, the likes of which we are unlikely to see again. The four games were watched by a total of 237,000 spectators. More than that, the unprecedented saga gripped the nation in a special way. Even those who had no interest in football at the start of the marathon battle, were captivated by it at the finish. TV viewing figures for the fourth game matched All-Ireland levels, despite the fact that it was on a Saturday afternoon.

In normal circumstances, a team would have won the Leinster title after four games. This time, Meath had played four games (two of which went to extra time) and were still only in the quarter-final against Wicklow. That too finished level. Meath won the replay, hammered Offaly in the semi-final and then comfortably beat Laois in the final, which was played on the second Saturday in August. Meath should also have lost the All-Ireland semi-final. Roscommon were all over them for much of the way but made the fatal mistake of glancing over their shoulders at a crucial stage in the second half to see how far Meath were behind. Meath were experts at spotting that sort of weakness in others and gradually hauled Roscommon back before eventually winning by a point, 0–15 to 1–11.

If Meath had made an art-form of great recoveries that year, they also had a fatal flaw, one which ultimately undermined them. Their inability to limit the damage during bad spells was inexplicable for a team with so much experience and so much talent. It was as if they wanted to play Russian roulette with themselves, rotating the barrel one more time every match they played. Eventually, the bang had to come. When it did, it was swift but nonetheless extremely painful. Down's charge before and after half-time in the All-Ireland took them into a 1–14 to 0–6 lead. Even for Meath that represented the tallest of tall orders. Once more, they summoned on all their survival skills and, as the finishing line beckoned, they were drawing alongside Down. But this time they didn't make it. Time ran out for Meath as Down held on to win by 1–16 to 1–14.

Then, and only then, did Meath get any idea of how Dublin felt on the first Saturday in July. Suddenly, Meath's contribution to a remarkable season counted for nothing. Their championship record read: Played: 10; Won 5; Drew 4, Lost 1. The pain of the defeat by Down still lingers among the Meath players who felt that, having survived for so long, their names were on the Sam Maguire Cup. They weren't, but their names are indelibly printed on the most remarkable first round game of all time. In future years, that will be worth something every time they dust down their scrap books and look back.

MEATH (third replay 1991): Mickey McQuillan; Bobby O'Malley, Mick Lyons, Padraig Lyons; Kevin Foley (1–0), Liam Harnan, Martin O'Connell; Liam Hayes, P.J. Gillic; David Beggy (0–1), Colm O'Rourke, Tommy Dowd; Colm Coyle, Brian Stafford (1–6), Bernie Flynn (0–2).
    Subs: Finian Murtagh for Padraig Lyons, Gerry McEntee for Murtagh, Mattie McCabe (0–1) for Flynn.

DUBLIN: John O'Leary; Mick Deegan, Gerry Hargan, Mick Kennedy; Tommy Carr, Keith Barr, Eamonn Heery; Jack Sheedy, Paul Bealin; Charlie Redmond (0–5), Paul Curran (0–2), Niall Guiden (0–4); Declan Sheehan (0-2), Paul Clarke, Mick Galvin (0–2).
    Subs: Ray Holland for Carr, Joe McNally for Clarke, Vinny Murphy for Redmond.

'There's Nothing To Equal A Cork-Tipp Munster Final'

Tipperary 4–19 Cork 4–15 (Munster Hurling Final Replay 1991)

All great rivalries come in cycles. While they may be bound together by a historical thread, they are very much dependent for survival on a set of circumstances which develop from time to time.

The truly memorable rivalries earn their stature simply because those circumstances come about often enough to leave an imprint on the memory. That has always been the case with Cork and Tipperary hurlers.

By the summer of 1991, their rivalry was in full, flowing tide. Tipperary's re-emergence from exile in 1987 had been achieved at Cork's expense. Not only that, but it had come in a replay against a Cork side which was defending the All-Ireland crown, while also bidding for a sixth consecutive Munster title. A year later, Tipperary had emphasised their new-found status with another victory over Cork in the Munster final. Waterford came between the duelling pair in 1989 when they beat Cork in the Munster semi-final but it was back to the 'Big Two' in 1990 when they again reached the final.

By now, Tipperary were All-Ireland champions, having won the 1989 title. They were also hot favourites to beat Cork, especially as the game was in Thurles. An inspired performance by Mark Foley, who scored 2–7, completely undermined Tipperary and Cork went on to win by 4–16 to 2–14. They crowned the season with an All-Ireland final success against Galway that September.

So when Cork and Tipperary reached the 1991 Munster final, there was a very definite winner-take-all undercurrent attached. Relationships between the counties were somewhat strained after the previous year's events, when it was alleged that Cork had deliberately misrepresented comments made by Tipperary manager, 'Babs' Keating. In the course of a TV interview before the 1990 Munster final, Keating, who regularly threw in horse-racing analogies in hurling discussions, was quoted as saying that 'donkeys don't win derbies.' Keating used it in a general sense but some Cork people chose to see it as an insult to their county and tried to whip up anti-Tipp feelings before the Munster final. It was suggested afterwards that Cork's turbo-charged performance in the final had been fired by the perceived insult. There were also claims that Cork had derived extra motivation from the fact that they were generally written off by the media in 1990.

A year later much had changed. Now Tipperary were outsiders heading into the Munster final, largely because they had to travel to Pairc Uí Chaoimh, a stadium which frowned dismissively on outsiders, even ones with a championship pedigree of Tipperary's calibre. Also, Cork were the defending All-Ireland champions.

The script looked to be going very much to plan for a long time. The Tipperary full-back line of Paul Delaney, Conor O'Donovan and Noel Sheehy were in all sorts of trouble against Ger Fitzgerald, Kevin Hennessy and John Fitzgibbon. 'Each time a ball flew in, prayer, you sensed, was all that might save Tipperary's last line,' wrote Vincent Hogan in the *Irish Independent* the following day.

It took a while for the prayers to be answered, however, as Tipperary were down 3–3 to 0–5 after just 18 minutes. Tipp did restore some equilibrium after that but lost it again early in the second half and, with just fourteen minutes remaining, they were 4–8 to 1–10 behind. Surely Cork would never surrender a seven-point lead on home ground? A leading Cork official had remarked to Galway manager, Cyril Farrell, after the previous year's All-Ireland final, that 'a good team should never lose a seven-point lead.'

Now his words came back to haunt him as Tipperary set about reeling in the champions. Point by point, they chipped away at Cork's lead and then struck for the match-saving goal with ten minutes remaining. Predictably, it was Pat Fox who scored it, darting on to a Michael Ryan clearance to whip the ball past Ger Cunningham. Two Michael Cleary points for Tipp levelled it up before Kevin Hennessy pointed Cork into the lead again.

Then came the incident which is still talked of to this day. Nicky English scampered clear, minus his hurley, but showed beautiful football skills to volley the ball goalwards. It seemed to fly well inside the post but, much to Tipperary's fury, the umpire signalled it wide. Thankfully for Tipperary — and indeed all those with a sense of fair play — there was one more throw of the dice and Pat Fox (who else?) managed to wriggle clear to angle over the equalising point. Cork 4–10 Tipperary 2–16. Back to Semple Stadium two weeks later.

Now the pendulum had swung Tipperary's way. They had survived the Pairc Ui Chaoimh test in style, recovering from a seven-point deficit in a truly magnificent game. Surely, things would be easier for them in Thurles. Or would they? The fact was that despite Tipperary's great pedigree they had not won a Munster title in Thurles since 1960, when they beat Cork by 4–13 to 4–11. That statistic looked more significant than it really was, since most Munster finals, involving Tipperary were played elsewhere. Nevertheless, it served as a reminder to the Tipperary team that Semple Stadium bestowed no obvious historical advantages despite the general assumption that it would.

That certainly looked to be the case when Cork recovered from an early three-point deficit to lead by 1–6 to 0–4 after John Fitzgibbon had scored the first of eight goals in the 18th minute. To add to Tipperary's problems, they had to line out without the injured Nicky English. By half-time it was 2–8 to 1–7 in Cork's favour. Twelve minutes into the second half it was 3–13 to 1–10 for Cork. Even Tipperary's most loyal fans were prepared for the worst, believing that a nine-point deficit was beyond the recovery powers of their side.

Scarcely a blue and gold flag rippled when Pat Fox fired over the first point in what was to launch one of the truly great comebacks of our times. Jimmy Barry Murphy, who was doing the analysis on RTE television alongside commentator Ger Canning, remarked that Fox might have gone for goal as Tipperary desperately needed something special to kick start them back into contention. Despite Cork's big lead, little things were beginning to happen which hinted at a real battle ahead.

John Leahy, who had moved to midfield, was picking and driving a lot of ball; Aidan Ryan, who had come on as a sub for Donie O'Connell was sniping into gaps which didn't appear to be there earlier on and Pat Fox was thinking and reacting that bit quicker than his markers. Fox's 52nd minute goal really ignited Tipp's comeback fuse. A few earlier Tipperary points, which seemed no more than a futile attempt at gaining respectability at the time, took on a whole new dimension when Fox out-thought, and out-ran the Cork defence to flick the ball one-handed to the net for a super goal. It was a typical Fox goal, conceived by speed of mind and executed with beautiful dexterity. Cork 3–13 Tipperary 2–13.

A couple of swapped points still left a goal between the sides with eleven minutes remaining. Then, as if on cue from the gods, Tipperary captain, Declan Carr somehow got his hurley higher than the thicket of ash which awaited a dropping ball in the Cork goalmouth to hook the sliothar past Ger Cunningham for the equalising goal. Aidan Ryan pointed Tipp ahead; Pat Buckley equalised and it was still all square with just two minutes to go. As in 1987, extra time beckoned, or so it seemed. But the drama was far from over in this amazing game. Cormac Bonner and Pat Fox drove over two points in a minute and, as the game headed into injury time, Aidan Ryan blocked down a Sean O'Gorman clearance, scooped the ball past another defender before picking it up and despatching it to the Cork net.

In the space of twenty-four amazing minutes, Tipperary had turned a nine-point deficit into a five-point lead, outscoring Cork by 3–7 to 0–2 in the process. And still the drama continued. A series of stoppages due to intrusions around the Cork goal in the second half meant that referee, Terence Murray played almost six minutes of injury time.

Cork re-grouped for one desperate fling and John Fitzgibbon drove in their fourth goal from a free to cut the lead to two points. This time though, there was to be no stopping Tipperary and Michael Cleary wriggled clear twice in the last minute to shoot two more points. Tipperary 4–19 Cork 4–15.

It truly was an amazing game, one which had provided 42 scores while a mere 19 frees had been conceded. Its satisfaction rating was all the higher for Tipperary because of the extraordinary manner in which they had come from so far behind to beat a Cork side which had shown themselves to be the masters of the comeback only ten months earlier.

'There's nothing to equal a Cork–Tipp Munster final. Everyone knows that and everyone envies us that,' remarked 'Babs' Keating afterwards. On the evening of 21 July 1991, few would have disputed his claim. Tipperary's amazing win gave them a 3–1 lead with two matches drawn in championship clashes with Cork since 1987. If Tipperary got the impression that they had established a psychological hold over Cork, they were badly mistaken. A year later, it was back to Pairc Ui Chaoimh for the Munster semi-final. Both sides had changed line-ups from the previous year. Richard Browne, Pat Hartnett (although he came on as a sub), Brendan O'Sullivan and Mark Foley were not in Cork's starting line-up, replaced by teenage sensation Brian Corcoran, Denis Mulcahy, Seanie McCarthy and Timmy Kelleher. Meanwhile Michael Ryan, John Madden and Donie O'Connell, all of whom had started for Tipperary in the famous 1991 replay, were replaced by George Frend, Nicholas English and Aidan Ryan, who had come on as a sub a year earlier.

Corcoran was designated to mark Fox, who was now regarded in Cork as more lethal than English. It worked to perfection. Corcoran's precocious skills were the ideal antidote to Fox's multi-talents. Fox was restricted to just two points, compared to the 1–5 he scored in the 1991 replay. English was held scoreless by Sean O'Gorman in the other corner while Cormac Bonner, the central fulcrum of what had been a deadly full-forward line was replaced at half-time. With this line completely tied up, Tipperary's scoring options were very limited. Not that things were going much better for Cork in the first half. Tipperary led by 0–6 to 0–5 at half-time but Cork increased the tempo on the re-start. John Fitzgibbon's goal started the Cork roll and they eventually won by 2–12 to 1–12. The margin flattered Tipperary somewhat as they trailed by eight points after Tomas Mulcahy scored Cork's second goal ten minutes from the end. Tipperary finished well but this time they lacked the drive and energy which rescued them in 1991.

TIPPERARY (v Cork 1991 Munster final replay): Ken Hogan; Paul Delaney, Noel Sheehy, Michael Ryan; John Madden, Bobby Ryan, Conal Bonner; Declan Carr (1–1), Colm Bonner; Declan Ryan (0–2), Donie O'Connell, John Leahy (0–2); Pat Fox (1–5), Cormac Bonner (0–1), Michael Cleary (1–7).

Subs: Aidan Ryan (1–1) for O'Connell, Joe Hayes for Madden.

CORK: Ger Cunningham; Sean O'Gorman, Richard Browne, Denis Walsh; Cathal Casey (0–1), Jim Cashman (0–3), Pat Hartnett; Brendan O'Sullivan, Teddy McCarthy; Tomas Mulcahy (0–1), Mark Foley, Tony O'Sullivan (0–6); Ger Fitzgerald (1–2), Kevin Hennessy (1–0), John Fitzgibbon (2–1).

Sub: Pat Buckley (0–1) for B.O'Sullivan.

Rebel Stand By Cork

Cork 5–15 Galway 2–21
(All-Ireland Hurling Final 1990)

Shortly before half-time in the 1990 All-Ireland hurling final, Galway centre-forward, Joe Cooney took a pass from Gerry McInerney, steadied himself and drove over his side's thirteenth point. As maroon and white flags danced in appreciation all over Croke Park, Cork centre-back, Jim Cashman banged his hurley in frustration off the ground.

It was turning into one of those days for Cashman. In fact, he was facing a crisis. A player of considerable skill and intelligence, Cashman was trying to devise some method of reducing Cooney's influence on the game. His earlier efforts had failed dismally. Cooney had already scored 1–6, (1–5 from play) in the sort of vintage performance which had almost guaranteed him the man-of-the-match rating even before the half-time whistle had sounded. It was all so horribly depressing for Cashman and, indeed, for Cork. Surely this could not be happening to them. Where was the power and poise which had enabled them to beat reigning All-Ireland champions, Tipperary in the Munster final?

By half-time, Cork were 1–13 to 1–8 behind and counting their blessings. The deficit could have been a lot more.

After a great start (Kevin Hennessy scored a goal in the very first minute), Cork had enjoyed a comfortable first-quarter before being swatted to one side by a rampant Galway side, presided over with elegance and cunning by Cooney. Galway won the second-quarter by 1–8 to 0–2, making Cork look like raw minors who had the audacity to challenge the big boys. Inevitably, Cooney had scored the goal. His initial effort had been smothered by Denis Walsh but Cooney reacted quickest and booted the ball to the net. Galway were dominant right through the field and really should have been miles clear at the break.

Only a few inches separated Noel Lane from a certain goal as he chased a through ball which ran on that little bit too far while Eanna Ryan actually had the ball in the Cork net, only to be whistled back and awarded a free. Cork were in chaos. The attacking machine which had scored 4–16 against Tipperary in the Munster final was getting little quality possession. Midfield was being conceded to Michael Coleman and Pat Malone while Cooney, Ryan and Lane were teasing the defence. Frankly, Galway could have led by 3–12 to 1–8 at half-time. The signs were ominous for Cork. They looked altogether like a side which had peaked for the Munster final and were now a notch off the pace against a Galway team which had timed its run perfectly for the final, having had little trouble in disposing of Offaly in the semi-final.

This was a really big final for Galway. They had raged against the GAA world after their three-in-a-row ambitions were shattered by Tipperary in controversial circumstances a year earlier. Tipperary had themselves been beaten in 1990 but Galway felt that the next best thing to beating Tipp was to oust the team which had ko'd the champions. Besides, Galway had beaten Kilkenny and Tipperary in successive All-Ireland finals in 1987–88. By beating Cork, they would have achieved a memorable treble over hurling's 'big three' in four seasons. That was a very definite motivation factor in the run-up to the final.

At half-time in the 1990 final, every Galway supporter in the 63,954 crowd believed Cork would go the same way as Kilkenny had in 1987 and Tipperary a year later. Frankly, the vast bulk of Cork fans thought it too, although they would subsequently deny that. Nobody had paid a whole lot of attention to the wind in the first half. It was behind Galway as they attacked the Railway goal but certainly did not appear to be exerting a match-winning influence on proceedings. When Galway maintained momentum to out-score Cork by 0–4 to 0–2 in the opening nine minutes of the second half, it seemed to support the belief that the wind was having no great bearing on affairs. Yes, Ger Cunningham's puck-outs were dropping very deep in Galway territory, forcing the half-backs close to their own goal but they had coped comfortably with a similar bombardment by Tipperary in the 1988 All-Ireland final.

So when Martin Naughton put Galway 1-17 to 1-10 ahead after forty-four minutes, it looked odds-on another western triumph, their third in four seasons. What happened in the next twenty minutes has gone down as one of the most dramatic turnarounds in modern GAA history.

At 45 mins Tomas Mulcahy, who had moved out to centre-forward, found a wide gap through a Galway defence which failed to tidy up a Ger Cunningham clearance. Goal. That was ominous for Galway as it was Mulcahy who played such a major part in master-minding Cork's win over Galway in the 1986 final, having galloped through for a crucial second-half goal at a time when Galway were very much in the game.

At 48 mins Galway centre-back, Tony Keady appeared to be fouled but didn't get a free. Instead he lost possession to Tony O'Sullivan. Point. Galway complained bitterly afterwards that this was one of the more important scores for while Cork only scored a point it kept their momentum going at a crucial time. Galway argued that Keady should have had a free out.

At 53 mins a poor sideline cut by Galway broke to Mark Foley, whose angled shot from way out on the right found the target. Point.

At 56 mins Kevin Hennessy found Foley, who threaded the ball to the Galway net. Goal.

At 60 mins Teddy McCarthy, with his back to goal, struck the ball over his shoulder. Point. By now the panic bells were ringing for Galway. Cork were in full sail and, just as had happened during Galway's dominant period in the first half, every break was favouring the attackers.

At 63 mins John Fitzgibbon reacted quickest in the Galway square. Goal.

At 64 mins Fitzgibbon again, put through by Hennessy. Goal.

That 4–3 scoring sequence by Cork was interrupted on only two occasions when Eanna Ryan and Noel Lane scored points for Galway. Now the score read: Cork 5–13 Galway 1–19. Galway scored 1–2 to 0–2 in the final five minutes but it was too little too late. Cork's super-blitz had won the day.

All sorts of theories abounded afterwards as to why the game underwent such an incredible turnaround. The most popular theory was that the Cork management gave the team such a 'roasting' at half-time that they dared not fail. It was also alleged that Galway became over-confident once they had established a seven-point lead. Then there was the question of Joe Cooney's second-half fade-out (he scored just one point, from a free).

All three theories are simplistic. First, there was no appreciable improvement in Cork's play for ten minutes of the second half. Second, Galway were most unlikely to develop any over-confident tendencies against a county which had won twenty-six previous All-Ireland titles. As for Cooney's 'fade-out', the truth is that it wasn't a forward failure which cost Galway this final. Besides, Cooney had done more than enough in the first half to justify himself.

More credence can be given to other considerations, however. Ger Cunningham's aerial bombardment on the Galway defence achieved a number of objectives for Cork. It forced the point of play right in front of the Galway goal. Tony Keady, who had stood so defiantly against a similar attack by Tipperary two years earlier, wasn't nearly as dominant this time, especially after Cork moved Tomas Mulcahy out to this area. Not that Keady should take all the blame. The rest of the defence weren't vigilant enough to cope with the amount of breaking ball which sprayed tantalisingly around their square. Two years earlier they had mopped up everything as Tipperary tried desperately to recover — this time the new-look defence was very sluggish.

By 1990, Sylvie Linnane and Conor Hayes were no longer on the team. This robbed the defence of the sort of instinctive cunning which dealt so admirably with crisis situation in previous years. Then there was the matter of Ger Cunningham's stunning save eleven minutes into the second half at a time when Galway were defending a four-point lead. The Cork revival was underway by then but it might have been short-lived if Cunningham hadn't saved Naughton's goal-bound rocket with the bridge of his nose, diverting the ball out over the endline. It probably was the real turning point of an amazing game. Cork got double value from Cunningham's save as, incredibly, the umpire signalled a wide rather than a Galway '65' so instead of still being on the defensive, Cork were allowed to resume the aerial attacks with a puck-out.

Galway manager, Cyril Farrell claimed that there was no great mystery surrounding the thirteen-point turnaround in twenty minutes. 'Most games have periods when one side or the other are in control. Ours came in the second quarter and early in the second half and, while we made reasonably good use of them, Cork took greater advantage of theirs later on, certainly when it came to scoring goals. 'We should have scored one or two more goals in the first half. We didn't and we paid the price,' he said.

The 1990 final represented the final fling for that particular Galway team. It had held together after the trauma of 1989, hoping to re-claim the No.1 spot in 1990. When it failed, the break-up accelerated, although it didn't become totally apparent until the 1991 All-Ireland semi-final, where Galway were well beaten by Tipperary.

It was ironic that Galway had launched a glory period with a great win over Cork in the 1985 All-Ireland semi-final and ended it with a defeat by Cork in 1990. While the Galway team of the 1985–90 period has gone down in history as the best ever produced by the county, it still failed twice to Cork in All-Ireland finals. 'That's one of our regrets, I suppose. We beat Tipperary, Kilkenny and Offaly twice in championship games in that period and while beating Cork in 1985 was sweet, we badly wanted to beat them in an All-Ireland final. We had the chances to do that in 1990 but didn't take them. That will always be a great regret from a great era in Galway hurling,' said Cyril Farrell.

Cork's reign as All-Ireland champions lasted until the following July when they lost to Tipperary in the Munster final replay.

CORK (1990 All-Ireland final): Ger Cunningham; John Considine, Denis Walsh, Sean O'Gorman; Seanie McCarthy, Jim Cashman, Kieran McGuckin (0–1); Brendan O'Sullivan, Teddy McCarthy (0–3); Ger Fitzgerald (0–1), Mark Foley (1–1), Tony O'Sullivan (0–2); Tomas Mulcahy (1–2), Kevin Hennessy (1–4), John Fitzgibbon (2–1).

Subs: David Quirke for McGuckin, Cathal Casey for B.O'Sullivan.

GALWAY: John Commins; Dermot Fahy, Sean Treacy, Ollie Kilkenny; Pete Finnerty, Tony Keady (0–1), Gerry McInerney; Michael Coleman (0–1), Pat Malone; Anthony Cunningham (0–1), Joe Cooney (1–7), Martin Naughton (0–4), 'Hopper' McGrath (0–1), Noel Lane (0–4), Eanna Ryan (0–2).

Subs: Tom Monaghan for Malone, Brendan Lynskey (1–0) for Cunningham.

Chapter 3

✤ ✤ ✤

Big Upsets

For some strange reason, hurling and football are not major betting mediums, certainly not at inter-county level anyway. The championships attract some attention on the gambling front but not to any great degree.

Stories of massive gambles usually surface around All-Ireland final time but, as often as not, they are the products of over-fertile imaginations. On a general basis, GAA fans prefer to spend their money travelling to games, rather than betting on them. Another reason for the lack of betting interest in Gaelic Games is the belief among fans that the odds on offer are very prohibitive. The reluctance by the bookmaking industry to take any chances is based on more than just current form. They follow very definite patterns, usually using history as the starting point. They operate in the belief that major upsets are rare, especially where counties with a tradition of success are involved. Nonetheless, there are occasions when the form book goes spectacularly wrong, days when underdogs snarl for their rights and insist on getting them.

This chapter is a celebration of some of the great outsiders who fought their way to the inside. For instance, Offaly footballers in 1982...the 4/1 outsiders who dared to defy Kerry just when the Kingdom was set to walk into a special place in GAA history. Much of modern-day GAA drama has centred on Offaly, who were at the painful end of an underdog's bite in 1989 when Antrim hurlers shocked them in the All-Ireland semi-final. Clare's win over Kerry in the 1992 Munster final may not have been a massive shock in pure football terms but was a positive earthquake when viewed in the context of a county which hadn't won the title since 1917.

Of course not all the great surprises were in finals. Wicklow footballers pulled off the major upset of 1986 when they knocked Laois out of the

Leinster championship at the quarter-final stage, just six weeks after Laois had won the National League title. Kerry hurlers stunned the hurling world by beating Waterford in Dungarvan in the first round of the 1993 Munster campaign to record their first championship win for 67 years. Donegal footballers reached the National League final in 1995, and then beat 1994 All-Ireland champions Down in the first round of the championship, but were the victims of a sensational upset against a Monaghan team who unleashed a powerful surge which stunned them in Ballybofey.

A Victory For The Small Man

Offaly 1–15 Kerry 0–17
(All-Ireland football final 1982)

Had Offaly lost the 1982 All-Ireland football final, team manager, Eugene McGee was planning to head for London on the Monday after the game to get away from it all. The prospect of heading into another round of endless post-mortems did not appeal to him.

McGee thought about things like that as the days counted down to the final. At face value it was odds-on that he would be on the plane for Heathrow on Monday evening. Kerry were bidding for a place in history by becoming the first team ever to win five consecutive All-Ireland football finals. Outsiders, Offaly, had lost to Kerry in both 1980 and 1981 and, however carefully one looked, it was difficult to see them making up the leeway in 1982. McGee and his team couldn't help but notice the apparent inevitability of it all. Switch on the radio and listen to the new song:

'And it's five-in-a-row, five-in-a-row
It's hard to believe we've got five-in-a-row.
They came from the South, from the North, East and West,
But to Micko's machine, they are all second best.'

Walk into the bookmakers and check the odds: Kerry 1/4, Offaly 4/1. Pick up the newspapers and read of the five-in-row industry which had suddenly taken on a life of its own. Bar a fall, Kerry were home and dry, or so it seemed. That stung McGee. A deep thinker on the game, he reckoned that the reality was a great deal different to the image which was being portrayed.

Deep down inside his psyche, McGee had a burning ambition. It was articulated in a comment made prior to the '82 final when he said that he would love to show 'some of the die-hards that a team can be trained by someone, who is not weighed down with All-Ireland medals.'

McGee was no Mick O'Dwyer or Kevin Heffernan, both of whom had enjoyed glorious inter-county careers, while the limit of his playing talents extended no higher than club level. Nonetheless, McGee believed that when it came to coaching he could match anybody. Kerry's dominance of Gaelic football at that time irritated McGee. It was nothing personal — in fact he got on well with the Kerry squad and Mick O'Dwyer — but he felt that their seemingly never-ending ascendancy was bad for football. It was most certainly bad for the Offaly team which he had built with such care and devotion through the late 1970s.

Offaly had run Dublin close in the 1978 Leinster semi-final with a team which included six U-21 players. Dublin were at their prime around then, having won the two-in-a-row in 1976–77. Thirteen months later, Dublin and Offaly would clash again, this time in the Leinster final. Offaly were a year older and a year wiser while Dublin, who had been thrashed by Kerry in the 1978 All-Ireland final, were beginning to lose altitude. In fact, Dublin seemed totally grounded when they trailed Offaly by five points with thirteen minutes remaining. To add to their plight, they were down to fourteen men, having had Jimmy Keaveney sent off just before half-time.

But in one final surge, Dublin rallied their forces to climb back within striking distance of Offaly and, in the very last minute, Bernard Brogan struck for the winning goal. Dublin 1–8 Offaly 0–9. McGee was well aware of the conventional wisdom which was circulating afterwards. Heffernan had out-smarted him tactically. How else could a fourteen-man team haul back a five-point lead?

That wasn't strictly true. Offaly were still in the formative stage and, as such, vulnerable to the sort of momentum which Dublin's experienced forces could whip up. It was different in 1980. Offaly beat Louth and Kildare convincingly and finally laid the Dublin bogey to rest with a 1–10 to 1–8 win in the Leinster final. Offaly thus became the latest in a long line of contenders who tried to end Kerry's reign.

The first of three Kerry–Offaly championship clashes in three years produced no fewer than eight goals in the All-Ireland semi-final. By modern standards that was a positive goal feast but then those were the hand-pass days, when Gaelic football was being played like a form of aggressive basketball. Kerry led by 1–9 to 1–3 at half-time but had stretched the lead to eleven points fifteen minutes into the second half. To their credit, Offaly didn't fold as some of Kerry's previous opposition had done and Matt Connor led the fightback. By the end, the gap was down to five points, Kerry 4–15 Offaly 4–10. It was wide enough to keep Kerry happy but narrow enough to suggest to McGee and Offaly that they were improving all the time.

While there was a justifiable air of satisfaction in Offaly at the end of 1980, McGee and his co-selectors still felt that the team needed strengthening, if they were going to push on in 1981 and win the All-Ireland final.

By summer '81, much had changed. Surgery had been performed in every outfield line. The Offaly team which reached the All-Ireland final showed no fewer than six changes from the side which lost to Kerry in the previous year's semi-final.

Offaly didn't have a particularly distinguished 1981 Leinster campaign. They beat both Westmeath and Wexford by five points before accounting for Laois in the final by 1–18 to 3–9. All were solid, rather than spectacular, performances. They beat Down by six points in a rather undistinguished All-Ireland semi-final. Kerry, meanwhile, had strolled effortlessly into the final, demolishing Clare (4–17 to 0–6), Cork (1–11 to 0–3) and Mayo (2–19 to 1–6).

An unusually small crowd of 61,489 turned up for the final. Clearly, there was no great faith in Offaly, who had the added burden of bidding for the double, as their hurlers had won the All-Ireland final a few weeks earlier. The record books show that Kerry won by 1–12 to 0–8 but the margin flattered them. Offaly had hung on tenaciously all the way and weren't finally buried until Jack O'Shea hit a thundering good goal three minutes from the end.

Offaly had a mixed League run in 1981/82 but it didn't bother them. The focus was very much on the championship which was regarded as a make-or-break campaign. The squad had been together for quite a few years and there was a feeling that another championship setback might just knock the heart out of them. That can happen. A team can tolerate a certain number of defeats during its learning curve but once it approaches a peak, it must deliver or else it will fall away pretty quickly.

This time, Offaly were sharper in Leinster. They hammered Louth by 0–17 to 0–8, out-goaled Laois by 3–13 to 1–15 in the semi-final and then destroyed Dublin by 1–16 to 1–7 in the Leinster final. Clearly, Offaly were a much better side than a year earlier. They had to be. Galway, who had won the National League title in 1981, only to blow their championship hopes in an awful display against Mayo, were back on top in Connacht. They showed both ambition and confidence for long stretches of the All-Ireland semi-final but Offaly's experience eventually proved decisive. They pared back Galway's five-point lead in the first half and eventually won by a point, 1–12 to 1–11.

Meanwhile, Kerry had swept Armagh off the pitch in the other semi-final. They won by 3–15 to 1–11 in a game watched by just 17,523 people. Such was Kerry's dominance at the time that very few neutral spectators even bothered to attend their All-Ireland semi-finals. In fact, not many Kerry fans made the journey either, opting to wait for the final. By now, Kerry had remained unbeaten in nineteen championship games, stretching back to 1978.

Eugene McGee pondered long and hard as to which tactics he would employ in the All-Ireland final. He decided to be bold. He had always felt that Kerry prospered against opposition which tried to be overly defensive. McGee also reckoned that irrespective of how they tried to disguise it, Kerry would be over-confident.

Offaly's formation had been designed earlier in the season with Kerry in mind. Sean Lowry was at centre-back, Richie Connor was at centre-forward, having made a remarkable recovery from a cartilage operation and Matt Connor was at full-forward. Kerry were without both Pat Spillane, who had knee ligament trouble, and Jimmy Deenihan, who had broken his ankle some months earlier. Nonetheless, the whole weight of evidence was very much in Kerry's book at they headed for Croke Park on 19 September.

Did Kerry fall or were they pushed? The argument rages on to this day. The only definitive statement which can be made about the final result is that it surprised everybody outside Offaly and a great many inside the county too. The wisdom of hindsight has spawned a whole network of theories as to how Offaly came to tear up the script. The most popular explanation points the accusing finger at Mikey Sheehy, who had his second-half penalty kick blocked by Martin Furlong at a time when Kerry were a point ahead.

Subsequent events suggest that the penalty miss was not all that important. Kerry, drawing on their vast experience, recovered from that disappointment and had built a four-point lead with just six minutes remaining. It was a familiar position for Kerry. Perhaps familiarity bred contempt. Either that or Offaly took inspiration from the magnificent comeback which brought their hurlers the All-Ireland title against Galway a year earlier.

Either way, the effects were the same. Matt Connor pointed two frees but Kerry were still two points clear with ninety seconds remaining. Then came the goal, buried in the Kerry net by Seamus Darby, who had come on as a sub earlier on. McGee's only instruction to him was to hang in around the goal in the hope that a chance would come his way.

The debate as to whether or not Darby pushed Tommy Doyle prior to gaining possession raged on for ages. As with all controversies of that type, there is no clear-cut answer. Some referees would have given a free against Darby. Others wouldn't. It was Offaly's good luck that Mayo's P.J. McGrath fell into the latter category.

Darby's goal gave Offaly a 1–15 to 0–17 lead. There was still time for Kerry to launch a survival bid but on this occasion it was without success. Having inched their way from the bottom to the top over long lonely years, Offaly were not going to let their place in history slip from their grasp. By any standards, it was one of the most dramatic victories in the history of All-Ireland finals. The scenes in Croke Park afterwards were unbelievable. It was difficult to work out who were more stunned, Offaly by the nature of their win, or Kerry by the nature of their defeat. All thoughts of a week away from it all in London were forgotten as Eugene McGee declared in a chaotic dressing-room that 'this was a victory for the small man'.

OFFALY: Martin Furlong; Mick Lowry, Liam Connor, Mick Fitzgerald; Pat Fitzgerald, Sean Lowry, Liam Currams; Tomás Connor, Padraig Dunne; John Guinan, Richie Connor, Gerry Carroll; Johnny Mooney, Matt Connor, Brendan Lowry.

Subs: Stephen Darby for Mick Lowry, Seamus Darby for Guinan.

KERRY: Charlie Nelligan; Ger O'Keeffe, John O'Keeffe, Paudie Lynch; Paudie Ó Sé, Tim Kennelly, Tommy Doyle; Jack O'Shea, Seanie Walsh; Ger Power, Tom Spillane, Ogie Moran; Mikey Sheehy, Eoin Liston, John Egan.

Sub: Pat Spillane for Moran.

'The Greatest Day In Antrim's History'

Antrim 4–15 Offaly 1–15
(All-Ireland Hurling Semi-final 1989)

Rarely in GAA history did All-Ireland semi-final day dawn to such an air of tension. As the 64,127 hurling fans entered Croke Park for the 1989 semi-finals, there was a very distinct impression that something dramatic was about to unfold.

What nobody could have anticipated was the amount of drama the afternoon of 6 August would produce. The entire focus was on the Galway–Tipperary semi-final. Their rivalry had enthralled the hurling world over the previous two seasons. It had started with a Galway win by six points in a smashing 1987 All-Ireland semi-final. It had gathered pace in the 1988 All-Ireland final when Galway again emerged as winners, this time by four points. By April 1989, Galway and Tipperary were still locked in a fascinating duel. Yet again, Galway prevailed, winning by two points in a great National League final. By August 1989, the rivalry was at its most intense. Only now, it was sprinkled with a dangerously explosive powder, provided by the controversial suspension of Galway centre-back, Tony Keady.

The Keady controversy, and its likely impact on the Galway–Tipperary game, dominated the previous weeks' agenda to such a degree that virtually no attention was paid to the other semi-final between Antrim and Offaly. Quite simply, the general perception was that Antrim would offer a brave but limited resistance to an Offaly team which had retained the Leinster title with a 3–12 to 1–14 win over Wexford in the final.

Eleven days before the semi-finals, Antrim had played Galway in a challenge game in Kells. Although it was merely a warm-up match, several journalists turned up, not to watch the match, but to assess the mood of a Galway camp which was fuming over the Keady affair. Galway easily beat Antrim, further fuelling the theory that the northerners had absolutely no chance of upsetting Offaly.

Had the Antrim–Offaly game been played on its own, the likely attendance would have been little more than 5,000. Two years earlier only 5,500 turned out in Dundalk to watch Kilkenny beat Antrim in the All-

Ireland semi-final and just 3,000 attended the previous Antrim–Offaly clash in the 1985 semi-final in Armagh. Antrim lost by fourteen points that day. A year later they scored 1–24 against Cork in the semi-final but still lost by five points. In 1987, Kilkenny had seven points to spare over Antrim while Tipperary beat them by eight points in 1988.

A common thread ran through all those games. Antrim performed solidly but at a lower level than their opponents. Yes, there were times when Antrim played well but they lacked the conviction and consistency necessary to cause an upset. As far as the hurling world was concerned, 1989 would be no different. Offaly, who had won six of the previous ten Leinster finals, were more experienced, more confident and more talented. It was amid such perceived wisdom that Antrim manager, Jim Nelson and his co-selectors set about their game plan.

He looked for optimistic signs and found them in events of some months earlier. Antrim had headed for Birr in March with their Division One League lifeline virtually severed. Five defeats from six games left them needing to beat Offaly to have any hopes of surviving in the group. It was the tallest of tall orders, especially in Birr. But, somehow, Antrim scaled it, helped there by a late goal from Olcan McFetridge, which gave them a two-point win. That set them up for a relegation play-off with both Wexford and Offaly. The first leg was a disaster. Wexford hammered them by fifteen points, leaving Antrim with a winner-take-all clash with Offaly in Dundalk. It was an amazing game. Antrim led by nine points at one stage but were hauled back and the game eventually finished level. It went into extra time and it was here that Antrim unveiled their fighting qualities. They also showed some excellent touches and eventually won by two points.

Games at the desperate end of the League campaign tend to be forgotten once the championship arrives in all its glamour and glitz. Not this time. Certainly not in Antrim, anyway. Jim Nelson repeatedly reminded his squad of their two earlier experiences against Offaly. Yes, Offaly would be better by August but so too would Antrim. On the weekend before the All-Ireland semi-final, Nelson took his squad away to a quiet location in Down for a two-day planning session. By then most of the hard work had been done but that weekend together worked wonders for the squad in terms of uniting them mentally and psychologically. They knew that nobody gave them a chance of beating Offaly but they reckoned that they could turn that to their advantage. After all, Offaly would be less than human if they remained unaffected by the all-embracing view that they were certainties to reach the final.

The Antrim players were surprised to find that they could back themselves at 4/1 in Belfast. Offaly were a punter-unfriendly 1/6.

There was nothing in the early stages of the game to suggest that the bookies, or indeed the tipsters, had got it wrong. Offaly were 0–6 to 0–2 clear after fifteen minutes. They weren't playing especially well but were still that bit ahead in most of the important areas. They were having problems with their shooting, however, and missed the target on no fewer than thirteen occasions in the first half. Nonetheless, they were pretty comfortable at half-time when they led by 1–10 to 1–6. Antrim read it differently. Yes, they were behind but they felt that Offaly's goal, scored by Vincent Teehan, was a giveaway and that they were unlucky to be four points adrift. Their own goal had come from an Aidan McCarry penalty.

Offaly's lead had been cut to two points thirteen minutes into the second half but they still looked to have something in reserve. As subsequent events proved, they hadn't. Antrim's rate of progress continued at an impressive rate. Dessie Donnelly led the defence heroically while Ciaran Barr's move out from full-forward was a master stroke. Barr hurled superbly out the field, leaving McFetridge and Co. to feast on the good ball he provided.

McFetridge's first goal was the signal for an Antrim stand which eventually devastated Offaly. McFetridge scored a second goal five minutes from the end and McCarry added another, followed by a Dominic McKinley point which left Antrim 4–15 to 1–15 ahead at the finish.

The scenes at the end will never be forgotten by those who witnessed them. Antrim's euphoria at reaching the All-Ireland final for the first time since 1943 lifted the county in a tidal wave of emotion. To their great credit, Offaly put their misery to one side and sportingly waited by the dressing-room entrance to applaud the Antrim team off the field. As the Galway and Tipperary teams emerged from their dressing-rooms for the second semi-final, they couldn't believe their eyes.

A joyous Antrim party was in full swing in the corridors while a disconsolate Offaly team trooped sadly into the darkest corners they could find. They had behaved with great dignity immediately after their defeat — now they simply wanted to be left alone to cope with their torment.

Offaly manager, P.J. Whelehan, father of current star Brian Whelehan, admitted afterwards that he would have preferred to meet either Galway or Tipperary in the semi-final. 'I felt Antrim's overall strength might prove too much for our young players and that's how it turned out. We lost it in the first half when we missed so many chances,' he said. Antrim goalie, Neilly Patterson, who was one of the team's great characters, captured the sense of euphoria better than most while also touching on a key ingredient in Antrim's shock victory. 'It's just like a dream. I have watched many finals and dreamt about playing in one. It's hard to believe that we won by nine points but it has happened. We were mentally right for this game whereas other times we might not have been. That was very important,' he said.

As events transpired, that game turned out to be Antrim's final. For while they prepared diligently for the final, the hype and atmosphere of the occasion appeared to paralyse them in the match and Tipperary galloped to the easiest of wins, 4–24 to 3–9. Nevertheless, the season was regarded as a great success in Antrim. For years, they had watched others enjoy success in Croke Park. At last they had enjoyed one great day when the hurling sun shone brightly on their backs.

Manager, Jim Nelson summed it up neatly and succinctly: 'it's the greatest day in Antrim's history,' he said.

Arguments rage in Offaly to this day as to whether over-confidence was the team's undoing. All concerned with the team believe that was not the case but sometimes over-confidence can seep into a squad's consciousness without warning. As often as not, the players don't even know it's there.

Naturally, Antrim took a different view of the day's events. They insisted that over-confidence had nothing to do with the result and that, quite simply, they had out-hurled Offaly. They also claimed that the media's attitude had been a prime motivator. Despite twice beating Offaly in the League, virtually no commentator predicted an Antrim win. This has always been a source of irritation in Antrim. They feel that because they are isolated from hurling's main strongholds, they don't get the attention they deserve. That is probably quite true but Antrim certainly made sure that they could no longer be ignored with that smashing win in the 1989 semi-final, one which will never be forgotten in either Antrim or Offaly.

ANTRIM: Neilly Patterson; Gary O'Kane, Terry Donnelly, Dessie Donnelly; James McNaughton, Dominic McKinley (0–1), Leonard McKeegan; Paul McKillen (0–1), Dominic McMullan; Brian Donnelly (0–1), Aidan McCarry (2–4), Olcan McFetridge (2–3); Donal Armstrong (0–2), Ciaran Barr (0–1), Terence McNaughton (0–2).
Subs: Danny McNaughton for McMullan.

OFFALY: Jim Troy; Aidan Fogarty, Eugene Coughlan, Martin Hanamy; Roy Mannion (0–1), Pat Delaney (0–3), Ger Coughlan; Joachim Kelly (0–1), Johnny Pilkington (0–1) Joe Dooley (0–3), Daithi Regan (0–2), Mark Corrigan (0–3); Vincent Teehan (1–0), Michael Duignan, Declan Pilkington (0–1).

Subs: Paddy Corrigan for Declan Pilkington, Danny Owens for Mark Corrigan, Brian Whelehan for Johnny Pilkington.

Clare's Kingdom Come

Clare 2–10 Kerry 0–12
(Munster Football Final 1992)

The words came in slow, measured tones. All his sporting life, Jack O'Shea had dreaded the prospect of this moment — now it was upon him and there was no turning back.

'That's it, I'm finished. I said before the start of the season that if we lost in this year's championship, I would call it a day. I have decided to do that. I've enjoyed some great times and I'm thankful for that. I was a little disappointed in my own performance today and I don't think I can go back and start again,' he said.

Journalists dashed from the Kerry dressing-room, preparing to file details of the final chapter of a great saga. Jacko was gone. It was the end of an era. In normal circumstances, the retirement of one of the greatest players in the history of Gaelic football would have been the story of the week but not this time. Jacko's farewell was over-shadowed by a new, exciting arrival.

Outside in the corridor of the Limerick Gaelic Grounds, a chaotic orgy of jubilation was underway. Clare had just beaten Kerry to win the Munster football final for the first time since 1917. It seemed as if every Clare person had somehow squeezed into the corridor and they were uncorking their emotions in a champagne explosion. For years, Clare followers had dreamed of winning a Munster title, only not in football. It was to their hurlers that they looked summer after summer in the hope of making that elusive breakthrough. Now the barrier had been sensationally broken by the footballers. Amazing!

Inside the Clare dressing-room, buried deep underneath a mountain of celebrations, the players and team management were trying to make sense of it all. Have we really won? Will we awake from a dream to see some Kerry player strolling casually by with the trophy tucked under his arm?

Out on the pitch thousands of Clare fans stood, wallowing in the delightful feeling of finally being winners. Many of the Kerry supporters hung around too, numb with disappointment at the defeat but deriving some consolation from being part of such a historic occasion. As the weeks passed, they would find it very hard to accept that their side had lost to Clare. It was a blot on their football pedigree, or so they thought. But for now, the sense of occasion was overwhelming, even for disappointed Kerry people.

The combination of circumstances which contrived to bring Clare to the Southern peak in 1992 was remarkable. Probably the two most significant factors were the introduction of the open draw in the Munster championship and the appointment of John Maughan as team manager. For years, long-time Clare selector, Noel Walsh and others had been coaxing, goading and gradually edging the Munster Council towards the introduction of an open draw. They argued that the seeding system, which kept Cork and Kerry apart, was unfair. It diluted the incentive for the other counties. The open draw brigade argued that even if one of the so-called weaker counties beat Cork or Kerry in a semi-final, they would still have to face the other in the final. It certainly was not much of an incentive for the weaker counties.

Eventually, the Munster Council relented and the open draw came into force in 1991. Ironically Clare, for so long the prime movers behind the idea, were drawn on the same side as Kerry and Cork. Kerry hammered them by 5–16 to 2–12 in Ennis. Still, all was not lost. Limerick took up the torch on behalf of the 'weaker' counties and ran Kerry to two points in the Munster final. The open draw decision had been vindicated. Limerick's brave performance (they scored three goals) silenced the cynics who claimed that the open draw would result in Munster finals being one-sided farces.

Clare's first round defeat had its consolations. It enabled them to enter the 1991 All-Ireland 'B' championship which they duly won. Further progress was made when they won promotion to Division One of the National League, which also earned them a League quarter-final clash with Meath in Ballinasloe in the Spring of 1992. They lost by two points to a team which had been sitting at the top table for almost six years.

It was an extremely significant performance for Clare, who had been a man down since the 10th minute after Gerry Killeen was sent off. Still, they hung on bravely and were two points ahead with ten minutes remaining. Meath, in a typically driving finish, squeezed home by 0–8 to 0–6. Meath were very impressed.

'You could see that day that Clare were very well organised and that they were fiercely motivated. Our experience took us through in the end but one couldn't mistake Clare's hunger or indeed their talent,' said Meath midfielder, Liam Hayes.

The Munster championship draw again pitted Cork against Kerry in the preliminary round. Kerry won easily but then left some unanswered questions in a moderate semi-final performance, where they beat Limerick by three points. Clare, Tipperary and Waterford were in the other half of the draw. The Clare squad saw this as their ideal opportunity to at least reach the Munster final. They achieved that with a four-point semi-final win over Tipperary, who had beaten Waterford. It was an impressive enough performance in its own way but it never even hinted at the volcano which was about to erupt. In the run-up to the final, the general view was that Clare would probably provide Kerry with as tough a game as Limerick had a year earlier but that the crafty Kingdom would prevail in the end.

Clare manager, John Maughan had a broader vision. He had enjoyed a reasonably rewarding playing career with Mayo, which had been short-circuited by a serious knee injury. When he took over as Clare manager in October 1990, he had two distinct assets. One, he was not conscious of the weight of negative history pressing down on Clare. Two, he was an army man, for whom discipline was an automatic part of life. Merging the two into a united force behind Clare football, he quickly got the entire squad in line and geared for the big challenge against Kerry, who were defending a title they won a year earlier after a five-year gap.

'There were only about twenty-six people who thought we could beat Kerry and they were all inside the Clare dressing-room,' declared Maughan afterwards. He was probably right. True, the Clare followers turned out in big numbers (they formed the majority of the 26,015 crowd) but they had no great confidence of victory. How could they? History's grim indicator pointed to Kerry as being some sort of superior force, who could always produce that little extra when required.

The script ran very much to order in the opening stages of the final. Clare enjoyed plenty of possession, earned mainly through the efforts of Tom Morrissey and Aidan Maloney at midfield, but their attack was nervy and inaccurate. Clare even wasted a penalty in the 6th minute when Peter

O'Leary had no great difficulty in saving Gerry Killeen's shot. In previous years, Clare heads might have dropped after such a setback. Not this time. Gradually, they dug in and while they continued to miss some opportunities, they also took some good scores to lead by a point (0–7 to 0–6) at half-time.

Their supporters gave them a standing ovation as they trotted to the dressing-rooms and while Clare had to face the wind in the second half, it was not sufficiently strong to cause them any great worry. They had coped quite well with Kerry and individually their confidence levels were rising. Could this be our day? Maybe Kerry aren't that good after all! Maughan outlined a very positive picture for them at half-time. Yes, they should have been more ahead but the important thing was that they had convinced themselves that Kerry were beatable. Build on that confidence and you will win — that was Maughan's message, issued with the sort of conviction which made the players feel very good about themselves.

Maurice Fitzgerald's opening two points of the second half hinted at a Kerry surge but it was at this stage that Clare showed their real merit. Instead of caving in under an inferiority complex hoisted on them by years of subservience in Munster, they took the game to Kerry. Seamus Clancy, Noel Roche, Tom Morrissey, Francis McInerney, Gerry Killeen and Aidan Maloney led the charge.

The decisive break came in the 51st minute when Colm Clancy scored Clare's first goal to put them three points clear. Jack O'Shea tried hard to be Kerry's reference point in a comeback but the magic of previous days was gone. Even the great Jacko couldn't muster any more energy from his body. Sensing their chance to take a place in Banner history, Clare built up more momentum and a 58th minute goal by sub Martin Daly, snatched expertly amid a posse of dithering Kerry backs, presented the Kingdom with an unattainable target. Clare goalie, James Hanrahan, made a great save from Pa Laide and while Kerry tried hard to haul themselves back into contention, they failed to get through for the goal they so badly needed. Clare bodies drove themselves through the pain barrier to hold onto the precious lead. Their supporters began urging referee, Paddy Russell to blow full time a full ninety seconds from the end, fearing that somehow Kerry would squeeze out of jail. They need not have worried. The Clare resistance was united and controlled and they easily held on for a truly incredible victory.

John Maughan realised the importance of allowing the players to celebrate before beginning preparations for the All-Ireland semi-final against Dublin. The panel travelled all over Clare in the following days in a sort of public relations blitz for the GAA which no amount of money could buy. It would have been easy to lose sight of what lay ahead but, in fairness, the squad behaved very maturely and trained diligently for the semi-final against a Dublin team which had finally escaped from Meath's clutches.

That too was one of the most emotional days in Clare football history. Rarely has a team got a more passionate welcome onto Croke Park. Dublin fans usually out-number rival forces in Croke Park but not this time. Clare people showed incredible resourcefulness to get their hands on priceless tickets and, having done that, made sure that the Clare shout was very much louder than the Dublin roar. Indeed, the supporters played a huge part in keeping the Clare team going right to the finish and while they eventually lost by 3–14 to 2–12 they had acquitted themselves exceptionally well. Ironically, Clare scored more against Dublin than any other team in the championship, including Donegal who won the final by 0–17 to 0–14.

Not that Clare were satisfied with that. Such was their confidence that they genuinely believed they would outwit Dublin. Beating Kerry in the Munster final had completely changed their outlook. Their days of being satisfied with second best were over. A new outlook had been born in Limerick on 19 July 1992.

CLARE: James Hanrahan, Ciaran O'Mahony, Gerry Kelly, Seamus Clancy; Ciaran O'Neill, J.J. Rouine, Frankie Griffin; Tom Morrissey (0–1), Aidan Maloney; Noel Roche (0–1), Francis McInerney (0-1), Gerry Killeen (0–4); Padraig Conway (0–2), Colm Clancy (1–1), Martin Flynn.
Sub: Martin Daly (1–0) for O'Neill.

KERRY: Peter O'Leary, Stephen Stack, Anthony Gleeson, Eamonn Breen; Liam Flaherty, Sean Burke, Connie Murphy (0–1); Noel O'Mahoney (0–1), Seamus Moynihan, Sean Geaney, Timmy Fleming (0–1), Maurice Fitzgerald (0–7); Karl O'Dwyer, Jack O'Shea (0–1), Billy O'Shea (0–1).
Subs: Ambrose O'Donovan for O'Dwyer, Pa Laide for Geaney, Noel O'Leary for O'Mahoney.

Kerry Hurlers End Sixty-Seven Year Famine

Kerry 4–13 Waterford 3–13 (Munster Hurling Championship 1993)

On the night before Kerry played Waterford in the first round of the 1993 Munster hurling championship in Walsh Park, Waterford, the Kerry squad stayed in a hotel in Dungarvan. Few people recognised them.

By a strange coincidence, 'Babs' Keating, who was then managing Tipperary, was staying in the same hotel that night. As Tipperary were due to play the Kerry–Waterford winners in the semi-final, 'Babs' had a special interest in the game. He got chatting to Kerry manager, John Meyler and was surprised to discover how confident the former Wexford and Cork player was.

'We'll be playing you in a fortnight's time,' were Meyler's parting words to Keating. Meyler's confidence was based on a solid conviction that Kerry were on the verge of producing something special. Their progress over previous seasons had been solid, even if it hadn't attracted much attention from the mainstream hurling world.

In 1990, they had lost to Cork by 3–16 to 3–8 in the Munster championship. The plus point from that game lay in the fact that Cork went on to win the All-Ireland final. Kerry could take being beaten by the best. A year later, Kerry had lost to Waterford in Killarney by 2–15 to 1–12 after leading by four points at half-time. Kerry were just one point down with five minutes to go so the final result flattered Waterford somewhat.

In 1992, Cork again beat Kerry by 0–22 to 0–8. A bad result for Kerry but at least they had the satisfaction of not conceding a goal. They did extremely well in the subsequent League, eventually winning promotion to Division One, before losing to Tipperary in the quarter-final by 0–14 to 0–5. Once again, they hadn't conceded a goal against another of Munster's top forces.

Unquestionably, Waterford were vulnerable as they prepared for the 1993 championship. They had lost a relegation game with Cork by a massive twenty-three points a few months earlier and looked in no way settled heading into the summer campaign. Nevertheless, the fact that the game was at home provided Waterford with a psychological boost. Also, they had a huge advantage in terms of championship success down through the years. In fact, statisticians had to delve back as far as 1926 to locate

Kerry's last win in the Munster championship. That was against Clare, whom they beat by 4–6 to 2–4 in Tralee.

Tradition's heavy hand weighed so heavily in Waterford's favour that despite positive comments from the team management, very few Kerry people expected their side to win. There were some optimists around, however. Somewhat prophetically, Kerry PRO, Eamonn O'Sullivan wrote in *The Kerryman* on the week before the game: 'we have a great chance of causing an upset'. Despite this, the Kerry public were not convinced.

So much so that when the Supporters' Club tried to organise a bus load of fans to travel to Waterford, there were only three takers. Not surprisingly, the bus was cancelled. Kerry trainer, John Meyler knew that outside of the squad, there was very little confidence in the side. It didn't particularly bother him. A veteran of many frustrating years with Wexford before switching to Cork and St Finbarr's, Meyler understood the underdog's role. This time he would use it to his advantage.

The hard work had been done. Kerry had trained on one hundred occasions since the beginning of the year, often in wet, miserable conditions out in Ballyheigue and Causeway. Meyler and his co-selectors, Eddie Murphy, Maurice Leahy, P.J. McInerney and Michael Hickey left nothing to chance. Indeed, some ten days before the championship game, travelled all the way to Walsh Park to watch Waterford play Kilkenny in a challenge game. Murphy's notes were added to Meyler's file.

And so when team captain, Nicholas Roche led Kerry out in Walsh Park everything was in order for the shock of the season as far as Kerry were concerned. Or was it? Twenty minutes into the game, Waterford looked to be galloping towards the mountain peak while Kerry were still lost in the foothills.

Waterford were leading by five points at that stage and showing no apparent signs of weakness. Paul Flynn's early goal had settled them into what appeared to be a match-winning routine. Flynn, who had been a star minor a year earlier, would eventually suffer the awful disappointment of ending up on the losing side, despite scoring 3–2.

Kerry stabilised in the fifteen minutes before half-time and, with their confidence rising, they clawed their way back and actually led by 2–8 to 2–7 at the break. Meyler was not happy with their first-half performance. He felt it had been patchy and not nearly good enough to sustain them in the second half.

'I said to them at half-time: are you men or mice. They gave me a pretty firm reply in unison and I told them to go out and finish the job. That's exactly what they did,' said Meyler.

Not that Kerry produced an instant surge. In fact, Waterford scored 1–4 without reply in the opening eleven minutes of the second half to lead by six points. J.P. Hickey pointed a '65' for Kerry but it still seemed as if frustration would again be their only reward for the day's activities.

It was at this stage that Kerry finally decided to break free from the binding shackles of history. Christy Walsh kicked a goal and suddenly Kerry began to dream. Waterford were still leading by three points with eight minutes to go but now all had changed. At last Kerry realised that they had the resources to win the game.

Jerry O'Sullivan came on in attack in what proved to be an inspired substitution while positional adjustments tightened the defence. Christy Walsh and O'Sullivan (twice) pointed to bring the sides level. Five minutes from time came the score which won the game for Kerry.

D.J. Leahy appeared to mis-hit a 35-yard free but, to his delight, it took a deflection off a Waterford defender and, helped by Joe Walsh, the ball spun into the Waterford net. Waterford tried desperately for the equaliser in the closing minutes but a disciplined Kerry defence held out.

The scenes afterwards were unbelievably emotional. The depression had been lifted after years of frustration and disappointment. Deep down the Kerry players knew that it was unlikely that they would progress any further (Tipperary awaited them in the semi-final) but that didn't matter. For rank outsiders, a first round win can be almost as enjoyable as an All-Ireland success. Kerry hurlers understood that as they joined in an impromptu celebration with the small band of loyal supporters who had travelled to Walsh Park.

The mood was vividly captured by John Barry, writing in the following week's *The Kerryman* newspaper. 'How do you do justice to a victory like this? Do you go searching for the finest superlatives in the book and use them liberally? Do you triumphantly shout to the hurling world over and over again: we've done it!. Or do you simply let your heart do the talking, allow yourself to get a little emotional and thank God you were in Walsh Park, Waterford last Sunday?

'The Rose of Tralee has rarely been sung so heartily as it was in the Kerry dressing-room after this great win. Everywhere there was euphoria — men not used to success revelling in the glory of it all. It was a victory which had been threatening and should probably have come two years ago against Waterford in Killarney but, very obviously, the extra dimension was there this time in the person of trainer, John Meyler,' wrote Barry.

Waterford were magnanimous in defeat. While they were bitterly disappointed, they readily acknowledged that Kerry deserved their win, an assessment which drew universal acceptance. John Meyler, and indeed his entire squad, knew full well that while a breakthrough of sorts had been made against Waterford, it would be a different story against Tipperary in the semi-final.

Tipperary had beaten Kerry by nine points in the League quarter-final a few months earlier and were likely to be even sharper ten weeks on. Also, the game was to be played in Thurles.

Kerry tried very hard to build on their first round success but were off the pace against a Tipperary squad which possessed far more big-time experience. Tipperary eventually won by 4–21 to 2–9. It was all rather disappointing for Kerry but reality was always likely to deal them a cruel hand after the Waterford game.

Nevertheless, nothing could ever erase the memory of that magic occasion when Kerry hurlers defied the odds so spectacularly in Walsh Park. Selector, Maurice Leahy summed it up perfectly in a boisterous dressing-room: 'If we never won another match, this one would keep me going.' The win over Waterford on 23 May 1993 really was that special for Kerry hurling.

KERRY: J.P. Hickey (0–2); Sean O'Shea, Mike Casey, Seamus McIntyre; Brendan O'Mahony, Seamus Sheehan, Martin McKivergan; Mike O'Shea, Nicholas Roche; Brendan O'Sullivan (1–2), Christy Walsh (1–1), Tom O'Connell; Tony Maunsell (0–3); Joe Walsh (0–1), D.J. Leahy (2–2).

Subs: Liam O'Connor for O'Connell, Jerry O'Sullivan (0-2) for O'Mahony.

WATERFORD: Ray Sheridan; Stephen Frampton, Damien Byrne (0–1), Mark O'Sullivan; Pat Walsh, Sean Cullinane, Fergal Hartley; Noel Crowley (0–2), Liam O'Connor (0–4); Paul Prendergast (0–2), Brian Greene, Billy O'Sullivan; Eamonn Cullinane (0–1), Sean Daly (0–1), Paul Flynn (3–2).

Subs: Pat Tobin for Mark O'Sullivan, John Meaney for Billy O'Sullivan.

Monaghan Flash, Donegal Crash

Monaghan 1–14 Donegal 0–8
(Ulster Football Championship 1995)

Less than a minute into the Ulster quarter-final at Ballybofey, Donegal fans were preparing to celebrate victory. Declan Bonner's red head was visible to everybody in the ground as he raced forward to take a penalty kick which, had it been scored, might well have short-circuited Monaghan's challenge even before they turned on the switch. Monaghan goalkeeper, John O'Connor, stood up strong and sturdy, however, to make a smashing save, deflecting the ball out for a '45'. Donegal fans groaned in disappointment but confidently expected Manus Boyle to compensate by pointing the '45'. He missed.

Monaghan players clinched their fists in a public gesture of defiance. They had survived the first test. Now let the game start again. This time, Monaghan would be better prepared. For months, Monaghan had looked ahead to the championship and could see only an Everest. The draw had pitted them against the winners of Down v Donegal, two teams who had won three of the previous four All-Ireland finals. Monaghan, meanwhile, had been scuffling in more modest surrounds.

In 1994 they had beaten Cavan, only to lose by six points to Down. A year earlier, they had also beaten Cavan but were eight points adrift of Derry in the Ulster semi-final. They derived some satisfaction from the fact that, in both years, Down and Derry went on to win the All-Ireland title. Still, it wasn't a whole lot for Monaghan to boast about, especially as they had dropped down to Division Four of the National League in early 1994.

The management team of Mick McCormack, Damien McBride, Philip Brady and Sean (Jack) McCarville were acutely aware of the need for a rapid improvement. Promotion from Division Four was absolutely vital. Better still if the team could finish on top of the group as that would earn them a League quarter-final clash with the Division One winners.

National media attention is rarely turned on Division Four. Match previews are usually no more than a few lines; similarly with match reports unless something startling happens. It's only when the winners emerge to play the Division One leaders in the quarter-final that Division Four comes under scrutiny. And so Monaghan toiled through the winter/spring campaign far away from the piercing spotlight which shone on teams like Down, Derry and Donegal. A defeat by Offaly in Ballybay pre-Christmas knocked Monaghan off line but they recovered well and crucial wins over Sligo and Wicklow in the spring not only ensured promotion but also earned them a League quarter-final tie with Laois in Croke Park on Easter Sunday.

Monaghan went into the game with the best scoring rate in the entire League but the value of that currency was somewhat spurious, given that it had been earned in Division Four which, for all its endeavour, is scarcely the mecca of defensive excellence. Monaghan played poorly against Laois. They raced into an early three-point lead but once Laois pressed the accelerator, Monaghan were off the pace and eventually lost by five points in a lifeless match. Suffice to say that nobody could have anticipated the important role which Monaghan would subsequently have in shaping the Ulster, and possibly, the All-Ireland championships.

Following the Laois game, Monaghan were installed as 12/1 sixth favourites to win the Ulster title with only Fermanagh and Antrim behind them. Frankly, nobody could see them beating either Down or Donegal. Down's elimination by Donegal changed nothing. The All-Ireland champions were gone but now Monaghan had to face their conquerors. Not only that but Donegal had earlier shown consistent form to reach the League final, which they lost to Derry. To add to Monaghan's problems, they had to go to Ballybofey!

Monaghan studied the difficult script but, far from dwelling on the more complex passages, decided to work on the positive aspects. They identified two possible areas of gain which they could exploit. One, Donegal may have peaked for the game against Down and, two, they may have been over-confident going in against a Division Four side.

Donegal team manager, P.J. McGowan talked non-stop, both privately and publicly, of the perils of complacency. He warned his players of the dangers of planning too far ahead while the Monaghan challenge was still to be seen off. The problem was that however hard the Donegal players tried they were living and listening in an environment which had jumped to the conclusion that, with Down out of the equation, a Derry–Donegal Ulster final was inevitable. Derry, of course, would subsequently fail to keep their part of the 'bargain' as well, falling victims to a Tyrone team which had been making steady progress in previous seasons.

The Monaghan team was ideally structured, both from a physical and mental viewpoint, for the Donegal test. The team management had put its trust in youth on the sound basis that young players will not be influenced by the form book in the same way as older players, who tend to allow their attitudes to fall into set patterns, which have been decided by previous events.

So when John O'Connor made that crucial penalty save, it was regarded as the most positive of signals by his colleagues. Gradually, they settled into a forceful rhythm and were rewarded in the 13th minute by a Declan Loughman goal. The finish itself was of a freakish nature, with the ball beating Gary Walsh off a post after taking a vicious dip. The odds against Walsh, one of the country's most experienced and reliable keepers, conceding that kind of goal were huge. But then it was one of those days for Donegal.

Monaghan grew in confidence with every passing minute while Donegal, who were having problems all over the place, looked edgy and uncertain. They badly needed a time-out to re-group. When it came at half-time they were 1–7 to 0–6 in arrears and while the margin was modest, Donegal accepted that they had serious problems. Monaghan were in full sail and Donegal knew well that they would have to improve dramatically to have any chance of making a recovery.

They had one crucial advantage over Monaghan in the area of experience and felt that if they could impose even a short, concentrated passage of power play on the game, it would raise enough doubts in Monaghan minds to give them a decent prospect of launching a genuine comeback. Monaghan started the second half well with a Declan Smith point but Donegal retaliated with two Manus Boyle points to leave just a goal between the sides with twenty-three minutes remaining. Amazingly, Donegal failed to score for the remainder of the game.

It all went horribly against them as bad luck combined with bad play to completely undermine them. Paddy Hegarty's flick crashed back off the upright — on another day it would have gone into the net. Manus Boyle, so often Donegal's match-winner from frees, spurned the chance to shoot for goal from forty metres, opting instead to try a short pass to Tony Boyle. It was cut out and Monaghan swept upfield to score a point, thereby extending their lead to five when it might have been down to three had Manus opted for a conventional kick at goal.

Monaghan's control of the final stages of the game was most impressive. Instead of falling back into defence in an attempt to defend their lead, a tactic which many teams would have opted for in the circumstances, they continued to pile forward and, in the end, had a full nine points to spare.

It was Donegal's heaviest championship defeat since Tyrone beat them by twelve points in the 1989 Ulster final replay. The fact that it was so unexpected made it very unpalatable to the supporters.

Almost inevitably, the rumour machine got into full swing in the subsequent weeks, claiming that all was not well in the Donegal camp prior to match. It was alleged that the players were unhappy with expenses payments and were also peeved by the small number of tickets they received for the glamour clash with Down a few weeks earlier.

Frankly, it is difficult to accept that even if there were rumblings of discontent over small issues, they had anything to do with Donegal's performance. The truth was that Monaghan were far better programmed mentally for the challenge. Not that any blame should be attached to the Donegal management in this regard. After all, there is only a certain amount that the team manager can do. Deep down, the Donegal players probably felt that there was no way that Monaghan could beat them and no amount of warnings could remove that dangerous assumption. Monaghan's perceived role as mere cannon-fodder for one of the championship favourites produced an effective cocktail of motivation and resolve. Monaghan also played extremely well from a technical viewpoint, leaving Donegal with a puzzle they failed to solve.

Donegal manager, P.J. McGowan summed it up perfectly: 'Monaghan played against us like we played against Down. That was the difference. It wasn't a characteristic Donegal performance at all,' he said.

Monaghan's victory sent expectations soaring in the county that the glory days of 1979/85/88 could be re-captured. That was inevitable but it was also very dangerous. Suddenly, players who were regarded a few weeks earlier as very ordinary mortals were being hailed as heroes who could look ahead to big days in Croke Park. Monaghan's new-found status weighed heavily on them against in the semi-final against Cavan. Chances were missed and mistakes were made while the air of authority which was so evident against Donegal was missing as Monaghan went down by 1–9 to 0–10. It was all part of the learning process for a young Monaghan team and while they were bitterly disappointed by the Cavan defeat, their performance against Donegal will long be remembered in the county and, indeed, far beyond.

MONAGHAN: John O'Connor; Eddie Murphy, David King, Noel Marron; Martin Slowey, Joe Coyle, John Conlon (0–1); Padraig McShane (0–2), Frank McEneaney; Peter Duffy (0–3), Michael Slowey, Gregory Flanagan; Stephen McGinnity (0–2), Declan Loughman (1–0), Declan Smith (0–6).

Sub: Ray McCarron for Flanagan.

DONEGAL: Gary Walsh; John Joe Doherty, Matt Gallagher, Barry McGowan; Mark Crossan, Noel Hegarty (0–1), Martin Shovlin; Martin Gavigan (0–1), Brian Murray (0–1); Mark McShane, James McHugh, Paddy Hegarty; Declan Bonner (0–1), Tony Boyle, Manus Boyle (0–4).

Subs: John Duffy for McShane, John Gildea for Bonner.

The Battle Of Aughrim

Wicklow 2–10 Laois 1–9
(Leinster Football Championship 1986)

Four weeks before Laois footballers launched their 1986 championship campaign, a crowd of over 8,000 turned up in O'Moore Park, Portlaoise to watch them play Kerry in a challenge game. It was a massive attendance for a tournament game but then it was a game of great significance for Laois.

It was, in fact, a celebration, an opportunity for the county's fans to reach out and say thanks to the players who had brought them so much delight the previous Sunday by winning the National League final for the first time in sixty years. All week the county had indulged in a non-stop party as fans relished the prospect of a sustained spell at football's top table.

The atmosphere in O'Moore Park for the clash with the All-Ireland champions, Kerry, was incredible. For while Kerry saw it as no more than a pre-championship warm-up, the Laois public attempted to turn it into a winner-take-all match between the All-Ireland and League champions. At one stage it looked as if the match would not take place at all as the Kerry players threatened to withdraw due to internal wranglings over a holiday fund. Thankfully, a compromise was reached and Kerry travelled in force.

In fact, eleven of the team which had won the 1985 All-Ireland final turned out in body, if not in spirit. Their minds were very much elsewhere but it hardly mattered to Laois who won in style by 2–13 to 1–7. It meant that in the space of three months, Laois had beaten Down (League quarter-final), Leinster champions, Dublin (League semi-final) Ulster champions, Monaghan (League final) and All-Ireland champions, Kerry.

Their status as potential Leinster and All-Ireland champions was gathering momentum by the day. After all, this was no mere sudden surge of form. The groundwork had been solid too. Laois had run into a progressive streak in 1985, reaching the Leinster final after comprehensively hammering Meath in the semi-final. Ironically, that game was to prove a watershed for Meath, who were extremely well-fancied to win the Leinster crown. Instead, they were thrashed by Laois, 2–11 to 0–7. That defeat convinced Meath of the need for a major overhaul which, when completed, enabled them to preside at, or near, football's summit for several seasons.

Laois lost the 1985 Leinster final to Dublin by 0–10 to 0–4. The margin of victory flattered Dublin. Laois had been in control for long stretches but couldn't match Dublin's capacity, as exemplified by Barney Rock, to convert chances into scores. Nevertheless, there were encouraging signs for Laois, especially in defence where team captain, Colm Browne, organised the resistance with admirable authority.

Also, Laois were without Tom Prendergast at the time. One of the best forwards the county ever produced, Prendergast was in self-imposed exile in 1985. He had grown disillusioned with the general set-up in 1984 and didn't return until early 1986. There are many people who believe that had Prendergast been playing in the 1985 Leinster final, Laois would have won.

Prendergast's return for the closing stages of the 1986 League had given a whole new impetus to the Laois attack. Laois were now a powerful force and while they were in Division Three of the League, it was no major surprise when they went on to actually take the title, beating Down by three points (after extra time) in the quarter-final, Dublin by two in the semi-final and Monaghan by one in the final. They surprised people by the level of their consistency but, under analysis, the team had a lot going for it.

Laois's progress was closely monitored in Wicklow, who were due to play them in the first round of the Leinster championship. Their glorious home-coming after the League final, the street parties, the celebrations....Wicklow watched from a distance and plotted. Wicklow were also a Division Three side but, unlike Laois, had remained in mid-table, taking eight out of a possible fourteen points, compared with Laois's haul of thirteen points from fourteen. Besides, Laois had beaten Wicklow by six points in a League game in Blessington in the previous February.

In the build-up to the championship game, Laois queried the suitability of Aughrim as the venue, claiming that it lacked the capacity to stage such an important game. Aughrim is a tight, compact ground where players sometimes get the feeling that the spectators are actually on the pitch. It has long been seen as a major plus for Wicklow teams. The fact that Laois asked for another venue went down badly in Wicklow. Initially, it was interpreted as élitism by the new League champions. Aughrim is not good enough for us! It quickly dawned on Wicklow that they could make extra capital out of Laois's reluctance to play in Aughrim. The players were repeatedly told that Laois wanted the game at a different venue, not because of crowd considerations but simply because they feared Wicklow in Aughrim.

A number of other developments were also combining to boost Wicklow's preparations. They had already played a championship game, beating Westmeath by 0–15 to 1–5 in Aughrim. The match report in the following day's *Irish Press* should have served as a warning to Laois.

> Wicklow offered enough evidence to suggest that they will provide a stern test for Laois. Wicklow were always enterprising and, when the occasion demanded, they showed plenty of intelligence too.

As the weeks passed, word began to filter through that Laois's preparations weren't going as smoothly as they might have. Yes, they were training hard but such was the hype in the county after the League success that the line between celebration and preparation tended to become blurred on occasions. Collectively, the players and management were doing their best to keep the focus right but, on an individual basis, it was proving very difficult not to let both feet drift off the ground on occasions. A county in celebration can be a very dangerous environment for players who are training for a championship game.

Sunday, 16 June was a scorcher. The influx into Aughrim began early. When the Laois team arrived there was a hot, claustrophobic atmosphere around the streets as 12,000 fans inched their way towards the ground. The odds against Wicklow were shortening all the time.

It would be stretching credibility for Wicklow to suggest that they didn't try to intimidate Laois. The venue had sown the seeds of doubt in Laois minds and pretty quickly there were doubts in Laois bodies too as they felt the force of a Wicklow team which had clearly decided that if they could win the physical battle, they would win the game.

Eventually, Wicklow ended up winning the physical and mental battles... and the game! Having gained so much big-time experience in the preceding months, Laois should have been able to cope. It wasn't the first time that a team with a big reputation had its mental resolve tested by underdogs. Really great teams survive. Others don't. In any event, Laois were strong enough physically to take care of themselves. For some strange reason though, they let Wicklow get to them.

Laois forward Willie Brennan and Wicklow defender Nick O'Neill were sent off by referee Carthage Buckley (Offaly) after just fourteen minutes. Advantage, Wicklow. Losing a forward is generally more damaging to a team than losing a back. A few minutes later, Laois were down to thirteen men when Christy Maguire was dismissed after an incident with Owen Doyle. Worse still, Laois were now left with four forwards.

It wasn't all going against Laois, however. They were far more inventive and incisive than Wicklow and seemed to be comfortable when they led by 1–8 to 1–2 at half-time. Wicklow re-grouped during the rest period and decided to use their sub, Pat O'Toole, as the spare man operating around centre half-back but with instructions to carry the ball forward and commit the Laois defenders, thereby creating overlap opportunities.

When Eamonn Whelan pointed for Laois to put them seven points clear, it looked all over for Wicklow. Amazingly, Laois failed to score for the remainder of the game. Wicklow kept plugging away and were rewarded with some points but it wasn't until Kevin O'Brien scored his second goal, thirteen minutes from the end, that they really took off. There was an element of luck to the goal. O'Brien's penalty shot was well saved by Laois goalie, Martin Conroy but the ball re-bounded into O'Brien's path and he flicked the ball to the net to level the game. Suddenly Wicklow were oozing conviction and drive. Laois buckled. Tom Prendergast was sent off after an off-the-ball tangle with Mick O'Toole and as Laois's game plan fell asunder completely, Wicklow scored four points to win an amazing game.

Referee, Carthage Buckley was immediately targeted by Laois supporters as they tried to come to terms with the shock defeat. Buckley was given a Garda escort to the dressing-room and had to remain there for another hour before attempting to leave. Even then, his car was kicked by the baying mob who had hung around. It was all quite shameful.

The unruly scenes took away from what had been a great achievement by Wicklow. Their tactics might have been questionable but that does not alter the fact that they played some fine football too. Laois only had themselves to blame for lacking the discipline to cope with the physical nature of the challenge offered by Wicklow. It was all very different in the semi-final. Meath were well able to stand up to Wicklow — physically and mentally — and won pretty comfortably.

Sadly for Wicklow, beating Laois in 1986 did not signal the start of a new era. The team began to break up after the defeat by Meath and a year later, Wicklow were hammered by Dublin in the Leinster semi-final. Nonetheless, nobody in Wicklow will ever forget their victory over Laois in 1986. In a county where success is rarely a visitor, beating Laois was a real triumph. The fact that it was a once-off, rather than the start of something exciting in no way dilutes the sense of pride felt by Wicklow people when they re-wind their memories to savour that roasting summer day in June 1986.

Losing the battle of Aughrim cost Laois dearly. Meath went on to win the 1986 Leinster final and had accumulated a heavy layer of confidence by the time they faced Laois in the 1987 championship. Laois's National League title had long since been surrendered after a poor Division Two campaign where they won just three of seven games. They were lucky enough to beat Carlow (1–12 to 2–7) in the opening round of the 1987 championship in Portlaoise but were beaten 1–11 to 2–5 by Meath, also in O'Moore Park, three weeks later.

The break-up of the Laois team speeded up after that and, in 1988, they failed to get past the first round of the Leinster championship, losing by 3–5 to 2–7 to Carlow. Unquestionably, that particular Laois squad peaked in 1986. However, they failed to cope with the different demands of a glorious League campaign and a championship test against Wicklow in Aughrim. Ultimately that was to prove their downfall.

WICKLOW (v Laois 1986): Dan Leigh; Owen Doyle, Pat Byrne, Nick O'Neill; John Darcy, Billy Kenny, Mick O'Toole; Seamus Morris, Pat O'Byrne; Robert McHugh (0–3), Kevin O'Brien (2–3), Pat Baker; Con Murphy (0–2), Tommy Murphy, Ashley O'Sullivan.

Subs: Pat O'Toole (0–2) for Doyle, Paul Tyrell for O'Sullivan.

LAOIS: Martin Conroy; Pat Dunne, Martin Dempsey, Eddie Kelly; Mick Ahearne, Pat Brophy, Colm Browne; Liam Irwin (0–3), John Costelloe; Gerry Browne (0–1), Tom Prendergast (0–1), Christy Maguire Michael Dempsey, Eamonn Whelan (1–3), Willie Brennan (0–1).

Subs: Noel Prendergast for G. Browne, Brian Nerney for Michael Dempsey, John Ramsbottom for Whelan.

Chapter 4

✤ ✤ ✤

Major Controversies

As the country's biggest sporting organisation, it is inevitable that the GAA will plunge headlong into controversy from time to time. For while its administrative structure is solidly based, there are always going to be occasions when the system breaks down.

Ironically though, some of the GAA's biggest controversies of recent times could have been avoided with some forethought. The RDS affair in 1991 started out as a molehill but kept growing until it became a great, big, ugly mountain. It centred on the GAAs late decision to withdraw permission for Down, the then All-Ireland champions, to play Dublin as part of a double-header in the RDS with a Bohemians–Shamrock Rovers League of Ireland soccer game. The pre-Christmas novelty was to have been one of the highlights of the Clan na Gael–Fontenoys GAA club's centenary celebrations. Instead it was turned into a nightmare, not only for the club, but also for the GAA itself which was left with a lot of explaining to do after withdrawing support for the double-header just eight days before it was due to take place.

While the GAA may have had very justifiable reasons for being sceptical of the whole business, the fact remained that they originally granted permission for it to go ahead, only to pull the plug later. Despite a belated public relations blitz, the damage had already been done. The GAA authorities were seen by many sports lovers, including some of their own members, as pandering to an anti-soccer mentality. The GAA's top echelons vehemently denied that but once a public perception gathers momentum, it's very difficult to keep control of it.

The famous Tony Keady saga of 1989 could also have been avoided. The Galway star was suspended for a year for playing in New York without the necessary clearances from back home. The GAA argued that rules were rules and that it was up to players to know, and abide by, them. Thus, Keady could expect little sympathy.

Galway argued on Keady's behalf that it wasn't that simple on the basis that (a) the proper disciplinary procedures had not been adhered to in New York (b) that other players had been equally guilty but had escaped (c) that a year's ban was excessive and (d) that no player should be used in what Galway claimed was a power struggle between the GAA authorities in Ireland and their counterparts in the US.

Despite a highly-publicised campaign by Galway, including a threat by the team management to withdraw completely from the All-Ireland semi-final against Tipperary, Keady lost his appeal against the suspension and had to sit it out while his colleagues lost an ill-tempered semi-final match against Tipperary.

While most controversies have a limited life span, the Rule 21 saga drags on from year to year. The rule which precludes RUC officers and members of the British Army from joining the GAA gets a lot more attention than it probably deserves. The official line is that it's not a big issue among ordinary GAA members.

Nevertheless, it is interpreted by many as a political statement by the GAA and, as such, is a subject that is fair game for regular debate. It was hoped that the 1994 ceasefire in the North would pave the way for the abolition of Rule 21. However, motions to this effect were not discussed at the subsequent GAA Congress in 1995 because of a Central Council proposal to hold a special Congress on a non-specified date to deal with the Rule 21 affair.

Senior GAA officials felt that a motion calling for the abolition of Rule 21 would have been beaten, thereby exposing the association to criticism from all quarters. By proposing a special Congress to deal with it, the GAA played for time. But how much time can they buy before facing up to making a decision?

Thre is a general public perception that hurling is a dangerous sport, but despite the huge number of hurling and football games played each year, serious controversies relating to actual matches are fairly rare. Two notable exceptions were the 1983 and 1995 All-Ireland football finals. In 1983, Dublin and Galway engaged in the most bitter final of recent times. It ended with just twenty-six players and led to weeks of controversy.

The RDS Affair

(A Christmas Cracker Explodes)

It started out as a Christmas gimmick and ended up as one of the most controversial episodes in modern GAA history. While the GAA have always insisted that their handling of the RDS affair in 1991 was no more than a minor hiccup, the wider view is that it seriously damaged their image, both internally and externally.

Quite how something as relatively unimportant as a challenge match between Dublin and Down footballers being played at the same venue as a Shamrock Rovers–Bohemians League of Ireland soccer game could develop into a veritable jungle of banana skins for the GAA still remains a mystery. But that is precisely what happened. It all looked relatively simple and straightforward when on, 8 November 1991, it was announced that a Gaelic football–soccer double header would be played at the RDS grounds in Ballsbridge, Dublin on 15 December as a joint venture involving Clanna Gael–Fontenoy's GAA club and Shamrock Rovers soccer club. The RDS was on lease to Shamrock Rovers for use as a soccer stadium.

Clanna Gael–Fontenoys are based in the Ballsbridge-Ringsend area and they decided to launch their centenary celebrations with the unique double header. Down had won the 1991 All-Ireland football title and were regarded as the prize catch for a challenge game against Dublin. Shamrock Rovers v Bohemiams always has been one of the top local derbies in League of Ireland soccer. Put the two games together in a one-off double event and you had the ingredients for a pre-Christmas sporting feast. At least that's what Clanna Gael–Fontenoys thought. They were extremely excited by the idea, not simply in terms of the money it would earn but because of the novelty value of the venture.

The GAAs response to the idea was less enthusiastic. Initially the GAAs Games Administration Committee refused to sanction the Dublin v Down game, on the basis that the RDS ground was not vested in the GAA. In lay terms, it meant that the GAA were not prepared to allow its players to play in a stadium which it did not own. That decision drew the first layer of wrath on the GAA authorities. However, following a serious of appeals and compromises, the GAC later decided to allow the game to go ahead. It stressed that this permission was given on the basis that conditions laid down regarding match expenses would be adhered to. This was believed to centre on the fact that Dublin and Down had each been promised seven thousand pounds as a match fee. The GAA were unhappy with this aspect, fearing that it could set a very dangerous precedent for other clubs organising tournament games in the future.

While the administrative rumblings kept the double-header to the forefront of the public consciousness, fears were being expressed in private by senior GAA officials about the overall wisdom of the venture. They could not understand why Clanna Gael had linked up with a League of Ireland soccer game to launch their centenary celebrations. It was felt that a Dublin v Down tournament game would draw a bigger crowd in its own right than a Shamrock Rovers v Bohemians League game. Clanna Gael's view was that the novelty aspect of the promotion would be of major value to the club.

Despite the early problems, the way seemed clear for the double-header when a final press conference took place on 4 December, at which it was announced that Tipperary Spring Water would sponsor the event. Advertisements were placed in the national newspapers, urging fans to buy tickets, which were priced at £8, £6 and £4, in advance. Everything seemed set for the big day.

The GAAs Central Council met on the following Saturday, 7 December. The agenda was of the routine end-of-season variety but, when the official business was over, journalists were asked to leave as a matter had come up which required to be dealt with in private. It transpired that the 'matter' was the RDS promotion. Later on, the GAAs Public Relations Officer, Danny Lynch issued a statement, outlining why Central Council had withdrawn its backing for the RDS event. This arose from a meeting of the Down County Board on the previous Thursday night where queries were raised as to whether or not the RDS fixture breached GAA policy.

The GAA's statement after the Central Council meeting was ambiguous. It read:

> At a meeting of the Central Council today, it was decided that the game planned for the RDS on 15 December between Dublin and Down could not go ahead. This decision was taken on the basis that conditions set out by the Games Administration Committee, with regard to the fixture, had been violated.
>
> Last Thursday, it emerged that the game, and its arrangements, were being billed as a joint venture involving Shamrock Rovers and that conditions relating to the collection and disbursement of monies

appeared not to be adhered to. The Dublin and Down County Boards, the GAC and the Management Committee were not informed or consulted in relation to these arrangements.

At a meeting of the executive committee of the Down County Board on Thursday night, they decided that they could not play the game on 15 December as they considered that they could be in breach of GAA policy, unless Central Council were able to confirm that no breach of such policy was involved.

If an application is received to play a game on an alternative date, it will receive every consideration. The association wishes to affirm that it has no objection to a game being played at the RDS under the control of a GAA unit and provided it conforms to GAA policy.

The statement was carried in all of the following day's newspapers but it confused, rather than enlightened. What exactly did it say? Why, specifically, were the GAA withdrawing support for the RDS fixture?

Suddenly, the affair had left the sporting arena and made its way onto the news pages. A dismayed public tried to read between the lines. Inevitably, the conclusion was reached that the GAAs decision was reached on the basis that they wanted nothing to do with soccer and were not prepared to see such prize assets as the footballers of Down and Dublin playing in a promotion which might, either directly or indirectly, earn money and prestige for soccer clubs.

Meanwhile, Clanna Gael were rooting through the debris, desperately seeking clues which, from their perspective, might bring sense to the whole affair. They issued a lengthy statement, putting their side of the story. They did not disguise their bewilderment.

The Dublin–Down match was a Clanna Gael–Fontenoy initiative and promotion. This was made clear in all applications, promotional material and tickets which have been issued. The club received no query from the Down County Board in this regard and dealt fully with the queries raised by the GAC.

The match could only go ahead with the active co-operation of Shamrock Rovers and the RDS. Neither Shamrock Rovers nor the RDS sought, or received, any control, over this match. Sales outlets were chosen because of the degree of control that the club could exercise over them. The club had agreed to have a full audit of the account of the money carried out by a named auditor, appointed by the GAA. No query was received from any quarter in this regard.

The club has given lengthy consideration to the rules, policies and aspirations of the GAA as expressed in the Official Guide. It is the expressed view of the club that this match was not in breach of the rules and was actively promoting the GAA and its aspirations.

The GAA could never have anticipated the reaction to its decision. Criticism deluged in from all sides. Among the most trenchant critics was Paddy Downey, the then GAA correspondent of *The Irish Times*, who described it as the blackest day in GAA history. 'Over the weekend gone by, the great and glorious times were not just devalued but virtually degraded,' wrote Downey.

Elsewhere GAA President, Peter Quinn was being targetted for severe criticism. Much of it was deeply personal and scandalously subjective. Quinn had taken over as President eight months earlier with a reputation for being one of the most progressive officials in the GAA. Now he was being depicted as an arch conservative, who would have no truck with soccer in any circumstances. The language used by some of Quinn's critics was highly emotive and way over the top. It was a very difficult start to Quinn's Presidency and his relationship with some sections of the media was never the same from then on.

The GAAs failure to explain immediately in clear, simple terms why it was withdrawing permission for the RDS venture was a mistake and fuelled the fires for days. The situation worsened when details of a letter sent by GAA Director General, Liam Mulvihill to the Dublin County Board on the Monday after the Central Council meeting were carried in the *Irish Independent*. It read: 'The Uachtarán has asked me to notify you of the official decision of the Central Council on Saturday last with regard to the above. There have been reports in the last 24 hours that the Leinster Council may be approached with regard to an alternative fixture. The Central Council have decided that games played on the same bill as a soccer game will not be allowed.'

The *Irish Independent* carried that letter in a report headlined: 'The Ban is Back — dark ages return as GAA bars all contact with soccer.' Senior GAA officials were furious when they read the report. They immediately issued a a statement, saying that the letter, details of which had been leaked, had been selectively interpreted.

The letter referred to was never intended to convey this message. It referred to a decision of Central Council on Saturday last, regarding the proposed game on 15 December. If a bone fide application is received from a GAA unit for the purpose of promoting Gaelic games and meets conditions already well publicised, there would be no reason why permission should not be granted for the playing of Gaelic games on the same date and venue as a soccer game.

The GAA still had a problem. Their initial failure to explain simply and in detail the reasons behind their unwillingness to allow Dublin and Down to play in the RDS had left the general public both confused and sceptical. Cut through the verbiage and you come down to the fact that the GAA wanted nothing to do with soccer. Rightly or wrongly that was the general view, not just among non GAA people but also among the ranks of the association's membership.

On the following Sunday, the GAA's top two officials went public on the background to the whole affair. President, Peter Quinn was interviewed by the *Sunday Independent* while Director General, Liam Mulvihill gave his version of events to the *Sunday Press*. Quinn refuted suggestions that he held an anti-soccer bias which lay at the heart of the controversy.

> It was a Greek philosopher who said that reality is what people perceive it to be. If people want to see me in that light (anti-soccer) there is not an awful lot I can do about it. I am not anti-anything, not anti-sport in any way. Those who heard me talk to school children in many counties this year know that I encouraged the kids to play sport, even if they didn't play our sport.

He said that the Management Committee's original decision to allow the RDS venture to proceed, subject to certain conditions, proved that the GAA had no fundamental objection to a joint venture with a soccer club. However, the GAA were unhappy with the concept of paying Dublin and Down match fees.

> It was a clear violation of the association's amateur status and it raised the possibility of a Kerry Packer type series developing. Clubs had, in the past, used intercounty games to raise money but this match was paying the teams. It would have been a bad precedent and I didn't want that.
>
> There was also the question of who was actually in control of running the RDS venture. 'I felt, as did the GAC, that Clanna Gael had to take control of all receipts accruing from the RDS promotion. This was agreed by Clanna Gael. It was also decided that control of receipts would be supervised by a member of the Dublin County Board and that a final balance sheet would be audited by an

independent party. We were concerned that if Clanna Gael was not in total control of the receipts, the fees which been originally promised to Down and Dublin might still be paid.

Mulvihill said that money, not soccer, was at the heart of the GAA decision.

> The whole thing was very complex but even a casual observer could see that all the information was not available. As far as the Clanna Gael-Fontenoy club was concerned, they were giving us all the information, as they saw it, but we were getting information in the papers which didn't tally with what the club was telling us. We had a major reservation that, from a financial viewpoint, there was no way the club's ambition could be realised and that, despite the excellent PR job they had done on it, it was unlikely to attract enough spectators to pay all the costs. Past experiences have shown that tournament games at this time of year were not great crowd-pullers and while this promotion had a novelty value, expert opinion was that the attendance would not be enough to pay for the commitments entered into to. Our decision to withdraw backing for the game was taken on practical, rather than idealistic grounds. There were certain aspects of the whole deal we found disturbing and these had nothing to do with an anti-soccer attitude.

Defending the vague wording of the Central Council statement withdrawing support for the game, Mulvihill said that because of the sensitive nature of the issue involved, the GAA had to be extremely careful. He continued:

> This may have led to the mistaken belief that we were simply being awkward for the sake of it, because soccer was involved. I can state categorically that is not the case. As for the nonsensical claims that we were trying to re-introduce the ban, all I can do is refute them as forcibly as possible.

Some months later, Mulvihill returned to the affair in his report to Congress. He said that while the GAA was not anti-soccer, it was unwilling to have its units used to raise funds for any professional club. In essence this seems to have been the crux of the matter, even if the GAA did not do a good job in conveying what was a reasonable argument.

The bottom line for the GAA was whether or not a professional soccer club (Shamrock Rovers) would benefit financially from the drawing power of Dublin and Down. The GAA felt that it would. In the circumstances, the GAA had a sound reason for not allowing the game to go ahead. Why should amateur players, who had already endured a long, hard season, contribute financially to professionals?

The GAAs failure to get that relatively simple message across was inexplicable. Blaming it on a public relations breakdown was not acceptable. In fact, it was unfair on PRO, Danny Lynch who, for the most part, was left in a very awkward position. Although not referring specifically to the RDS affair, Lynch noted in his subsequent report to Congress that 'no public relations or image enhancing efforts can be effectively applied without base corporate policy: direction, logic, consistency, structure, organisational loyalty and discipline,' he wrote.

Most of those took a severe knock during the RDS affair.

The Keady Affair

(The American Dream Turns Into an Irish Nightmare)

If, at the beginning of 1989, a League table had been compiled of players who were likely to figure at the epicentre of a GAA earthquake, Tony Keady's name would have been a long way down the list. The Galway centre-back stood high on hurling's peak at the time, having been chosen as Texaco Hurler of the Year for 1988, after a series of stunning performances, climaxing in a super show against Tipperary in the All-Ireland final.

Keady's brushes with the GAA disciplinary powers were extremely rare and never serious. An occasional booking perhaps, or maybe the odd argument with a referee who caught him mischievously trying to move the ball closer to the opposition goal while lining up a long range free — otherwise Keady didn't occupy officialdom's time very much. So when word broke in June 1989 that Keady was facing an investigation for allegedly playing illegally in New York, it caused some surprise. Keady had travelled to the US with the Galway squad which had won the National League title in April. He had stayed on afterwards and lined out with Laois against Tipperary.

Those who are unfamiliar with the detailed workings of the GAA may find that difficult to comprehend. How could a Galwayman play for Laois? Simple really. Things are different in New York. A player can declare for any 'county' he chooses over there, irrespective of his place of origin. The only stipulation is that his transfer — whether permanent or temporary — must be properly sanctioned by the GAA authorities in Ireland.

That was Keady's first problem. He had no intention of remaining on in New York for the summer. He planned to play a game or two while extending his visit and then return home to begin training with Galway, who were bidding for the three-in-a-row. Keady claimed that he believed all the necessary paperwork had been cleared by the Laois officials who asked him to play. It wasn't. Nor was Keady the only Galway player in trouble. Two other squad members, Aidan Staunton and Michael Helebert, were also in the dock charged with playing without the proper clearance. However, the main focus was on Keady because of his high profile.

The scene in New York had long been a minefield in terms of eligibility. It was well known that dozens of Irish-based players travelled out to play there every summer. Some stayed for months while others made weekend trips, flying out on Friday evening and arriving back on Monday. The GAA authorities were unhappy with the situation, not least because they believed that some players were being paid for playing in the US. They were right, of course, but it was very difficult to prove, since brown envelopes stuffed into pockets in dark corners are easily disposed of, once emptied.

The GAA's answer to the problem was to impose a rule whereby players could not play in the US unless they had lived there for a certain period of time. This effectively ruled out the weekend junkets. It was Tony Keady's bad luck that the GAA chose the summer of 1989 to step up its campaign. The first inkling of trouble came when an objection was raised against Keady in New York. The New York Board, anxious to appease the GAA authorities in Ireland, while at the same time being sympathetic to 'visitors' came up with a novel solution. Keady was suspended for two games.

That meant absolutely nothing as it only applied to New York and, by then, Keady was back home. Besides, the GAA's official rule book does not allow for match suspensions.

Unhappy at the manner in which New York handled the affair, the GAA's Games Administration Committee launched its own investigation and stunned the sporting world by banning Keady, Helebert and Staunton for a year.

There were claims that Tipperary people in New York had availed of the opportunity to report Keady to the authorities in the hope that he would be suspended for the All-Ireland semi-final. In fairness, there was no evidence to support that. Quite the contrary, in fact.

In any event, it was irrelevant. Galway's problem now centred on how to get the Keady ban overturned. It would not be easy, despite the fact that there was a great deal of public sympathy around for him. From a procedural viewpoint, an appeal to the GAA's Management Committee was the obvious step. Privately, those close to the Galway team thought it would be a waste of time, believing that Management would not overturn a decision by one of its subsidiary bodies.

The Galway view was that an appeal to Central Council might stand a better chance of success. Central Council has representatives from all thirty-two counties and Galway believed this would be a help in the Keady case. Problem was that Central Council were not scheduled to meet until after the All-Ireland semi-final. While Galway were deciding on its course of action a story appeared in the *Irish Press* that they were considering withdrawing from the semi-final in protest at the Keady suspension. It was a well-placed 'leak', designed to re-open the affair in the public mind. It was also a sensational development in a saga which had come to dominate the sporting headlines. Suddenly, the picture had changed. What if Galway carried it out and allowed Tipperary a walkover?

The possibility of a boycott had been discussed by the Galway management trio, Cyril Farrell, Phelim Murphy and Bernie O'Connor. Technically, they were not entitled to withdraw the team from the semi-final but they reckoned the mere mention of a boycott would bring the Keady affair back into its sharpest focus so far.

The threat to withdraw was taken seriously by the GAA. For while they knew that it was unlikely to happen, it had hoisted the Keady story back into the limelight. Acres of newsprint were devoted to it, while radio and television also dealt extensively with the case, both on news and sports programmes. It was reflecting badly on the GAA. Despite their adherence to the official line, i.e. that Keady and Co. had broken the rules, a year's ban simply for playing a game in New York seemed disproportionate.

Amidst all the furore, the GAA's Management Committee decided to make a gesture by calling a special meeting of Central Council to hear the Keady appeal on the Tuesday night before the semi-final. Frank Burke, Jimmy Halliday and Joe McDonagh presented Galway's case. By then, all the delegates knew the details anyway, so it was unlikely that they would be swayed one way or the other by the arguments offered. Although not admitting it openly, some delegates were not not prepared to back the Keady appeal on the basis that, if it was successful, Galway's threat to withdraw from the semi-final would have been seen to have worked.

Others felt it would be wrong to overturn a decision made by the GAA, irrespective of the circumstances.

Galway had another disadvantage, one which was ultimately to prove the most serious of all. Five members of the Games Administration Committee, which had made the original decision to ban Keady, were also on the Central Council and obviously had to support their own original ruling. This meant that Galway were five votes down from the start. The flaw in the appeal system, whereby members of the committee which made a decision could also sit in on an appeal, was rectified a few years later. However, it took a High Court action by the then Waterford County Board chairman, Eamonn Murphy, to force the GAA to change its regulations on who could adjudicate on an appeal. Despite the odds being stacked against them, Galway presented a good case which drew considerable support. The appeal was debated at length but, in the end, was voted down, 20 to 18. Keady would miss the semi-final and would not, in fact, be eligible to play until the following year's championship. Galway were disgusted. Cyril Farrell commented:

> I would love to have asked the twenty delegates who voted to keep Keady out of hurling for a year if they knew of anybody in their own counties who had played illegally in the US and got away with it. It's easy to be self-righteous when you are dealing with a player from another county. What also annoyed us was the fact that we did not get the support of all the Connacht delegates. As Galway are the only county flying the hurling flag at the highest level, one might have expected more support but no, we could go to hell as far as some from the west were concerned.

Farrell and his co-selectors came in for some criticism afterwards for their handling of the controversy. They were accused of merely whipping up resentment by even hinting at a boycott but they felt that they had to threaten something drastic to even get the debate re-opened after the initial GAC decision. There was another route open to Galway which, in hindsight, might have been more effective, if even more controversial. Galway had argued that, from a technical viewpoint, there were flaws in the original disciplinary procedure because the objections to Keady and Co. playing in New York had not been lodged inside the stipulated seven days. Had they put that to a judge in a Court hearing a few days before the semi-final, the chances are that they would have been granted an injunction preventing the GAA from implementing their decision to ban Keady until a full court-hearing was held. The use of the courts in sporting matters is generally frowned upon but in cases where natural justice is under threat, it remains the only option. Certainly in the Keady case, a Court ruling on the procedures used to suspend him would have been very interesting.

Keady's suspension had deep ramifications. Apart from having to cope without their star No.6, Galway also had to face up to the psychological fall-out from the case. Irrespective of how they tried to disguise it, the affair had distracted them somewhat that summer. To add to their worries, they lost Martin Naughton with a bad knee injury and couldn't call on super-sub, Noel Lane, who had been so effective as a replacement in 1987–88. He was ruled out with a long-term injury.

In the space of a few weeks, it had all gone horribly wrong for Galway. Psychologically, doubts began to set in, fuelled by the impression that, for whatever reason, the gods had decided that it was time to end their reign. Meanwhile, Tipperary, who had been locked in Galway's grip for the previous two years, were improving all the time. To what degree the Keady affair shaped the 1989 All-Ireland semi-final is uncertain. However, there is enough evidence to suggest that it played a major part in Galway's downfall, not just in terms of missing a star player but as an eroding agent which gnawed away at the team's confidence. Sean Treacy did a fine job as Keady's replacement at centre-back but it wasn't enough. Keady had a sense of presence which bothered Tipperary.

The odd thing about the 1989 semi-final was that Galway might have won despite being almost totally inert in the first half. Two Eanna Ryan goals, at the start and end of the half, had them just two points adrift of Tipperary at half-time. That was a near miracle, as Tipperary had controlled most of the thirty-five minutes with astonishing ease. Second-half events are still discussed, mostly for the wrong reasons. Pat Fox's goal gave Tipperary a vital break but an even more significant development was the dismissal of Galway corner-back, Sylvie Linnane, who was deemed to have struck Nicholas English. That infuriated Galway and, in their anger, they began to believe that they were the victims of a conspiracy to prevent them winning the three-in-a-row. The siege mentality was further reinforced when Michael 'Hopper' McGrath was sent off for a foul on Conor O'Donovan.

Despite the chaos, Galway managed to rattle Tipperary. After two seasons under Galway's thumb, Tipperary's respect for them was so great that even when they had two extra men, they feared a Galway tornado.

Galway eventually managed to come within three points of Tipperary but time ran out on them. Their title was gone.

The Keady affair took a new twist shortly after the All-Ireland semi-final. Rumours gathered momentum that all had not been well with Paul Delaney's transfer to a London club a year earlier. Fearing that they might be disqualified if they played him in the All-Ireland final, Tipperary left a bitterly disappointed Delaney out of the team for the match against Antrim. Galway insist to this day that they had no intention of objecting to Delaney on the basis of eligibility. 'There was no way we would attempt to inflict the sort of pain Keady had experienced on another player. Nor indeed would we have done anything to damage Tipperary's chances in the All-Ireland final. We had a great rivalry with them but it never extended beyond the playing fields,' said Cyril Farrell.

As the turbulent autumn '89 days gave way to winter, the Keady affair continued to cause unease. A growing volume of GAA people were unhappy with the suspension as it was well known that several others were as 'guilty' as Keady but had escaped undetected. The GAA authorities then took an unusual step. They announced that an amnesty would be granted to players who came forward and admitted playing illegally, either in the US or Britain. Quite a few availed of the opportunity but their identities were not revealed. In effect, they were suspended and reinstated on the same night without having their names revealed to anybody other than the investigating committee.

It was all rather infuriating for Keady and Galway, especially since the GAA took no action against the officials in New York, who told Keady that they had cleared the way for him to play in the previous May. Galway argued that if Keady had such a serious case to answer then those who persuaded him to play in New York in the first place were even more guilty.

It was a great pity that the affair should have overshadowed the Galway–Tipperary semi-final. By then, their rivalry had developed into a total fascination and while Galway had held the upperhand through 1987–88, many believe that even without the Keady suspension, Tipperary would have beaten them in 1989. Sadly, the Keady business interfered with what had become a gripping saga and in the end it, served nobody well. Certainly not Galway, who had to field a weakened team. Not Tipperary, who had to live with claims that they won a devalued All-Ireland title that year and very definitely not the GAA who somehow contrived to attract all sorts of negative publicity over a relatively trivial issue.

Rule 21

(Sport and Politics: An Uneasy Mix)

By now, it is as predictable as ticket touting on All-Ireland final day. No sooner does the GAAs County Convention circuit swing into operation in December than the debate over Rule 21 begins its raging season. Rule 21 of the GAAs official guide decrees that members of the British Army or RUC are not allowed to become members of the GAA.

It further states that any GAA member who participates 'in dances, or similar entertainment promoted by, or under the patronage of, such bodies shall incur suspension of at least three months'. That particular section of the rule causes no problems, unlike the first part which has become the GAAs annual banana skin. Those who are not closely involved in GAA affairs find it almost comical that such a rule exists. However, it is far from comical to a great many members of the GAA, who steadfastly adhere to the belief that British Army personnel or RUC members should not be allowed to join the association.

The remarkable aspect of the controversial rule is that, of all the regulations laid down by the GAA, this is the one which is least likely to face a challenge since British Army or RUC personnel are not exactly queuing up to join the GAA. Nevertheless the rule gets more public airing than any other. It also causes more problems for the GAA in a PR sense than any other rule.

In order to understand its significance, it is important to acknowledge the GAAs basic aim, as expressed in its official guide. 'The Association is a National Organisation which has, as its basic aim, the strengthening of the National Identity in a thirty-two-county Ireland through the preservation and promotion of Gaelic Games and pastimes.' The guide also states that the association shall be non-party political. The significance here is that it leaves the GAA open to express views of a political nature, provided they are not aligned to a particular party.

Basically then, the GAA is more than a sporting organisation. It sees its role in a broader context, particularly on the question of Irish unity. And while many will argue that it should concentrate solely on its sporting ideals, the fact remains that the GAA has always had a political dimension in Irish life. Nowhere is this better characterised than in the Rule 21 saga. For many years, efforts have been made to get rid of the rule. Motions have been passed by various County Conventions, calling for its abolition but they have never come remotely close to succeeding at annual Congress.

That would suggest a great groundswell of opinion in favour of keeping the British Army and the RUC at arms length. In reality, thousands of GAA members couldn't care less about the rule and would scarcely even notice if it were removed. However, the rule does have a great significance for many GAA members in Ulster generally and in the six counties, in particular. They see it as a valid stance against an army and police force which they deem to be seriously hostile. Stories of harassment of GAA members by the RUC and British Army are well documented. Because of its nationalist tradition, the GAA has been a target for unfair attention by the security forces. GAA players have been stopped on their way to training and to matches for no apparent reason, other than to delay and infuriate them. Relationships between the GAA and the RUC, in particular, have not been good down through the years. The problem was exacerbated when the British Army commandeered part of the Crossmaglen Rangers club grounds in Armagh.

In fact, this has been the single biggest obstacle to an improvment in relations between the GAA and the security forces. Crossmaglen Rangers have argued for years that the British Army were behaving disgracefully, not only in commandeering part of the club's premises but also by being deliberately provocative, often ruining games by flying helicopters needlessly low over the pitch while a game was in progress. The GAA made every effort to persuade the British Army to vacate the Crossmaglen club premises but to no avail.

Against this background, calls for the removal of Rule 21 generally met with a very negative response from GAA members in the six counties. This effectively set the tone for Congress debate on Rule 21, since many of the southern counties took their cue from views expressed by their northern counterparts. The extent to which this is true was underlined by a Galway motion in 1995 which asked that the Ulster Council be given the task of reviewing sections of the Official Guide 'that are relevant to recent developments in the six counties and to formulate a policy initiative in response to these developments for sanction by Central Council.' Stripped of its official language that translates into: 'let Ulster decide on the Rule 21 issue.' The motion was not discussed, having been withdrawn because of earlier development, relating to Rule 21.

When the IRA ceasefire came into effect in August 1994, it was inevitable that the Rule 21 question would surface in a different form. In the new spirit of reconciliation, pressure grew on the GAA to be seen to make some gesture towards helping the peace process. Abolishing Rule 21 was regarded by many as a very obvious way of achieving that. Sligo, Carlow and Dublin, who were always to the forefront of calls to abolish the rule, all passed motions calling for its abolition. However, it was the decision by the Down County Convention to urge the abolition of Rule 21 which really put a new complexion on the situation. For the first time, one of the six counties was supporting the call. That was regarded as especially significant.

Senior GAA figures were worried, however. They felt that the timing of the motion was wrong and that it could prove very divisive at Congress. Also, they felt that despite Down's attitude, the motion might be defeated. This decision would have sent out a negative signal at a very delicate time in Northern Ireland affairs.

In an effort to stave off possible embarrassment, it was decided to discuss the matter at the Central Council meeting, which was held on the eve of Congress. The upshot was that Central Council agreed to introduce a special motion of its own, which would be taken before the call for the abolition of Rule 21. The Central Council motion read:

> That motion 42 (the call for the abolition of Rule 21) on the Congress Clar not be moved on condition that Congress deputes to Ard-Chomhairle authority to call a special Congress to deal with Rule 21, should the circumstances in the Six Counties call for such action. The Association takes this opportunity of reiterating its commitment to contribute meaningfully to the cause of reconciliation and peace, based on mutual understanding and respect.

Standing orders were suspended to discuss this motion. Realising the consequences, Dublin objected to the suspension of standing orders but it was pretty clear that the vast majority of the delegates were happy to row in behind the Central Council motion, which was duly passed, thereby avoiding the need to debate the Rule 21 issue. No date was set for the special Congress.

The manner in which Central Council succeeded in stifling debate on Rule 21 angered many GAA members. However, the counter view was, that in the circumstances, it was better not to debate the matter at all than to discuss it and then opt to retain Rule 21. That would have left the GAA open to accusations of narrow-mindedness at a time when a spirit of reconciliation was sweeping the country.

Would the motion have been defeated? Most likely. The strange aspect of the Rule 21 affair is that if it were put to the 300 Congress delegates without debate, the odds are that the majority would vote for its abolition. However, some of those opposed to its abolition are experts at arguing their case, often in the sort of emotional language which tends to sway the non-committed delegates. By not debating the motion to drop Rule 21 and thereby risking defeat, the GAA avoided the embarrassment of being depicted as narrow-minded. However, it could be a case of merely postponing the problem.

In the near future the special Congress will have to discuss Rule 21. Inevitably, it will be a very high-profile affair, subjecting the GAA to the sort of piercing inspection which few other sports organisations have to endure. Meanwhile, of course, the Rule 21 saga will drag on as there is nothing to stop a County Convention from calling for its abolition on a yearly basis.

It is unfortunate for the GAA that it has become tangled over an issue which, in practical terms, is irrelevant. While the ban on the security forces is regarded as very important by some in the six counties, it is not a big issue elsewhere. The fact that the rest of the country doesn't vote it out of the rule book is a matter of deference to those for which it is an essential principle.

The anti-Rule 21 brigade insists that by abolishing it, the GAA would benefit, both North and South. They contend that part of the reason for the British security forces' antipathy to the GAA is the existence of Rule 21 so that by abolishing it, GAA members in the North would have a far more comfortable existence. They also insist that the GAA as a whole would benefit from the inevitable goodwill which would accrue.

From a GAA viewpoint, the most unfortunate feature of the entire Rule 21 debate is that it refuses to go away. Worse than that, it is used by the GAAs critics as an example of how backward the association can be in certain policy areas. Rule 21 represents only a tiny part of the GAAs philosophy but because of its emotive nature it continues to pop up year after year. All the evidence suggests that it is a counter-productive rule for while there may well be justifiable historic reasons for its presence, it scarcely has much relevance anymore. Apart from anything else it fails the key test of any good rule — does it enhance the image and running of the organisation?

The Good, The Bad And The Very Ugly

(All-Ireland Football Final 1983)

On the day after the 1983 All-Ireland football final, the air was thick with tension at the reception for the teams in Dublin's Burlington Hotel. As usual, the morning and evening newspapers had devoted several pages to the final, only this time it wasn't the actual game which dominated the agenda.

Instead, the whole focus was on the many, and varied, negative aspects of an extraordinary clash between Dublin and Galway. Virtually all of RTEs morning radio programmes had also concentrated on follow-up reaction as the GAA world tried to come to terms with a final which had trawled every available depth before finishing up with just twenty-six players — twelve Dubs and fourteen Galwegians. Both teams were rather self-conscious as they arrived for Monday's reception. Few players greeted each other. It was all very awkward, even for those who knew opposing players well on a personal level. The final had soured relationships on all fronts. The respective officials were also conscious of the strained atmosphere — indeed some had contributed to it by making inflammatory statements in the immediate aftermatch of the match.

Dublin, although triumphant, were not triumphalist. For while they had won the All-Ireland title, there was a sense of disappointment that far from being remembered as a great game, the final would be recalled as one of the most controversial in GAA history. Dublin were annoyed that their success had become almost a secondary sideshow to the controversies. Besides, Brian Mullins, Ciaran Duff and Ray Hazley had all been sent off and would face disciplinary action.

Despite the tense atmosphere and the unfortunate backdrop, Dublin were however, jubilant. They had won the game with twelve players after staging one of the most defiant second-half efforts ever seen. Galway were in a state of bewildered confusion. Their failure to exploit a two-man advantage with a gale force wind left them open to ridicule. Performances, both on and off the field, were open to justifiable criticism. Galway had lost All-Ireland finals in 1971, 1973 and 1974 but this was the ultimate loss, one which would go down in history, for all the wrong reasons.

Somewhat surprisingly, it was difficult to find traces of embarrassment in the Galway camp. Instead, there was a tendency to rage against Dublin, accusing them of intimidatory tactics. Several Galway officials had cut loose in post-match interviews, depicting Dublin as a squad of hitmen who had no regard for decency or fair play. That analysis was, to say the least, over the top. The fact that midfielder, Brian Talty was unable to play in the second half after an incident in the tunnel on his way to the dressing-room at half-time was used as evidence by Galway to support their 'dirty Dublin' campaign. Certainly, the Talty incident brought no credit on Dublin but to use it as an excuse for Galway's defeat was childishly simplistic. Talty's leadership qualities were undoubtedly missed as Galway thrashed about without focus in the second half but Dublin were missing an equally influential figure in the form of Mullins, who had been sent off in the 23rd minute for a retaliatory foul on Talty.

Just before half-time Ray Hazley (Dublin) and Tomás Tierney (Galway) were sent off after a rather harmless wrestling match. It was their bad luck that, by then, the mood had soured to such a degree that Antrim referee, John Gough was making no allowances for misbehaviour, however trivial it might appear. Gough's willingness to send players off was further underlined just after half-time when Dublin's Ciaran Duff was dismissed for swinging his boot dangerously close to Pat O'Neill's head. The incident probably looked worse than it really was but, in the volatile climate, Gough's decision was understandable. Dublin were leading by 1–7 to 0–2 at the time but despite the eight-point deficit, Galway looked absolutely certain to overtake them. How could they possibly fail? On a day which September had borrowed from dreariest winter, a howling gale was blowing relentlessly into the Railway goal. It was very much behind Galway backs. Besides, they had fourteen players to Dublin's twelve.

All seemed to be going to plan for Galway when Stephen Joyce scored a goal and Mattie Coleman pointed to cut the lead to just three points with almost twenty minutes left. Surely Dublin could not hold out! The next fifteen minutes has gone down in history as one of the greatest survival acts by any team. Dublin's four-man forward line improvised magnificently. Veteran, Anton O'Toole played a central role in holding the ball up any time he got possession; Barney Rock exploited every chance he got while teenagers, Tommy Conroy and Joe McNally played as if they hadn't even spotted the odds stacked so high against them.

Without Talty's calming influence, Galway grew ever more desperate and disjointed. Instead of building slowly and carefully, they rushed their moves. Passes were misdirected (they kicked several over the sideline) as panic took over and with Tommy Drumm and Pat Canavan presiding with shrewd authority over Dublin's resistance, they held on to win by 1–10 to 1–8.

Barney Rock had scored 1–6 for Dublin, with his goal in the 10th minute ultimately proving to be the match-winner. Typical of the 1983 final it was wrapped in controversy. Rock had responded smartly to a poor free out against the wind by Galway goalie, Padraig Coyne and showed a precise touch to hoist the ball into the Galway net from 40 yards as Coyne back-pedalled furiously. Galway protested strongly that the goal should not have been allowed, claiming that Dublin manager, Kevin Heffernan was interfering with play as he attended to the injured Joe McNally. The referee did not agree and Galway were made to pay for a woeful defensive blunder. Given the wind conditions, it was crazy to bring the goalie out to take a free, especially when his line was left unprotected. Besides, Galway full-back, Stephen Kinneavy, was one of the longest kickers of a dead ball at the time, yet he did not take the free from just outside the 21 yards line. It was another example of Galway's questionable appreciation of the tactical demands.

The fall-out from that final lasted for ages. Duff was suspended for a year, Mullins got five months, while both Hazley and Tierney were banned for a month each. Galway centre-back, Peter Lee, although not sent off, was subsequently suspended for a month after an investigation while Kevin Heffernan was suspended for three months for coming onto the pitch too often.

It is impossible to locate the exact source of the ugliness which marred the 1983 final. There was no history of violence in previous Dublin–Galway matches. Nor had there been any provocative statements made by either camp in the run-up to the final. Galway did have some residue of resentment, dating back to the 1974 All-Ireland final when they felt that they did not get as many frees as they deserved against Dublin and that certain players, notably John Tobin, had been subjected to intimidatory tactics, which went unpunished. However, the sides had later met in the All-Ireland semi-final in 1976 and while the exchanges were very tough, there was no great problem in a low scoring game (Dublin 1–8 Galway 0–8).

The truth is that there was no one reason why the 1983 final boiled over. Instead, a whole set of circumstances conspired to turn it into an ugly encounter which reflected very poorly on all concerned. The bad weather conditions ensured that the physical battle would be more intense than usual. A high wind played all sort of tricks with the ball, leading to inevitable frustrations as players tried to cope. While the weather was a factor, it would be silly to blame it for all the problems. For whatever reason, personal antagonisms gathered momentum at an alarming rate until they were eventually out of control.

The controversial final tended to overshadow Dublin's great achievement that year in coming from way off the championship pace to actually take the title. They had started out with no great hopes of dethroning Offaly in Leinster. A year earlier, Dublin had been wiped off Croke Park by Offaly in the Leinster final, eventually losing by 1–16 to 1–7 after trailing by 1–9 to 0–3 at half-time. Dublin had looked spiritless and leaderless that day, yet a year later they would win the All-Ireland final with a team which contained nine of the side hammered by Offaly in 1982.

The irony of the 1983 final was that both Dublin and Galway were extremely lucky to be in it all. Meath, in their first season under Sean Boylan's management, had pushed Dublin to the limit in the quarter-final. The sides drew 2–8 each in Croke Park and it took extra time in the replay before Dublin finally squeezed through by 3–9 to 0–16. Dublin held a huge psychological edge over Meath in those days. Meath had failed against Dublin in the 1974–76–77 Leinster finals, before heading into a trough where even routine first round games against modest opposition became too much for them. By 1983, Meath were beginning the slow haul back up the rankings but still lacked the mental resolve to cope with a far more self-assured Dublin team. Nonetheless, Meath's energetic surge had come very close to squeezing them through.

Dublin fans felt that their side might have used the season's luck quota against Meath but that wasn't the case. After ending Offaly's reign as All-Ireland champions with an impressive performance in the Leinster final, Dublin were out-played for long periods by Cork in the All-Ireland semi-final. Indeed, they looked dead and buried when Cork led by three points as the game ticked to a conclusion. Then up popped Barney Rock to score the equalising goal. The recovery was a tribute to Dublin's never-say-die spirit but it must be said that Cork's failure to make more of their dominant periods was a major factor in enabling Dublin to hang on before finally striking for the equalising goal.

The replay in Pairc Ui Chaoimh a week later was one of the season's highlights. It was also one of Dublin's best performances for years. The general view was that Cork would exploit home advantage but they were never allowed to settle into a rhythm and Dublin romped home by 4–15 to 2–10. If Dublin had some lucky breaks *en route* to the final, the same applied to Galway. In fact, they should never have survived the first round of the Connacht championship against Leitrim in Carrick-on-Shannon. With Mickey Quinn producing a truly outstanding performance at midfield, Leitrim controlled much of the game but, like Meath against Dublin, they lacked the self-belief necessary to beat Galway. If ever there was a case of tradition playing a big part in deciding a game, this was it. Over the years, Galway had almost always beaten Leitrim. With history's heavy hand bearing down on them, Leitrim needed to be five or six points better than Galway to actually win in 1983. Alas for Leitrim, they eventually ran out of personal resolve and were beaten by 1–8 to 1–6.

Galway deservedly beat Mayo by three points in the Connacht final but rode their luck to hell and back in the All-Ireland semi-final against Donegal. Once again, tradition seemed to play a major part. Donegal led for most of the way but failed to shake off a Galway team, which was not playing particularly well. Almost inevitably though, the county with a big tradition will finish better in such circumstances. Luckily for Galway, Donegal did not capitalise on their superiority and a late goal by Val Daly edged Galway home by 1–12 to 1–11.

The odds favoured Dublin going into the final. Apart from anything else, they had a great record against Galway, having won six of the eight championship games between the sides. In fact, Galway hadn't beaten Dublin in the championship since the 1934 All-Ireland final.

Whatever the reason for the breakdown in discipline, the sad reality was that the 1983 All-Ireland final cost the GAA dearly in terms of public relations. Gaelic football was depicted as a brawling mess where the protagonists not only thumped each other on the field but also took their grievances into the tunnel at half-time.

The GAA authorities, shocked by the manner in which one of their showpiece games had disintegrated into an embarrassing shambles, should have acted quickly. Instead, they took weeks to sort out all the disciplinary matters arising from the final. That was another public relations disaster as it ensured that the ugly game held centre-stage for far longer than it should have. The GAA have always contended that procedures must be followed and that it takes time to deal with disciplinary matters in a fair way. However, given the bad publicity the 1983 football final continued to attract in the subsequent weeks, it was imperative to have acted much quicker than they did.

Dublin felt aggrieved by the eventual outcome of the GAA's deliberations, believing that they were handed far too much of the responsibility for the controversies. Ultimately though, it didn't matter to Dublin; they had the Sam Maguire trophy while Galway were left with a horrible sense of loss.

DUBLIN: John O'Leary; Mick Holden, Gerry Hargan, Ray Hazley; Pat Canavan, Tommy Drumm, P.J. Buckley; Jim Roynane, Brian Mullins; Barney Rock, Tommy Conroy, Ciaran Duff; John Caffrey, Anton O'Toole, Joe McNally.
Subs: John Kearns for Conroy, Frank McGrath for Caffrey.

GALWAY: Padraig Coyne; Johnny Hughes, Stephen Kinneavy, Mattie Coleman; Pat O'Neill, Peter Lee, Seamus McHugh; Brian Talty, Richie Lee; Barry Brennan, Val Daly, Brian O'Donnell; Tomás Tierney, Gay McManus, Stephen Joyce.
Subs: Michael Brennan for Talty; Billy Joyce for Lee, John Tobin for Hughes.

Chapter 5

✥ ✥ ✥

Managers

One of the most dramatic changes in hurling and football over the past twenty-five years has been the arrival on the scene of team managers, many of whom have total control of selection and tactical policy.

Prior to that most teams were looked after by selection committees who were voted into office. While a team trainer was usually appointed to oversee the preparations, decisions were taken on a collective basis. Big selection committees were not unusual. For instance, at one stage during Galway's All-Ireland football three-in-a-row run in 1964–65–66, there were as many as eleven selectors choosing the team.

The switch to more centralised management was a direct follow-on from the upsurge of interest in English soccer. The television age had brought English soccer into Irish homes for the first time in the late sixties and early seventies so it was inevitable that some of its influence would rub off. The team manager syndrome was about to take off in the GAA.

Events in Dublin and Kerry ensured that the cult of the manager gathered rapid momentum. They were first to vest almost total power in managers with the appointment of Kevin Heffernan and Mick O'Dwyer. Both enjoyed great success and other counties followed suit.

Nowadays, virtually all teams operate with a team manager. In many cases the team manager is allowed to choose his own selectors which, of course, increases his power and influence. The upsurge in media interest in Gaelic Games has further raised the team manager's profile. The managers, rather than the players, are the first people journalists turn to for comment before and after a game.

It has now become accepted that the manager can make or break a team, which is why the more successful managers are sought after well beyond the

A man with a vision... Kevin Heffernan took team management onto a new level back in the 1970s.

Breaking the mould... Manager, Dermot Healy, switched from Kilkenny to Offaly and guided them to a double All-Ireland success in 1981–85.

The day Kerry's five-in-a-row dream died. Offaly were the team to finally end Kerry's bid for a place in history in the 1982 All-Ireland final. Johnny Mooney (Offaly) has possession, watched by team mate, Matt Connor, while Kerry's Paudie Lynch and John O'Keeffe close in.

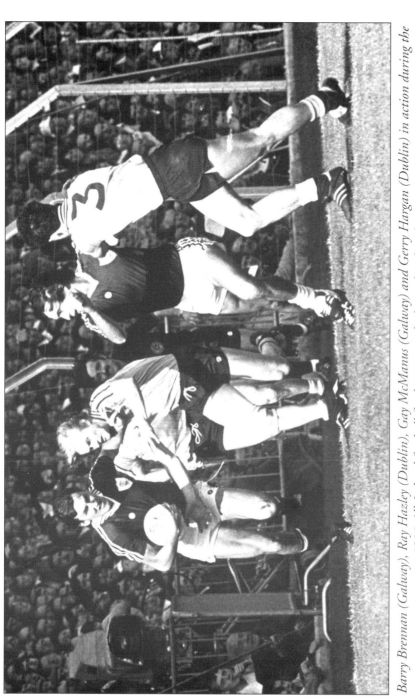

Barry Brennan (Galway), Ray Hazley (Dublin), Gay McManus (Galway) and Gerry Hargan (Dublin) in action during the 1983 All-Ireland football final, a game which was laced with controversy.

The Galway–Tipperary rivalry of the 1980s produced some great battles. Nicky English and Pat Fox (both Tipperary) and Galway's Conor Hayes all played crucial roles at various stages.

History in the making... Cork are on their way to their first ever All-Ireland football double in 1990. To make it all the sweeter, they beat old rivals Meath. Colm O'Neill (Cork) and Gerry McEntee (Meath) tangle for possession, watched by Dave Barry (Cork), Martin O'Connell (Meath), Mick Lyons (Meath) and Larry Tompkins (Cork).

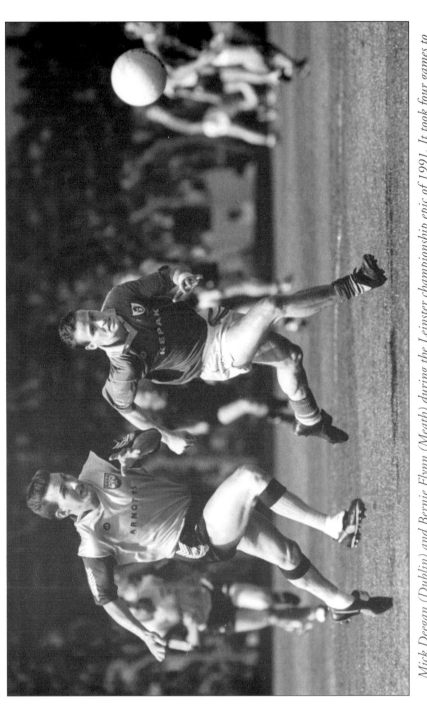

Mick Deegan (Dublin) and Bernie Flynn (Meath) during the Leinster championship epic of 1991. It took four games to separate them, with Meath eventually winning by a point.

Brian Corcoran (Cork), on the right, burst onto the championship scene in 1992 with a series of great performances but Eamonn Morrissey had the last laugh as Kilkenny beat Cork in the All-Ireland final.

*Cyril Farrell was re-appointed as Galway team manager in September 1996
for the third time. He is one of the most successful managers in hurling history,
having previously guided Galway to All-Ireland successes in 1980–87–88.*

confines of their own counties. Several high-profile managers have crossed over achieving glory with their adopted counties.

This chapter looks at a range of managers over the years under various headings. Kevin Heffernan and Mick O'Dwyer were very much the trend-setters, setting standards for others to follow. Cyril Farrell, Dermot Healy, Ger Loughnane, Eamonn Coleman and Brian McEniff were the mould-breakers, men who refused to accept that a losing tradition was a barrier to success in counties which hadn't achieved a whole lot down through the years.

The power of persistence was typified by Sean Boylan, Billy Morgan and Pat O'Neill, all of whom experience heartbreaking failures, prior to making the breakthrough. Hurling success always came naturally to Kilkenny, Cork and Tipperary but there are times when even the super-powers needed special managerial skills. Pat Henderson, 'Babs' Keating, Johnny Clifford and the late Ollie Walsh provided those skills in glorious abundance.

The ability to maximise a county's asset is one of the most important talents a manager can possess — as instanced by the success rate of Eugene McGee, Peter McGrath, John O'Mahoney and John Maughan. There are many who claim that far too much responsibility is thrust upon team managers and that they get too much credit in victory and too much criticism in defeat. Then there are the cases of managers who did nothing wrong but still ended up as losers. Luck is always the unpredictable ingredient, over which no manger has control. Tom Heneghan, Sean McCague, Christy Keogh, Gerry McCaul and Seamus McCarthy are amongst the managers who, for various reasons, could consider themselves unlucky not to have achieved more than they did.

The Trend-setters

(Kevin Heffernan, Mick O'Dwyer)

When Kevin Heffernan took over as Dublin football team manager in 1973 nobody could possibly have envisaged that his appointment would lead to a fundamental overhaul of the manner in which GAA teams were looked after. Heffernan was, in effect, the first man to be given complete control of affairs.

Television's increasing influence on sporting life had introduced the GAA to the cult of the manager. English soccer, in particular, was taken as the role model. If one man could take full charge of a professional soccer team, with all its attendant pressures, surely the same could be tried in Gaelic football and hurling.

At the time of Heffernan's appointment, there was something of a quiet desperation prevailing in Dublin football. Not alone had Dublin failed to win an All-Ireland title since 1963, they were no longer serious contenders. In fact, they hadn't even reached a Leinster final since 1965. Meantime, Meath and Offaly had dominated Leinster, and even Longford had got in on the act, having won the title in 1968.

The GAA authorities were worried about the state of football in Dublin. For while Dublin may believe that the other thirty-one counties want to see them down, those who possess a broader vision for Gaelic football know that a healthy, vibrant Dublin scene is good for the game. The Dublin County Board turned to Heffernan in their hour of need. A man with a great playing career behind him, he was fiercely proud of Dublin football and all it stood for. The challenge of trying to hoist it back up to its rightful status excited him. His appointment as Dublin manager didn't make very big headlines. For while he was highly regarded as a shrewd judge and an able tactician, it was felt that Dublin lacked enough players of genuine quality to seriously challenge for the game's top honours.

The significance of his appointment wasn't apparent at the time. However, it would change forever the structure under which GAA teams operated. The age of the manager had arrived. Heffernan had full control of affairs, although he did place a great deal of trust in his co-selectors, Donal Colfer and Lorcan Redmond, certainly when it came to making an assessment of a player.

When Mick O'Dwyer took over as Kerry manager early in 1975, there was an air of gloom hanging over the Kingdom. Outsiders would find it hard to understand why there should be despondency in a county which had completed yet another two-in-a-row just five years earlier and which had won four consecutive National League titles in 1971–74.

Things were different in Kerry. They expected success. Not just any success but the ultimate accolade, i.e. the All-Ireland title. National League titles were all very fine for filling in the days in the run-up to the championship but the real test of a Kerry team was whether or not they were in Croke Park in September.

It is quite probable that Dublin's 1974 success under Kevin Heffernan was central to Kerry's decision to adopt a more streamlined sideline structure. There had been criticisms of sideline performances in the previous seasons and it was decided at the start of 1975 to vest most of the power in O'Dwyer, the newly-appointed team manager. Dublin's success under Heffernan was even mentioned at the Kerry Convention that year.

Unquestionably, Heffernan and O'Dwyer were the trend-setters when it came to team management. Their first priority was to raise fitness levels. The theory was simple. A team manager may have no control over the quality of players at his disposal but he can very definitely influence their fitness levels.

The duration of championship games had been increased from sixty to eighty minutes in 1970. That was quite a change and required a whole new approach to training methods. When O'Dwyer and Heffernan came face to face with each other for the first time as managers in the 1975 All-Ireland final, the duration of championship games had been cut back to seventy minutes but, by now, the emphasis was very much on acquiring levels of fitness which were unprecedented in the GAA.

Both O'Dwyer and Heffernan also decided that super-fitness could be used to exploit the change of rule which allowed the use of the hand-pass. For several years, it wasn't a hand-pass at all but rather a basketball-like throw. It made for speedy games but there was very little actual football on view.

Neither O'Dwyer nor Heffernan saw that as their problem. The GAA had devised a set of rules and they would exploit them to the maximum. Indeed it was quite common for Kerry players to test out the referee's reaction to a questionable hand-pass early on in a game. If the referee allowed it, then it would become the norm for the day; if he penalised it, then Kerry would use a more refined, if less effective, version.

It was typical of O'Dwyer's meticulous attention to detail that he would think of such a ploy but so great was his psychological battle with Heffernan that both men were trying to out-manoeuvre each other all the time. Neither would admit to that, claiming that their only motivation was to get the best out of their players, but there can be no doubt that they derived a lot of satisfaction from devising way of out-flanking each other.

O'Dwyer started and finished on top of the duel. His young tigers ripped Dublin apart in 1975 and, took complete control in the late seventies, beating Dublin by seventeen and eleven points respectively in the 1978–79 All-Ireland finals. O'Dwyer's men also held the upperhand over Dublin in Kerry's second coming in 1984–85.

But in between, Heffernan had masterminded a great success. That was in 1976 when Dublin avenged the 1975 defeat by Kerry with a comprehensive 3–8 to 0–10 win in the All-Ireland final. Eleven months later, Dublin again beat Kerry — this time in the All-Ireland semi-final — and while it was regarded as one of the greatest games in the history of Gaelic football, it almost cost O'Dwyer the team manager's job. Coming on top of the 1976 defeat, the 1977 setback led to criticisms of O'Dwyer's management within Kerry. The reaction convinced O'Dwyer of one thing — it doesn't matter what you achieve, the critics are only a few defeats away from full voice. It was something he would never forget.

Heffernan's grip on the Dublin public was tighter. They accepted defeats under his reign as if they had nothing whatsoever to do with him. In a sense Heffernan enjoyed the best of both worlds. When Dublin won he got the credit, when they lost the players took the blame. That was not the case in Kerry where it was generally believed that the county had so much talent that O'Dwyer's role was merely to apply an organisational role.

That was only partially true. For while he was lucky that his term as manager coincided with the arrival of an incredibly talented collection of athletes, his sharp football brain, allied to a willingness to experiment with new techniques, was critical in harnessing those special talents. His boundless enthusiasm was also central to Kerry's amazing success run between 1975 and 1986.

The Kerry players readily accepted that this was one of his greatest attributes. It takes a special managerial talent to keep a squad together for so long. O'Dwyer achieved it, year after year after year. O'Dwyer has one great regret about his managerial career. He would have dearly loved to have been part of history but was denied in the most dramatic circumstances by Offaly who shattered the five-in-a-row dream in 1982.

While both Heffernan and O'Dwyer very much set the trend in the managerial stakes, they had different approaches to off-field activities. O'Dwyer believed that success should be exploited in a positive way so that GAA players could reap some commercial benefits from their achievements. Kerry were generally one step ahead of the GAA guidelines on amateurism and O'Dwyer, a shrewd businessman, was assumed to have been at the heart of the shift towards a more commercial-friendly environment.

O'Dwyer's biographer, Owen McCrohan wrote that O'Dwyer 'had sailed close to the wind; so close in fact that he might, with justification, have been charged under the most emotive rule in the book, that of bringing the Association into disrepute.' O'Dwyer's view was the time was ripe for players to exploit their success. Owen McCrohan quoted him thus in the biography: 'Realistically, all we did was show the GAA how easy it was to get money. In doing so, we helped a lot of people to grow up. We opened up new horizons and, where we led, others have followed. Nowadays, nobody bats an eyelid if some county team decides to take a foreign holiday. There is no longer an outcry over the wearing of specific sportswear. If this shows that some people have matured, then that is a good thing and we must claim credit for it. It was, of course, unfortunate that that we were made scapegoats for the growing pains within the GAA. It is also regrettable that so many guardians of morality begrudged us a sunshine holiday.'

Although the GAA authorities never acknowledged it publicly at the time, they were suspicious of O'Dwyer's efforts to open the door to commercialism. Ten years on, they are knocking on every door themselves in an effort to capitalise on sponsorship opportunities. O'Dwyer, the trend-setter, had shown them how.

Kevin Heffernan showed little interest in this side of affairs. However, he had his own run-in with the GAA authorities when he was suspended for encroaching on the pitch during the 1983 All-Ireland final against Galway. Two years later, the GAA selected him ahead of O'Dwyer to manage the Irish Compromise Rules team for the tour to Australia. It was the first time that a decision had to be made as to the relative abilities of the trend-setting pair and, for whatever reason, the GAA came down on Heffernan's side. O'Dwyer was both surprised and disappointed. The GAA gave no reason for the decision.

It was always going to be a tough choice but, on the evidence of his record, O'Dwyer appeared to be the logical candidate, even allowing for Heffernan's great managerial skills. O'Dwyer may well have paid the price for his out-spoken attitude and for his views on commercialism within the GAA. Heffernan was seen as the safer option and, together with assistant coach, Galway's Liam Sammon, presided over an Irish team which beat the Australians 2–1 in the three-test series.

Heffernan's reign as Dublin manager (he had opted out for a period in the 1970s with Tony Hanahoe taking over) finally ended in January 1986. It seemed like an odd time to quit, as team managers normally step down after a championship campaign. That would have been easy in Heffernan's case as Dublin lost the 1984–85 All-Ireland finals to Kerry. However, Heffernan stayed for a few months after the second defeat. The inside view was that the timing of his resignation was linked to changes within the Dublin County Board.

O'Dwyer stayed at the helm in Kerry until the third consecutive Munster final defeat by Cork in 1989. Just over a year later, he took over as Kildare manager in a high-profile move. He succeeded in raising the county's football awareness and took them to two Leinster finals and a National League decider but lost all three to Dublin. His great dream of making the breakthrough with an adopted county did not materialise. Nonetheless, he had achieved more than any other manager in the history of Gaelic football.

O'Dwyer and Heffernan will go down in GAA history as the men who changed the whole approach towards the preparation of teams. Their methods were rapidly copied by others but, as is the case with all good managers, they kept devising new ideas all the time. They really were trend-setters in every way.

Mould-breakers

(Cyril Farrell, Dermot Healy, Ger Loughnane, Eamonn Coleman, Brian McEniff)

Between 1923 and 1979 Galway hurlers didn't win a single All-Ireland senior hurling title. They won three of the next nine. Offaly hurlers had won no All-Ireland title up to 1981. They took two of the next five. At the start of 1995, Clare hurlers had gone eighty-one years without winning an All-Ireland title and sixty-three years without winning a Munster final. By the end of the year, they had won both.

Derry footballers failed to win an All-Ireland senior title in over one hundred years of the competition and, as they headed into the 1993 championship, they hadn't even reached a final since 1958. All changed in September '93 when they beat Dublin to win their first ever senior final. A year earlier, Donegal had scripted their own piece of history, also winning the All-Ireland final for the first time.

Five counties, five tales of how they broke free from the shackles of history to take their place at the top table. In all cases, the main credit has to go to the players who succeeded where their predecessors had failed but there is also the story of the managers, five men who helped make all the difference in tight situations, where steely nerves, tactical sharpness and good decision-making were required.

Ironically, Cyril Farrell, who managed Galway and brought them hurling glory in 1980–87-88 and Dermot Healy, who was at the helm when Offaly won in 1981–85, had never reached any great heights as players. Like Eugene McGee and Sean Boylan, in football, they proved that the secret of being a good manager has nothing to do with success as a player. Not that it is an hindrance either. Clare's Ger Loughnane was one of hurling's most distinguished wing-backs for several seasons and, by a curious coincidence, Brian McEniff played in the same position for Donegal footballers for many years, prior to turning his fertile brain to management. Eamonn Coleman, Derry manager in 1993, had also been an inter-county player.

The first link in the mould-breaking chain is self-belief. Without it, there is no possible chance of success. Individuals acquire it in different ways. Cyril Farrell acquired it by adopting a near-paranoid stance, based on the belief that outsiders saw Galway hurling as a sort of warm-up act, which would never prove good enough to command centre-stage on its own.

His thought process was helped in no small way by the decision to bring in 'Babs' Keating to coach the Galway team in 1979. Farrell was trainer but had no real power and was absolutely devastated when Galway lost the All-Ireland final to Kilkenny. He was given sole managerial charge for the following season. Otherwise he would have walked away from it.

Farrell has always believed that the west has been badly treated. Years of neglect by governments and other agencies had, according to Farrell, drained people's self-confidence. That created an inferiority complex which manifested itself in many ways, not least the manner in which some good Galway hurling teams had allowed their resolve to be drained away when confronted with the likes of Tipperary, Kilkenny or Cork.

Farrell saw three things as essential to a Galway breakthrough when he took over in 1979. He would have to banish the squad's insecurities; fitness levels would have to raised (shades of O'Dwyer and Heffernan in football) and specific plans to suit the Galway style would have to be devised.

That he achieved all three in less than ten months is a compliment to his persuasive skills, not to mention his tactical appreciation, plus an ability to get a team physically geared for the most stern tests. It all came right for him in September 1980 when Galway buried the ghosts of past failures, beating Limerick in the All-Ireland final by 2–15 to 3–9.

It was to be the start of a great decade for Galway, a period in which they won more All-Irelands than Cork, Kilkenny or Tipperary, hurling's three great powers for so long. Farrell's mould-breaking continued in 1987–88 when Galway won their first ever two-in-a-row, and he was also in charge when Galway won their first-ever All-Ireland minor title in 1983.

Farrell's contribution to the liberation of Galway hurling was immense. While it couldn't have been achieved in an era when Galway had less talent coming on stream, there is no doubt that Farrell's methods, allied to his incredible self-belief, provided the vital spark which lit Galway's brightest fires.

Kilkenny man, Dermot Healy was brought in as Offaly coach in 1979 for two reasons. Firstly, he had proved himself an accomplished coach at under-age level and secondly, Offaly felt that the time had come to look for outside assistance. Ironically at a time when Galway were dispensing with that idea, Offaly were adopting it. It was to work well for them.

Offaly was the ideal setting for Healy to test his coaching skills at the highest level. Genuine progress was being made but the view was that it would take something a little extra to make the long-awaited breakthrough. Healy provided that extra ingredient. For while he had no big-time experience with Kilkenny, the Offaly players still regarded him as something of a Messiah. Who better to coach us than a man who was brought up in the heartland of our long-time bogey team?

When Healy guided Offaly to their first Leinster title win in July 1980, there were many who thought that it was merely a question of catching Kilkenny on a bad day. Few Offaly fans will admit as much nowadays but the fact that only 9,000 attended the game suggests that not even Offaly fans held out much hope. Fourteen months later Offaly's following had grown dramatically as the team reached the All-Ireland final where they staged a remarkable comeback to beat Galway by three points. Healy, the Messiah, had delivered in a very short space of time. The basis of his managerial success centred on superimposing the Kilkenny style and approach on Offaly's game plan. Men like Andy Gallagher had toiled long and hard to haul Offaly to the top and while his role should never be overlooked in the breakthrough, it was quite natural that most of the public acclaim should go to Dermot Healy.

If the 1981 success was sweet, the 1985 All-Ireland triumph was equally satisfactory. Winning the second All-Ireland in the space of four years established Offaly as a genuine hurling force, something they badly wanted to achieve after a rather disappointing effort against Cork in the 1984 All-Ireland final in Thurles.

To this day, Dermot Healy's name is spoken with reverence in Offaly. When things were going badly for Offaly at the start of the 1996 championship, manager Eamonn Cregan, invited Healy to talk to the Offaly squad. It typified the respect in which Healy is held in Offaly. Indeed it is a position he is likely to occupy all his life. Mould-breakers are never forgotten.

Ger Loughnane looked a most unlikely candidate for mould-breaking status a few years ago after a highly-fancied Clare U-21 team, which he was managing, failed to deliver. Loughnane's stewardship came in for a lot of criticism and it seemed as if his ambition to take over the senior team in the future would never be fulfilled. However, he eventually did get his chance, initially serving his time as a selector under Len Gaynor's managership. Loughnane's single-mindedness was underlined by the fact that he only agreed to become a selector on the condition that when Gaynor resigned as manager, he would take over. His chance came in the autumn of 1994 and less than a year later, Clare were celebrating a famous All-Ireland success.

In many ways, Loughnane resembled Cyril Farrell in Galway. Loughnane always believed that bringing in an outside manager was not appropriate. Clare would win an All-Ireland title in their own right if they were good enough. Looking across borders for help may have been understandable but it was not necessary. Loughnane's selectors, Michael McNamara and Tony Considine were of like-mind. Loughnane brought one vital ingredient to the Clare mix. He wasn't just ambitious, he was also extremely confident of his own ability. Nobody can be quite sure whether or not Clare's 1995 training regime was tougher than any other county but Loughnane and Co. very cleverly gave the impression that it was. Tales of 7 a.m training sessions gradually wafted all over the country and while there is absolutely no evidence to suggest that a morning session is any better than an evening one, the important thing from Clare's viewpoint was that a message was sent out that they meant business.

Loughnane's capacity to convince his players that they really could beat the best was critical. So too was his ability to keep them going after winning the Munster final. Critics predicted that the celebrational trail would swamp the team after the Munster final, leaving them easy pickings for Galway in the All-Ireland semi-final. It was to Loughnane's credit that he succeeded in keeping the balance between celebration and ambition just right. Some managers — and indeed players — might have been happy to have won a Provincial title for the first time in sixty-three years. Not Loughnane or his players. They rightly regarded it as no more than a stepping stone to bigger things.

Loughnane's self-belief was perfectly illustrated on the day of the All-Ireland final when he almost climbed into an RTE camera lens on his way back out of the dressing-rooms after the half-time break to tell the nation: 'we are going to win'. Clare were trailing at the time but there was such passion and sincerity about his statement that nobody could possibly believe it wouldn't prove accurate. It did. Loughnane and Clare had broken the mould.

If Ger Loughnane had to recover from a bad experience with an U-21 side before re-launching his career at senior level, Donegal's Brian McEniff had to re-launch himself on no fewer than three occasions before finally placing the flag on the management summit. It's difficult to think about Donegal football without McEniff. He has always seemed to be part of it, first as a player, then as a player-manager and finally as a manager who had the resolve, persistence and know-how to lead Donegal to their first ever All-Ireland success in 1992.

McEniff's greatest asset was his passionate love of football. It wasn't something merely to occupy his spare time but rather a way of life, an expression of his personality. Few people would want to come back for more after being removed as team manager on three occasions but McEniff had such a sense of pride in Donegal football that the political side didn't bother him.

Nor did he subscribe to the view that Donegal would always fall short of the required level to make the breakthrough. That wasn't easy, given that fate seemed to deal Donegal a bad hand on the really big days. Donegal seemed to be heading into their first All-Ireland in 1983 when they led

Galway for most of the way in the semi-final only to get caught by a late Val Daly goal. Early in 1992, they led Dublin by four points with just a few minutes to go in the National League quarter-final but were beaten by two late goals.

Nonetheless, McEniff retained faith in the squad and steered them through to the All-Ireland final less than six months later. Many managers are inclined to deal in total isolation, refusing to listen to any outside opinion. McEniff was different. Before the 1992 All-Ireland final he decided to speak to several people who had been through the big-day experience, including Pete McGrath, Larry Tompkins, Jack O'Shea, Art McRory and Ogie Moran. He wasn't necessarily going to follow their advice but he took it all on board, mixed it with his own views, and produced the final blueprint which would lead Donegal to the promised land.

McEniff would have to figure very high on any list of great managers, not least because of his willingness to battle on despite suffering so much frustration. He finally achieved his goal of winning an All-Ireland final but whether or not that has dulled him ambitions remains to be seen. Given his past record, very few people would bet against him making another comeback as Donegal manager some time in the future.

While McEniff left the Donegal job in the most harmonious of circumstances in 1993, Derry's Eamonn Coleman had a much different experience a year later. Coleman, one of the most colourful managerial characters of recent times, was removed as Derry manager by the County Board a few months after losing to Down in the 1994 Ulster championship. His dismissal led to bitterness, division and acrimony, with the Derry squad threatening to go on strike at one stage. It was all a far cry from the glorious summer and autumn of 1993 as Coleman led Derry to their first ever All-Ireland success.

Coleman was very much a players' man and always said that he would prefer to be down at the back of the bus with the players than up front with County Board officials. It was a policy which endeared him to the squad but which created a divide between him and the Derry County Board. Ultimately he would pay a heavy price for not forming a better relationship with officialdom.

Coleman gave the impression of being abrasive and unfriendly and liked nothing better than to publicly chide journalists who had dared to predict that Derry were going to lose a game. Beneath the gruff exterior lay a mischievous individual with a great sense of fun, a man who, like McEniff, would listen to other people's opinions before making up his own mind.

Coleman took Derry from being an enthusiastic bunch of naive hopefuls to a stage where they were the best-organised, most highly motivated team in the country. They won the 1993 title the hard way, beating Down, the 1991 All-Ireland champions, Monaghan, Donegal, the 1992 All-Ireland champions, Dublin and Cork. Up to 1993, Derry did not have a particularly good record in Croke Park. In fact, they were regarded as a county which lost its resolve once they faced serious questions in Croke Park. Eamonn Coleman worked hard at changing the attitude and the extent to which he succeeded is underlined by the fact that Derry came back from five-point deficits in both the All-Ireland semi-final against Dublin and in the final against Cork. The refusal to accept defeat was one of Derry's trade marks in that remarkable season and Coleman's contribution to the players' new-found self-belief possibly ranks as his best achievement.

Unquestionably, Donegal's breakthrough in 1992 provided Derry with great encouragement once they got their chance the following year but they were lucky to have had a man like Eamonn Coleman in charge. Mould-breaking seemed to come natural to the Ballymaguigan man.

If At First You Don't Succeed....

(Sean Boylan, Billy Morgan, Pat O'Neill)

At the end of the 1985 championship season, Sean Boylan was faced with a dilemma. This was to have been the year when Meath pressed on and won a Leinster football title. Instead, they didn't get past the semi-final where they were hammered 2–11 to 0–7 by Laois in Tullamore.

It was all very bewildering. The script never allowed for such a setback after the two previous seasons when Meath's graph line had been rising rapidly. They had fallen in the first round of the 1983 championship but the circumstances were comforting enough to suggest that there were better times ahead. Meath had, in fact, forced Dublin into extra time in a replay before losing by three points.

In 1984, Meath won the special Centenary Cup competition which was introduced to mark the GAAs 100th anniversary, beating Monaghan in the final. Later on they reached the Leinster final where they played well below par but still ran Dublin to four points. Everything seemed right for 1985, the year in which Meath would finally end their fifteen-year barren run in Leinster.

Not so. They were positively taken apart by Laois. The nature of the defeat shattered the Meath squad. Questions were asked about Boylan's managership and he even had to survive a vote at a County Board meeting to remain in office. Boylan was very keen to stay on. The Laois experience had been devastating but it had served a very valuable purpose. A narrow defeat might have given the false impression that there wasn't much wrong with the overall structure. A ten-point defeat left nobody in any doubt that major surgery was required.

With his fresh mandate, Boylan set about re-organising the squad and by the time Meath won the Leinster final thirteen months later, there were wholesale changes on the team. Meath went on to win four of the next five Leinster titles and also won two All-Ireland finals in the greatest run in the county's history.

It would have been easy for Boylan to have walked away after the Laois defeat in 1985, especially as he came under pressure from factions within Meath who felt that he would never achieve anything with the side. Boylan saw it differently. He had come into a Meath camp in the autumn of 1982 to be met with a dispirited squad who had lost first round Leinster championship games to Wexford and Longford in 1981–82. He reckoned that considerable progress had been made in his three years in office and he was extremely reluctant to hand over at a time when things were coming right.

The 1985 defeat by Laois was, according to Boylan, simply part of the learning process. Once the lesson had been learned, it could quickly be forgotten. Boylan's persistence paid off and he went on to become one the most successful managers in the history of Gaelic football.

Boylan's managerial qualities were enhanced by his stewardship in the 1995–96 seasons. After losing to Dublin by ten points in the 1995. Leinster final, Boylan had to survive an election. With a fresh mandate and new selectors Boylan re-built the side and was rewarded with another All-Ireland success in 1996.

When Billy Morgan took over as Cork manager in 1986, few people realised that things were about to take a dramatic change in Munster football. Kerry's dominance had gone unchecked between 1974 and 1982 and while Cork had won the 1983 final with a smash and grab effort, Kerry had returned to the winners' bay a year later, a position they continued to occupy in 1985–86.

It was always only a matter of time before Morgan took over in Cork. Even as a player, he had often been involved in managerial duties and found it all came very naturally. Nonetheless, Morgan could never have imagined how quickly Cork would have won a Munster title under his guidance. A draw with Kerry in the 1987 final seemed to hand the initiative to the Kingdom but the bell finally tolled for an aging team when they were swept aside by Cork in the replay in Killarney. A new era had been launched.

Cork lost the 1987 Munster final to Meath and, while they retained the Munster title in 1988, they found Meath again too good for them in the All-Ireland final. Admittedly, it was desperately close with Meath scraping home by a point in a controversial replay. It was at this stage that Morgan's resilience came under scrutiny. Unquestionably, Cork had made great progress but had still lost two consecutive All-Ireland finals.

Morgan decided that a change of strategy was needed. Cork had never been known as League specialists but Morgan decided that it was vital to win a national title to restore confidence. Cork put in a really big effort for the 1988/89 League and were rewarded with a final win over Dublin.

That victory served two purposes. Not only did it give Cork a national title, it also put down a marker which would be extremely important later in the year when they met Dublin in the All-Ireland semi-final. They almost blew that game, allowing Dublin into a big early lead. Indeed, were it not for two giveaway goals by Dublin, Cork might have been in serious trouble. As it was, they won by four points, beat Mayo in the final and completed the county's first-ever All-Ireland double a year later, beating old rivals Meath.

It had been a long haul for Cork but they had finally proved themselves to be a truly great team. Morgan's constant belief in his players had been crucial. Always regarded as the ultimate players' manager, Morgan didn't always have a good relationship with County Board officials but he never lost sight of the real goal and his dogged persistence was eventually rewarded.

When Paddy Cullen was appointed Dublin manager in 1990, he was joined as selectors by former colleagues, Pat O'Neill and Jim Brogan. At first, everything went well. The championship saga with Meath in 1991 had so much drama and excitement packed into it that, although Dublin lost, there was no sense of despair. Dublin believed that their time would come, a view which seemed well-founded when they reached the 1992 All-Ireland final. They went into that game as red-hot favourites. Nobody disputed Donegal's talents, it was more a question of whether or not they could overcome the burden of history. After all, Donegal had never won an All-Ireland final.

That unenviable record was shattered in 1992 when Donegal produced a great performance to beat Dublin by four points. As Donegal celebrated, the fall-out in Dublin was pretty heavy. It quickly became apparent that all was not well with the management team. Paddy Cullen eventually resigned and Pat O'Neill took over as manager. Dublin's reign continued in Leinster but there was a major setback in the 1993 All-Ireland semi-final when Derry hauled back a five-point lead to beat Dublin by a point. That was a massive blow to O'Neill. Still, he had only been in the manager's chair for a year and felt that it would take another season to really get things right.

He was wrong. Dublin reached the 1994 All-Ireland final but this time they found Down too good for them. Down were hanging on in the end but a penalty miss by Charlie Redmond blew Dublin's final chance. It was at this stage that O'Neill's powers of persistence were tested. While he still had a year of his term to run, he knew full well that many Dublin fans were questioning his capacity to lead his team to that elusive All-Ireland win.

Nevertheless, when he looked at the situation in a cool, clinical way, he would point to the fact that Dublin's only championship defeat in three years had been to the eventual All-Ireland champions. Dublin must be doing something right. He would give it more go in 1995.

O'Neill's decision to continue coincided with the arrival on the scene of a youngster with a special talent, Jason Sherlock. Sherlock had played on the 1994 minor team which lost the All-Ireland semi-final to Galway and although of slight physique, he clearly possessed that little extra which can unlock defences.

As the summer of 1995 progressed, Sherlock's importance to the Dublin set-up became increasingly clear. O'Neill took the bold gamble of playing him at full-forward, on the basis that you place your deadliest sniper closest to the target. It worked perfectly. Sherlock scored the goal which beat Cork in the All-Ireland semi-final and set up the all-important goal for Charlie Redmond in the final against Tyrone. In the end, Dublin were hanging on for survival — and were extremely lucky to attain it — but it didn't matter. Sam Maguire was back in the capital after eleven years. O'Neill's persistence had paid off.

He might well have walked away after the defeat by Down a year earlier but deep down he believed that there wasn't a whole lot wrong with the set-up. He was proved right. If O'Neill showed that he could be as persistent as was required in a tough, lonely business he also proved that he could take brave decisions. O'Neill became the first manager in GAA history to resign after winning an All-Ireland title. Many of them had talked about it but had always been persuaded to continue. Not O'Neill.

He took the unusual decision of staying on until after Dublin's first game of the new National League against Leitrim. Efforts to persuade him to remain failed. Just as he stood by his own convictions after the defeats of 1993–94, he now stood by the belief that the time was right to stand down. He had gone out as a winner. Very few managers in any sport can say that.

Maximising Their Assets

(Liam Griffin, Eugene McGee, Peter McGrath,
John O'Mahoney, John Maughan)

If the real test of managers is whether or not they get the maximum return from available resources, then Liam Griffin, Eugene McGee, Peter McGrath, John O'Mahoney and John Maughan are Grade A material.

All five drained the last drop out of their talent pool. For Griffin, McGee and McGrath the reward was All-Ireland titles. Both O'Mahoney and Maughan guided Mayo into All-Ireland finals while also claiming unexpected provincial successes with 'adopted' counties.

Liam Griffin took over in Wexford at a time when there was no great rush towards the hot seat. Things looked pretty bleak in the autumn of 1994 as Wexford surveyed the wreckage of yet another Leinster final defeat. There was hope after the 1993 campaign. Wexford had lost National League and Leinster finals in replays and while the dejection had lasted for several months, there was a feeling that luck was the only absent ingredient in both of those campaigns.

It was different after the 1994 championship. Wexford had lost the Leinster final to Offaly by 1–18 to 0–14. There could be no excuses. There weren't. Nor was there any big demand for the team manager's job. When Liam Griffin was eventually appointed it didn't exactly lead to a flood of money being put on Wexford for the 1995 campaign. He was regarded in Wexford as a passionate enthusiast who would give everything to the job. The trouble was that wouldn't be enough, according to the sceptics. The talent wasn't there.

When Griffin's first championship campaign ended with a 2–14 to 1–10 defeat by Offaly in the 1995 Leinster semi-final, the cynics chuckled. They felt vindicated. Griffin, the enthusiast, was out of his depth. And yet odd little things were going on. They didn't seem very important at the time but their significance would emerge later on. George O'Connor, who had flirted with retirement, decided to continue. So did Billy Byrne. Why?

In reality, both felt that Griffin's way represented as good a chance as any. His passion for hurling and his obsessional confidence in Wexford people was infectious. It galled him to hear the knockers talk of O'Connor and Byrne as 'has-beens'. It riled him to hear criticisms of Tom Dempsey, Martin Storey, Liam Dunne etc. No, they hadn't won a major title but they had kept battling away, proving to Griffin that their resolve was very much intact, despite what the critics said.

In March 1995, Meath beat Wexford in a League game in Enniscorthy. Seventeen months later, eleven of that Wexford team climbed the steps of the Hogan Stand on All-Ireland final day. The turnabout was a triumph for Griffin and his capacity to get the best from available resources. It wasn't as if a new generation of Wexford whizz-kids had come along. No, this was essentially the same faces which had failed so often in previous years. The likes of Gary Laffan and Rory McCarthy were new to the scene but the core was the same as in 1993–94–95.

Griffin's greatest strength was his power of persuasion. His pride in Wexford rubbed off on his players. It persuaded them that all the effort would be worth it if they trusted him. If Wexford lost a game, Griffin's philosophy was: 'forget about it and win the next one'. If a player made a mistake either in a match or training, Griffin's advice was 'next ball'. It was always 'next ball' and 'next match'. There would be no looking back.

Griffin became a cult figure during the 1996 campaign. His self-belief was the constant factor, right from the build-up to the first championship game against Kilkenny. Once that was safely negotiated, he worked even harder at taking control of the players' minds. He sensed that in terms of overall talent, there was very little between all the top teams. The Leinster and All-Ireland titles would go to those who most wanted them. It was his job to convince the Wexford players that they wanted success more than their rivals. Ultimately, he achieved that, proving in the process that even players who are deemed to have failed too often can turn things round if the attitude and approach is right.

Eugene McGee achieved his first managerial triumphs with UCD. His progress was noted in Offaly who saw him as the man to take on the power of Dublin and Kerry in the late 1970s. It was an awesome task. The 'Big Two' were setting new standards and seemed in a different League to most of their pursuers. The Offaly two-in-a-row team of 1971–72 had broken up and the re-structuring task had been progressing slowly.

When McGee agreed to accept the Offaly challenge he knew that he would have to maximise his assets in a very thorough way. For while Offaly had a good football tradition, it was operating from a small population base. There was plus side to that too. The larger counties often have difficulty in deciding on their best panels and end up chopping and changing far more than is either necessary or desirable.

McGee had no such luxury. His panel base was small but he was lucky that his term in charge of Offaly coincided with a period when a whole series of brothers were all up to top inter-county standard. He could call on the three Lowry brothers, Sean, Mick and Brendan; the Connor brothers, Matt and Richie and their cousins, Liam and Tomás; the Fitzgeralds, Pat and Mick and the Darbys, Seamus and Stephen.

Of the seventeen Offaly players used in the 1982 All-Ireland finals, no fewer than eleven came from just five families. It really was a remarkable family collection and underlines the theory that it's not always necessary to draw from big numbers to win an All-Ireland title.

It took Eugene McGee a few years to get things right. Even when Offaly took over from Dublin as Leinster's top team in 1980, they were still some way short of the high standard set by Kerry. They narrowed the gap in 1981 but McGee still wasn't satisfied that the balance was right. The most interesting adjustment concerned Sean Lowry and team captain, Richie Connor. Lowry, who was at centre-half-back when Offaly won the 1972

All-Ireland final, was at full-forward in the 1981 final with Richie Connor at centre-back and Matt Connor at right full-forward.

Things had changed for the 1982 final. Lowry was restored to centre-back, Richie Connor was switched to centre-forward and Matt Connor was at full-forward. It was all part of McGee's attempts to extract the absolute maximum from his resources and it worked extremely well as Offaly never allowed Kerry to get too far away from them and then struck for the famous winning goal a few minutes from the end. It is quite likely that with a less shrewd manager that particular Offaly team would never have won an All-Ireland final. It was Offaly's good fortune that McGee was so smart at striking the right balance.

Peter McGrath was equally successful in making the best of his hand in Down. His team seemed to have quite a few suspect areas when they set sail in the 1991 Ulster championship. The full-back line looked some way off the championship pace while midfield seemed unlikely to win consistent ball against the better pairings. On the plus side, there was an exciting dimension to the attack but could they compensate for other weaknesses? The summer of 1991 proved that they could. Clever tactical ploys, allied to a very high work ethic took them all the way to All-Ireland glory.

Having done it once, Down assumed that the same format would work again. It didn't. They lost to Derry in 1992 but treated it as if it was a one-off mistake. They retained the same basic formula in 1993 and were hammered by Derry in Newry. Pete McGrath reached some very public conclusions after that game and while they weren't to the liking of some of his players it was pretty clear that a new game plan was required.

McGrath showed his tactical expertise for the 1994 championship. He was no longer happy with Eamonn Burns and Barry Breen at midfield. He also needed extra power in the half-back line to counteract Derry's physical strength. And so he dropped Burns and Breen into the half-backs, switched big Conor Deegan from full-back to midfield alongside Gregory McCartan. The new set-up was designed specifically with Derry in mind. It worked to perfection and Down dethroned the reigning All-Ireland champions in a great game in Celtic Park. There was now no turning back. If the new-look line-up was good enough to beat Derry it could probably cope with anything. McGrath was right. The team went from strength to strength and climaxed a great season with an All-Ireland final win over Dublin. Once again, McGrath had got the most from his squad.

John O'Mahoney may never have coached a side to All-Ireland glory but he achieved a rare double by managing to maximise his assets in two counties, Mayo and Leitrim. O'Mahoney's leadership in Mayo's 1989 championship campaign was crucial in getting a rather ordinary team all the way to an All-Ireland final. Indeed, were it not for some bad luck in the final against Cork (remember Anthony Finnerty's missed goal chance in the second half?) Mayo might have pulled off a famous win.

His part in Leitrim's Connacht final win in 1994 was even more significant. For several years, Leitrim had promised a great deal but always lost direction at a vital crossroads. They seemed paralysed by tradition, especially when they were playing Roscommon or Galway. O'Mahoney played a big role in lifting that particular cloud. In fact, it may have been the missing link which finally fit into place as Leitrim ended years of misery with a Connacht final success in 1994.

O'Mahoney's fellow Mayoman, John Maughan achieved an even greater triumph in Clare in 1992. This was the ultimate in terms of getting the best out of available resources. Maughan's army-style discipline, allied to his constant reminders to the Clare squad that they would be every bit as good as Cork or Kerry if they believed in themselves, finally did the trick. Clare threw tradition to one side in the 1992 Munster final and produced a performance which left Kerry stranded. It was as much a victory for Maughan's persuasive powers as for the Clare team's talents.

Maughan's talents were again in evidence in 1996 when he presided over a Mayo team which made remarkable progress in a few short months. Mayo may have ultimately failed to win the All-Ireland final but they proved that they were a team of real substance. Maughan's determined hand was very much at the heart of the improvement.

Hard Luck Stories

(Tom Heneghan, Sean McCague, Christy Keogh, Gerry McCaul, Seamus McCarthy).

Tom Heneghan stood and watched his dream exploding. It was the closing minutes of the 1980 All-Ireland football final and Kerry had locked onto victory mode. Roscommon's early rebellion had been quelled and while Kerry had found it impossible to completely shake off their pursuers, they were still quick enough to maintain a decent lead.

In the end, Kerry clinched the three-in-a-row with a three-point win. Nine months later Roscommon lost to Sligo in the Connacht championship, thus ending a four-year period of dominance in Connacht. When it all started back in 1977, Heneghan was a player, a tough corner-back who made life miserable for defenders. Three seasons on, Heneghan was still a member of the panel but was also the team manager. Right through the 1977–80 period, Roscommon reigned supreme in Connacht. In 1977 they lost the All-Ireland semi-final in a replay against Armagh and a year later were hammered by Kerry in the semi-final.

Despite this setback, Roscommon retained their sense of ambition, primed mainly by men like Heneghan and Dermot Earley. They won the National League title in 1979 and were well fancied to beat Dublin in that year's All-Ireland semi-final. Dublin were in sharp decline at that stage after reaching heady heights in the mid-seventies but they somehow managed to outwit Roscommon, winning by a single point.

By 1980 Roscommon had reached make-or-break time. Once again, they won the Connacht title and this time they finally got it right in a All-Ireland semi-final, beating Armagh by 2–20 to 3–11. Their preparations for the All-Ireland final were the most meticulous ever undertaken in the county. Heneghan left nothing to chance as Roscommon sought to devise a plan which would curb the mighty Kerry team which had won the previous two finals.

The Heneghan plan almost worked. Roscommon shot into an early lead and had Kerry reeling for a time. However, Kerry, in typical fashion, fought back and drew on all their vast array of skills and experience to edge home by three points as winners in a bad-tempered game, where most of the emphasis was on the negative. Roscommon were understandably angry at post-match reports that they were solely responsible for the poor quality and that they had set out to intimidate Kerry. They claimed that their game plan of trying to cut down the space for the Kerry forwards, using the closest of close marking techniques, was perfectly valid.

In the end, it didn't work. It was Roscommon's and Tom Heneghan's bad luck that their spell of dominance in Connacht should have coincided with a period when Kerry had possibly the best team in the history of Gaelic football. It is quite likely that had Roscommon not peaked for a few more years, they would have won an All-Ireland title. There is absolutely no doubt that the Roscommon team of 1979–80 would have won at least one All-Ireland had they been around in the 1990s. Tom Heneghan was an extremely good manager but was unlucky enough to have been leading his side at a time when Kerry were so dominant.

The same applies to Sean McCague, the man who did so much to modernise Monaghan football. Prior to 1979, Monaghan football had a reputation for being rough and uncouth with inter-club rivalries running so deep that players from certain clubs wouldn't co-operate with each other when playing for the county side. It was a standing joke in other counties that a tackle wasn't deemed late in Monaghan football provided it happened on the same day as the match.

It was against that background that McCague went to work with the Monaghan team of 1979. Using man-management rather than team management techniques, McCague brought about a complete overhaul of the county scene. The innate talent which the county always possessed was now being harnessed in a positive way. So much so that Monaghan won their first Ulster title for forty-one years in 1979. They were hammered by Kerry in the All-Ireland semi-final but the breakthrough had been made. Monaghan football was on the way up.

They lost the Centenary Cup (a special open draw competition to mark the GAAs 100th anniversary) final in 1984 but a year later they won the National League title and doubled up with an Ulster championship success. The Monaghan team which faced up to Kerry in the 1985 All-Ireland semi-final was a whole lot better and more mature than the 1979 side. Meantime, Kerry, who had lost out in 1982–83, had re-charged their batteries and were back at No.1.

Monaghan produced a splendid performance to draw with Kerry in the semi-final but lost their way in the replay and lost by five points. Just as Roscommon had experienced in 1980, Monaghan had become victims of the great Kerry team. Sean McCague and his players can consider themselves unlucky that their challenge for major honours came at a time when Kerry were so awesome. In another era, notably the 1990s, McCague would have been celebrating an All-Ireland win with that Monaghan side.

When Brian Mullins, Robbie Kelleher and Sean Doherty stood down as Dublin selectors after the 1986 Leinster final, the Dublin County Board replaced them a lower-profile management team, headed by Gerry McCaul. He had shown himself to be an excellent manager at club level and was now given his chance to test his skills on the inter-county scene. It all seemed so easy at first. Dublin galloped through the 1986/87 National League season, eventually winning the final by beating All-Ireland champions, Kerry. Dublin's future looked extremely bright. McCaul looked certain to be an All-Ireland winning manager.

It was his bad luck that he should have taken over at a time when Meath were on a rapid upward curve. Having finally broke free of Dublin's chains in 1986, Meath were in no mood to get caught again. And so began another chapter in the intense Dublin–Meath rivalry, one in which Meath generally held the upperhand. Meath beat Dublin in the 1987–88–90 Leinster finals and also overcame them in a replay in the 1988 National League final. It was all very frustrating for McCaul and Dublin, who could argue with a degree of credibility that they were the second best team in the country in 1987–88.

Dublin did manage to beat Meath in the 1989 Leinster final but then made a serious of stupid errors against Cork in the All-Ireland semi-final which completely undermined them. McCaul had one more throw of the dice in 1990 but lost out to Meath again. In another era, McCaul would almost certainly have enjoyed much more success with Dublin. Luck was rarely his friend during his four seasons in charge, not least that Meath were so strong at that time.

Tipperary's Seamus McCarthy suffered from a more fundamental type of bad luck. Quite simply, he was a great manager in a county which lacked the resources to seriously challenge Kerry or Cork. McCarthy's love affair with football was so passionate that, up to his retirement as senior team manager in May 1996, he had been involved as a player and administrator for more than 25 years. One of his proudest moments came in 1984 when he managed Tipperary to glory in the Munster minor football championship. They beat Roscommon in the All-Ireland semi-final but lost the final to Dublin by 1–9 to 0–4.

McCarthy progressed through the ranks with that minor team, many of whom went on to become excellent senior players. He was in charge of the two senior teams which reached the 1993–94 Munster finals, where they lost to Cork on both occasions. McCarthy's managerial skills were widely acknowledged all over the country but unfortunately for him, Tipperary lacked the player base to enable him to show his talents at the highest level.

McCarthy had the consolation of knowing the reasons why he couldn't make the breakthrough, something which did not apply to Wexford hurling manager, Christy Keogh, who suffered the cruellest of luck in 1993. It was as if the fates got together and decided to deal Keogh and his Wexford players the worst possible hand. It all started out so promisingly when they reached the National League final against Cork in Thurles. It was a game they should very definitely have won but they missed several good chances, including a last minute close-in free, and were held to a draw, 2–11 each. The replay also finished level, after extra time, and once again it was Wexford who felt the greater sense of loss as they had continued on their wasteful way. The initiative was very much with Cork going into the third game and they duly delivered, winning by five points.

If luck deserted Wexford in the League final, it also checked out on them in the 1993 Leinster final against Kilkenny. They seemed to be on their way to their first Leinster title since 1977 when they led Kilkenny by four points as the game headed into the closing minutes. Kilkenny battled back to cut the lead to a single point in the final seconds. Wexford got a great opportunity to seal the game but Billy Byrne's shot for a point was charged down and Kilkenny swept upfield in a flowing move which presented Eamonn Morrissey with the equalising chance. He gleefully accepted. Once again, luck had deserted Wexford. Their chance had gone. The replay was an anti-climax as Kilkenny took a grip early on and ran out winners by seven points.

It could be argued that Wexford contributed handsomely to their own bad luck in both the League and Leinster finals. Nevertheless, Christy Keogh and his players had every reason for believing that the fates had conspired against Wexford in a most unfair way. Certainly, Keogh would never consider himself a lucky manager after the experiences of 1993.

Heroes From Hurling's Super Powers

(Pat Henderson, 'Babs' Keating, Johnny Clifford, Ollie Walsh)

When Dermot Healy became Offaly manager in 1979 he said that one of the prime reasons he took the job was because it represented the sort of challenge he could never get in his native Kilkenny where winning All-Ireland titles was seen as much a right as an aspiration.

Kilkenny expect to win All-Ireland finals at regular intervals. The supporters become very impatient if they have to wait very long. Sometimes they become impatient after just a few years away from the All-Ireland podium. That was very definitely the case at the start of 1982.

Kilkenny had won an All-Ireland final in 1979 so it wasn't as if they were out of the limelight for very long. What annoyed them was that they had been overtaken by a new force in Leinster. Not just once but twice! Kilkenny did not take kindly to being behind Offaly for so long. Pat Henderson, a veteran of many great Kilkenny days, was now in charge of the team and was fully aware of the responsibilities which were being placed upon him.

There wasn't any great optimism in Kilkenny at the time. The team looked solid enough without in any way suggesting that it would develop into one of the highest achievers of modern times. By the end of 1983, Kilkenny would have won an All-Ireland and National League double and Henderson would be elevated to the status of a really great manager. Henderson's finest hour came in the 1982 All-Ireland final against Cork. Kilkenny went into that game as rank outsiders after Cork had scorched their way through Munster as if they were on a different planet to all the other contenders. Kilkenny, meanwhile, approached from the opposite direction, combining good luck with an ever-improving game plan. They were very fortunate to beat defending All-Ireland champions, Offaly in the Leinster final, courtesy of a goal which is still shrouded in controversy to this day. That didn't matter to Kilkenny. The important thing was that they were back on top in Leinster.

Pat Henderson was unimpressed by all the hype surrounding Cork going into the All-Ireland final. He reckoned that apart from the fact that Kilkenny almost always acquitted themselves well in big games, Cork were over-rated. In Henderson's opinion, it hadn't been a particularly good Munster championship.

He was proved right. His carefully charted plans worked to perfection. Kilkenny pumped ball after ball down on new full-forward, Christy Heffernan who positively thrived on the big occasion. In the end Cork were routed. A year later, Pat Henderson's tactical awareness was put to an even more searching test. Kilkenny were defending their All-Ireland crown against Cork on a stormy day in Croke Park. They had built up a decent lead with the wind in the first half and struck for a goal immediately after the break but had to withstand a fierce Cork barrage for the remainder of the game.

The pressure on the Kilkenny defence was sustained and heavy. Much of the ball was coming straight down the middle. Ger Henderson was magnificent at centre-back and his one man-show, allied to a shrewd defensive strategy whereby Kilkenny crowded the area as much as possible, left the Cork attack totally frustrated and Kilkenny held on for a two-point win.

Kilkenny won no more All-Ireland titles under Pat Henderson, although they reached another in 1987 where they lost to Galway. There was only one occasion when Henderson was out-witted tactically. That was in 1986 when Galway crowded midfield and used a two-man midfield in the All-Ireland semi-final. It worked to perfection and Kilkenny were beaten out of sight.

That tactic may have beaten Kilkenny but it didn't fool Cork in the final, thanks mainly to the sharp hurling brain of another great manager, Johnny Clifford . He had studied the Galway plan in detail and decided that he would not change his formation. Galway could do what they liked — Cork would play in the traditional formation. That meant that Galway had a spare man out the field while Cork corner-back, Johnny Crowley, was left on his own. Clifford's gamble worked. Galway, all nervy and unsure, couldn't exploit the outfield situation while Crowley thrived in his 'sweeper' role. Clifford's tactical analysis was a clear winner on the day.

Apart from his tactical genius, Clifford also had a great manner with players. As far as he was concerned, a Cork hurler was a special person and deserved endless respect. The players loved him and would do anything for him. Not surprisingly, the excellent rapport between manager and players made for a very settled and successful camp.

Settled and successful camps were pretty rare in Tipperary in the late seventies and early eighties. The county's hurling stock was trading at its lowest ever value. A good performance in the 1984 Munster final against Cork did not bring about the expected upturn and, by the autumn of 1986, Tipperary were still in a deep depression. The arrival of 'Babs' Keating as manager changed everything. Apart from a wealth of hurling knowledge, 'Babs' also brought a style and personality to the job which helped to raise Tipperary's profile. He made it fashionable to be involved with Tipperary and, through the Supporters' Club, a great amount of money was raised to ensure that the players were looked after like never before.

Keating's impact was almost immediate. Tipperary won their first Munster title for sixteen years in 1987, thus launching a period of great success for Keating, who presided over five Munster title wins, two All-Ireland and two National League triumphs. Keating's managerial style didn't always endear him to people outside Tipperary. A straight talker who never hedged his bets, Keating believed that Tipperary were best and never tired of telling the world that. He had a great presence both in the dressing-room and on the pitch. There were times when Keating looked almost like a sixteenth player as he stalked the sidelines urging his men on. Unquestionably, Keating's very presence on the sidelines had the dual effect of boosting the Tipperary players' morale while slightly intimidating less-experienced opposition.

Keating got in trouble on a few occasions for being critical of his own players and also ran into a controversy in 1998 over the omission from the All-Ireland final team of captain Pat O'Neill. He fell foul of Cork fans in 1990 when they mistakenly assumed that he was talking about their hurlers when he commented that 'donkeys don't win derbies'. Keating was quite upset at the manner in which what he regarded as an innocent comment was portrayed. He believed it was done deliberately to discredit him. Nobody could ever deny that Keating was the man who brought the pride and the passion back into Tipperary hurling. He did it with style and vigour and can rightly take his place among the great managers.

The late Ollie Walsh had a much different management style but it was no less successful. Indeed, he achieved something Keating failed to do, i.e. winning the two-in-a-row with Kilkenny in 1992–93. Somewhat like Pat Henderson a decade earlier, Walsh took over at a time when Kilkenny hurling was very much second in line to Offaly in Leinster. Offaly had won three successive Leinster titles in 1988–89–90, much to the dismay of Kilkenny fans who could never have envisaged such a scenario.

Walsh turned the tables in his first season in charge, guiding Kilkenny to the 1991 All-Ireland final, where they lost by four points to Tipperary. That would be Kilkenny's last defeat in the championship until 1994 when they were finally dethroned by Offaly. In between, they had captured the 1992–93 All-Ireland finals. Walsh tended to keep a low profile as a manager, allowing others to make most of the public statements but when it came to strategy there was no sharper mind in hurling. Coaching a team to a double All-Ireland success is still a fairly rare achievement. How ironic that two former colleagues, Pat Henderson and Ollie Walsh should achieve it within ten years of each other. It was a fitting testimony to their prowess as managers.

Chapter 6

✣ ✣ ✣

Football's Order Of Merit

(All-Ireland Champions Parade 1971–96)

There can be no arguments about the top two football teams in the last twenty-five years. In fact, irrespective of the time scale, there can be no serious debate as to the No.1 team. Kerry's incredible record of eight All-Ireland titles between 1975 and 1986 entitles them to the undisputed title as the best team in the history of Gaelic football. Obviously there were several changes to the Kerry team as it evolved but, for rating purposes, it's impossible to categorise the team from year to year except to say that, for sheer power, poise and invention the 1978–79 side explored new peaks.

The Dublin team of 1974–76–77 are a clear second to Kerry. Apart from rescuing Dublin from eleven years in obscurity, Kevin Heffernan's squad goes down in the history as the launch pad for the new approach to football, one in which physical fitness and planning were taken to unprecedented levels. Kerry not only borrowed Heffo's professional prototype but moved it on to a stage where nobody — including Dublin — could compete for several seasons.

It was Dublin's bad luck that a very special Kerry squad should emerge at a time when they looked set to dominate the latter half of the 1970s. That does not alter the fact that the Dublin team of 1976–77, in particular, was extremely formidable, combining all the important ingredients in a potent mix which left most others trailing helplessly in their wake.

So if Kerry and Dublin are the undisputed top two of modern football, which of the other contenders would be best placed to challenge them? The Meath team of 1987–88 probably fits that particular bill best of all. When it came to self-promotion and public relations, Meath were seriously different, despite the affable front presented by manager, Sean Boylan and a few of his players. Meath seemed keen to present a sullen, distant image which certainly did nothing for their general popularity. However, that should not cloud over the truth, which was that Meath were an outstandingly efficient side whose line in self-belief was pretty staggering.

After years of subservience to Dublin it was as if they became new people once they won the 1986 Leinster final. All the old doubts and inhibitions flooded away to be replaced by a confident, determined side which made an art out of dogged persistence. If Meath had one fault it was that they never seemed to be able to put the opposition away. Thus, games which they should have won easily were alive right to the finish, even if Meath usually did manage to scrape through. Ultimately, Meath's dice-with-death mentality cost them dearly for after running the ultimate survival show in 1991, they ran out of time after giving Down a ridiculously generous headstart in the All-Ireland final.

Dublin apart, Cork were Meath's great rivals in the 1987–90 period. Their championship duel eventually finished 2–1 in Meath's favour with one drawn, a statistic which entitles Cork to fourth spot in the ratings. While some may query the quality of their performance in the 1989 All-Ireland final against Mayo, they had earlier beaten Dublin in fine style after a disastrous start in the semi-final. In a sense, it was a performance worthy of an All-Ireland final. A year later, Cork proved just how mature they had become when they out-pointed Meath in the sort of game they might well have lost a few seasons earlier. By 1990, they were able to adapt their game to any circumstances.

It's very difficult to separate Down 1991–94 and Offaly 1971–72 but the nod goes to the northerners on the basis that the opposition was stronger than that encountered by Offaly. Despite their dual success, Down were a real enigma. They came from virtually nowhere in 1991 to win the title, slipped back alarmingly in 1992–93, and just when it was assumed that their best days were behind them they re-emerged to win the 1994 championship. They were a team of peaks and valleys. At full throttle, they were very exciting but were incapable of surviving on a day when everybody wasn't performing at full efficiency. That failure to improvise was very evident in League campaigns where they struggled badly. Nevertheless, Down probably deserve fifth spot in the All-Ireland rankings ahead of Offaly 1971–72 who are in sixth position.

The 1971–72 Offaly team created all sorts of records in the county but are just squeezed out of the top five. They had the added distinction of being the first Offaly team to win an All-Ireland final and the manner in which they held their resolve to win the two-in-a-row suggests that they were a special side. The only question mark against them is the level of opposition they encountered. They beat Cork, Galway, Donegal and Kerry in the 1971–72 All-Ireland semi-finals and finals. History suggests that there was nothing special about that quartet.

Cork did go on to win the 1973 All-Ireland title but by then the side was a lot more developed and far more experienced than the team which lost the 1971 semi-final to Offaly by five points. Galway promised plenty in the early 1970s but when the pressure came they always found an escape chute and ended up losing three All-Ireland finals in four years, a tragic triple loss which probably contributed greatly to the county's subsequent slide down the rankings. Donegal were new to that level of competition in 1972 while Kerry, who held Offaly to a draw in the final, were heading into a decline which lasted until 1975. The extent of the transition in Kerry football in the first half of the 1970s is underlined by the fact that only three of the 1972 team (Paudie Lynch and Brendan Lynch and John O'Keeffe) were still on board when Mick O'Dwyer set sail with his new side in 1975.

The 1982 Offaly team comes next (seventh) in the ratings. Like so many other sides they were unlucky to be around when Kerry were at their peak; unlike other teams they never lost confidence in their ability to beat Kerry and were eventually rewarded with that sensational win in 1982. It was their third championship shot at Kerry, having lost in 1980 and 1981 but in circumstances which provided justifiable nourishment for their belief that they would finally get it right. They did just that in 1982.

Cork 1973 has gone down in history as a team which short-changed itself. Having won the All-Ireland title that year, after scoring a total of thirteen goals in three games against Kerry, Tyrone and Galway, they seemed set for a lengthy spell on top, especially when they hammered Kerry in the 1974 Munster final. Whether or not they began to believe the rave reviews before the All-Ireland semi-final is uncertain but there was evidence that Cork went into the game against Dublin with a less than focused attitude. That was fatal against a Dublin side which majored in ruffling opponents' feathers, especially those of the fancied opposition.

The Dublin team of 1983 come next in the ratings. Unfortunately for that team, the ugliness of the All-Ireland final against Galway has tended to devalue their achievement in a remarkable championship. But when you scratch below the surface, you find that Dublin conducted a very solid campaign with a new-look side. They could have fallen at any number of hurdles (they drew with Meath and Cork and beat defending champions, Offaly) but they never lost faith in themselves, a virtue which was put to the ultimate test when they had to face a Galway team with two extra men in the final. They rose to the challenge with relish.

Donegal 1992 come next in the ratings. Their campaign was conducted with admirable organisation, self-belief and style. Their critics claim that they got into the final by beating a very poor Mayo side in the semi-final. Earlier though, they had showed great resilience to beat Derry in the Ulster final, having been reduced to fourteen men just before half-time. In the All-Ireland final, they conceded the early initiative to Dublin but regained their composure and gradually wore down opponents who had gone into the final brimming with confidence.

Donegal's historic success smoothed the path somewhat for Derry in 1993. The psychological barrier had been broken by Donegal, who proved that, yes it was indeed possible for a team with no All-Ireland pedigree to make the breakthrough. That stood to Derry, particularly in the All-Ireland semi-final against Dublin. Purely on the basis that they broke the psychological barrier first, Donegal deserve to be rated ahead of Derry.

Both rank ahead of Dublin 1995. Dublin were one of the most consistent championship sides for the previous three years but just couldn't reach the promised land. They finally did it in 1995, only to find themselves confronted by questions as to the overall quality of the campaign. Not that it mattered to Dublin who were delighted to have finally won the title. It was a case of never mind the quality, look at the cup. However, it has to be said that the 1995 championship was not as good as its immediate predeccesors. The 1996 campaign, while providing quite a few shocks, some interesting games and plenty of controversy, also had question marks against it in terms of overall quality. However, Meath's stubborn persistence against both Dublin and Mayo, allied to some very inventive play against Carlow, Laois and most especially Tyrone, entitles them to be rated ahead of Dublin 1995.

How The Football Champions Rate (1971–96)

1. Kerry 1975–86
2. Dublin 1974–76–77
3. Meath 1987–88
4. Cork 1989–90
5. Down 1991–94
6. Offaly 1971–72
7. Offaly 1982
8. Cork 1973
9. Dublin 1983
10. Donegal 1992
11. Derry 1993
12. Meath 1996
13. Dublin 1995

Football's Greatest Era

(Kerry's Eight Plus Dublin's Three)

Between 15 June 1975 and 21 September 1986, Kerry footballers played forty-eight senior championship games, winning forty-one, drawing three and losing four. They won eight All-Ireland titles, were beaten in two finals, one semi-final and also lost a Munster final to Cork.

Their right to be regarded as the best team in the history of Gaelic football is as unquestionable as is Mick O'Dwyer's right to be recognised as the most successful coach of all time. Amazingly, Kerry could have taken an even bigger haul of titles.

Despite the scoreline, they were very little behind Dublin in playing terms in the 1977 All-Ireland semi-final, a game which has gone down as one of the best in history. Had they beaten Dublin, it is a virtual certainty that they would have handled Armagh in the final just as easily as Dublin did. In 1982, Kerry came within minutes of clinching the record-breaking five-in-a-row, only to lose out to a Seamus Darby goal for Offaly. A year later, Kerry had cranked up the championship machine again, but were beaten by Tadhg Murphy's late goal for Cork in the Munster final. A Kerry win there would almost certainly have catapulted them to another All-Ireland title, as they were infinitely more experienced than any of the other remaining contenders. Effectively then, Kerry can consider themselves unlucky not to have won every All-Ireland title between 1977 and 1986.

Between 26 May 1974 and 16 September 1979 Dublin played thirty-two championship games, winning twenty-nine and losing three. They won three All-Ireland finals and were beaten in three others. All three final defeats were inflicted by Kerry. Unlike Kerry, however, Dublin could have no arguments about any of the finals they lost as they were well beaten each time; by seven points in 1975, by seventeen points in 1978 and by eleven points in 1979. If Dublin had any complaints they could only be on the basis that fate had dealt them a cruel hand by making them contemporaries of the best team Gaelic football has ever seen. In a less competitive period, Dublin might well have picked up four, or possibly even five consecutive titles.

In terms of championship clashes between Kerry and Dublin, the score stood at 3–2 to Kerry at the end of their five-year struggle for supremacy. One of the most amazing aspects of the intense rivalry was the fact that while the sides seemed so evenly matched, the margins of victory were often quite high on one side or the other.

1975 — Kerry 2–12 Dublin 0–11 (All-Ireland final).
1976 — Dublin 3–8 Kerry 0–10 (All-Ireland final).
1977 — Dublin 3–12 Kerry 1–13 (All-Ireland semi-final).
1978 — Kerry 5–11 Dublin 0–9 (All-Ireland final).
1979 — Kerry 3–13 Dublin 1–8 (All-Ireland final).

Those scorelines look so cold and stark on the record books and in no way even hint at the incredible drama which lay behind them in five seasons of unrelenting passion and excitement. In the end, the advantage lay very definitely with Kerry and as subsequent events proved, they were merely reaching their peak when that particular Dublin team signed off in 1979.

One of the more curious aspects about the emergence of Kerry and Dublin in the mid-seventies was that neither had shown any sign that they were about to unveil such a stunning array of talent. Kerry had come off a disappointing (by their standards) run for while they had won four consecutive National League finals in 1971–74, they had failed in all four corresponding championships, including 1972 when they lost an All-Ireland final replay to Offaly. Cork had beaten them in the 1971–73–74 Munster finals.

Dublin's previous All-Ireland success had been in 1963 and they hadn't even contested a Leinster final since 1965. Nor were they making much of an impression on the League either, spending the 1973/74 season in Division Two where they were beaten by Kildare in the final, having earlier lost to Clare.

Cork, Galway and Offaly were the most fancied teams going into the 1974 championship but all three were to fall victims to the new force which had arrived on the scene. It was a fate they were to experience several more times for the remainder of the decade and beyond. Other contenders suffered similar treatment at the hands of the 'Big Two.'

Ironically, it was a Cork win over Kerry which was to shape the Kingdom's future. It came in the 1974 Munster final when Cork, the defending All-Ireland champions, beat Kerry by 1–11 to 0–7 in Killarney. Ten of the Kerry team which lost that day would feature on the team which routed Cork a year later but much had changed in the interim. Kerry were disgusted by the 1974 defeat and decided it was time for serious action. They appointed Mick O'Dwyer, who had resigned from a distinguished playing career a few months earlier, as team manager for the 1974/75 season. O'Dwyer had been playing for Kerry for eighteen years and knew just about every angle, having been both a forward and a back. Now, at the age of 38, he was ready for a new challenge. Nobody could have possibly envisaged the changes O'Dwyer would bring about. A fanatic for fitness, his regime was the most 'professional' Kerry had ever seen. O'Dwyer had studied Dublin's emergence closely and decided that a great deal was down to their super-fitness. If, and when, the opportunity arose, O'Dwyer vowed that Kerry would be even fitter. He underlined his commitment to fitness by bringing the team together for twenty-seven consecutive nights training before the 1975 Munster final. It worked — Kerry hammered Cork by 1–14 to 0–7.

It was the start of the big time for O'Dwyer's men. Meanwhile, Heffo's Army was still in charge in Leinster, having won the 1974 All-Ireland final with a great win over Galway. The change in Dublin football had been remarkable. In the space of four months they had gone from no-hopers to title winners. The upturn was due almost entirely to the organisational and motivational skills of Kevin Heffernan, who had Lorcan Redmond and Donal Colfer as his selectors.

The 1975 All-Ireland final was the start of fascinating duels between Dublin and Kerry and, on a more personal level, between O'Dwyer and Heffernan, both of whom spent many hours trying to devise tactical variations which might prove crucial in a tight game. O'Dwyer drew first blood in the 1975 final with his young lions combining at breathtaking speed to out-run Dublin. Even the loss of captain, Mickey O'Sullivan early on in the game didn't upset Kerry. If anything, it prodded them on as they were most unhappy with the tackle which ended O'Sullivan's participation in the game. Kerry eventually won by 2–12 to 0–11 and O'Dwyer announced in the dressing-room afterwards that 'this is the best Kerry team of all time.'

In a county which had won twenty-two All-Ireland senior titles up to then that was really saying something but, as events transpired, O'Dwyer was proved right. The problem was that some of O'Dwyer's young heroes may have taken the master's words too literally and felt that rewards would continue to mount up without living by the strict personal discipline code they had adhered to for the 1975 campaign. They should have paid the penalty in the 1976 Munster final in Pairc Ui Chaoimh. The match ended level but, in the replay, which was also played in Pairc Ui Chaoimh, Cork led by seven points at one stage in the second half before being hauled back and eventually beaten in extra time, 3–20 to 2–19.

Meanwhile, Heffernan was re-gathering his forces. There was a feeling in Dublin that perhaps he had been too loyal to the 1974 team and paid the price in the 1975 final. Even for a manager of Heffernan's ability, the dilemma of when to discard the loyalty card is always a problem. It was especially difficult for Heffernan in 1975 as he had a great sense of affection for the team which had emerged from the wilderness a year earlier. It would be different in 1976 — new players had to be brought in. Dublin introduced a complete new half-back line in Tommy Drumm, Kevin Moran and Pat O'Neill. That was to prove crucial. They cut off Kerry's supply of quick ball and consequently reduced the number of scoring chances. Meanwhile at the other end, the Dublin forwards were slicing through the Kerry defence, using angles of attack which mesmerised their markers. Dublin won well, 3–8 to 0–10.

The 1977 All-Ireland semi-final has gone down in history as one of the best games ever played. The speed was electrifying, made all the more possible by the style of hand-pass which was allowed at the time. Critics felt that it had robbed football of its basic skills but it didn't matter to Kerry or Dublin who hand-passed their way to glory on alternate years. It was Dublin's turn in 1977, coming from behind in the final six minutes to score two goals. Dublin 3–12 Kerry 1–13. That was possibly the high point of the Dublin–Kerry rivalry. The pace was unrelenting, the moves well planned and speedily executed and the tension unbearable. Kerry seemed to have hit the front at the vital time but goals by David Hickey and Bernard Brogan snatched victory.

While Dublin went on to win the final with an easy win over Armagh, O'Dwyer was facing a crisis in Kerry. For the first time, his judgement was being questioned and were it not for the persuasive powers of County Board chairman, Ger McKenna, O'Dwyer might have been replaced. He was re-appointed but went into 1978 under enormous pressure. Another defeat would have meant the end of the line. O'Dwyer's critics claimed that it had been a mistake to play Jack O'Shea and Paudie Ó Sé at midfield in the 1977 semi-final and that not enough was done to close down Anton O'Toole, who had a great game. O'Dwyer headed into the new campaign very much on trial.

By the end of 1978 it was 2–2 in the Kerry–Dublin saga after a truly amazing All-Ireland final. By now, the rivalry had taken on a life of its own. Such was their dominance over the rest of the contenders that Kerry and Dublin could almost hold back on their training programme in order to ensure that they peaked for the All-Ireland final. Dublin had eleven points to spare over both Kildare in the 1978 Leinster final and Down in the All-Ireland semi-final. Kerry, meanwhile, beat Cork by seven points (Cork were flattered to be so close) in the Munster final and Roscommon by twelve points in the All-Ireland semi-final. The scene was set for the decider.

The 1978 final is guaranteed a place in GAA folklore. Dublin, all swagger and poise, built up an early lead but Kerry came back with a John Egan goal, followed by Mikey Sheehy's goal-in-a-million from a free as Paddy Cullen back-pedalled furiously towards his goal and then the 'Bomber' struck. Eoin Liston was Kerry's new full-forward but he played like a veteran, scoring an amazing three goals in a second half which Kerry won by 3–8 to 0–2. Dublin's demise had no basis in logic. A team which had shown itself to be so committed, so proud and so damned hard to beat for four years folded meekly once Sheehy chipped the ball over Cullen's head for that astonishing goal. It was as if Dublin had given Kerry their best shot in the first twenty minutes but, like Muhammed Ali against George Foreman four years earlier, the challengers waited their chance before stepping in to deliver the knock-out punches in the form of five stunning goals. The winning margin of seventeen points sent statisticians dashing to their record books to find out how long it had been since an All-Ireland football final had produced such a big winning margin. In fact, it had not happened since 1946 when Mayo beat Laois by 4–11 to 0–5.

The degree to which Kerry were so far ahead of their rivals in the late 1970s was underlined in 1979 when they again reached the All-Ireland final by virtue of a 5–14 to 0–7 win over Monaghan in the semi-final. Dublin had a more troubled route, having to come from behind to catch Offaly on the line in the Leinster final and then having just a point to spare over Roscommon in the All-Ireland semi-final. By then, Dublin were a pale shadow of the 1976–77 sides but were still good enough to beat the rest of Leinster and Roscommon, who were appearing in their third consecutive All-Ireland semi-final. However, Dublin were most certainly not good enough to cope with Kerry, who easily beat them 3–13 to 1–8 in the final.

Kerry were now at the peak of their awesome powers. They had such a strong panel to choose from that they could afford to be without one of two top stars on a given day and still cope quite comfortably. In the 1979 final, they were minus Ger Power (hamstring injury) but still clicked quickly into an impressive momentum and were 1–7 to 0–3 ahead at the interval. Their only scare came when Paudie Ó Sé was sent off in the second half as they had also lost John O'Keeffe through injury. Dublin cut the lead to five points but, without Jimmy Keaveney, suspended after being sent off in the Leinster final, the attack was very weak, as their final tally of 1–8 testifies. The 1979 final really was the last stand for that particular Dublin team. For while most of them were still around in 1980, they lost the Leinster final to Offaly and were beaten by Laois in the Leinster semi-final a year later.

It was a pity for Dublin that their contribution to a truly great rivalry should have ended in two huge defeats. In so many ways, the 1978–79 games against Kerry were not a fitting epitaph for a team which brought such magic to Gaelic games earlier in the decade. In full flow, the Dublin of 1976–77 was a joy to behold. Paddy Cullen, Gay O'Driscoll, Sean Doherty, Tony Hanahoe and Jimmy Keaveney were all around long enough to recall the bad days and savour the good ones. Their desire to winkle some success from their careers was a central plank in Heffernan's strategy. Despite being beaten for eleven goals in five championship clashes with Kerry, Cullen was a great goalie. The high goal rate of that era has to be viewed in the context of the hand-passing game where it was possible to virtually 'walk' the ball into the net. Nowadays the hand-pass is far more restricted in general play and cannot be used to score a goal, making life far easier for goalkeepers. O'Driscoll and Doherty were out-and-out stoppers, backs who saw their main duty as preventing their opponents from scoring. They were deadly effective at doing that. Left corner-back, Robbie Kelleher was a more adventurous sort, who liked to move out with the play.

Paddy Reilly, Alan Larkin and George Wilson comprised the Dublin half-back line in 1974–75 but were replaced on bloc in 1976 by Tommy Drumm, Kevin Moran and Pat O'Neill. The new trio were altogether of a more attacking inclination, especially Moran whose surging runs forward brought a new dimension to centre-back play. Midfield was invariably anchored by Brian Mullins, the St Vincent's giant who was very much the Dublin engine. He was one of the truly great midfielders of modern times, combining strength, energy and commitment with an unyielding determination to never accept defeat. Above all, he had an instinctive eye for an opening and his ability to (a) spot a team mate who had stolen a yard on his marker and (b) thread the ball through to a well-placed colleague, was the foundation stone for many Dublin scores.

Steve Rooney was Mullins' partner in 1974–75 but was replaced by Bernard Brogan in 1976. Brogan was a perfect foil for Mullins, possessing lots of mobility and a great technical ability to carry the ball at high speed. Brogan's soloing style was matched only by Kerry's John Egan. Both could gallop on a solo run, with the ball never passing more than a few inches from hand to foot, making them almost impossible to dispossess. Tony Hanahoe and Jimmy Keaveney were the key figures in the Dublin attack. Hanahoe had a low scoring rate, mainly because his job was to act as a decoy, dragging the centre-back into all sorts of positions while leaving the middle free for the runners to exploit. Bobby Doyle, Anton O'Toole, John McCarthy and David Hickey did the running job extremely well, inter-passing with breathtaking sharpness. While all this movement was very impressive it could only be productive if the attack had a deadly opportunist and a reliable free-taker to capitalise on the openings. Jimmy Keaveney filled both roles admirably.

He had been coaxed back into the Dublin panel in 1974 by Heffernan precisely for those two reasons. His strike rate from frees was incredible. Long or short, they were all the same to Keaveney. With Dublin moving the ball so quickly in attack, it was inevitable that defenders would give away frees under pressure, which made Keaveney's role ultra-important. Of course, his contribution was not merely confined to free-taking. He had an innate sense of positioning which presented him with many openings which a lesser full-forward would never have spotted.

Heffernan's role in stitching the whole thing together cannot be over-emphasised. In a sense, he can be credited with bringing a new respectability into football in Dublin at a time when it had lost virtually all of its previous appeal. Thankfully for Dublin, it has held on to its status ever since. As football bade farewell to the Dublin team of the '70s, Kerry were merely getting into their awesome stride. They had seen off the

Dublin challenge and now turned their attentions to the new line-up of contenders, led by Offaly and Roscommon, who emerged as major threats in 1980. Offaly knocked four goals past Kerry in the All-Ireland semi-final but also conceded four and were eventually beaten by 4–15 to 4–10. The final was a much different affair, tense, low-scoring and, at times, very rugged. The outcome was the same, however, as Kerry won by 1–9 to 1–6. Those two games epitomised the sheer flexibility of the Kerry team. One day conceding 4–10 and winning, the next, scoring just 1–9 and still winning. At that stage, Kerry could adapt to any type of challenge.

A year on and the story was the same. This time Mayo took their turn in the All-Ireland semi-final queue but were neither mentally nor physically up to the challenge and were hammered by 2–19 to 1–6 after failing to register a single score in the second half. Improving Offaly were by far a tougher opposition in the final, eventually losing by 1–12 to 0–8. Significantly though, Offaly had hung on until near the end when Jack O'Shea scored a thundering goal. Kerry's seven-point win looks comfortable on the record books; in reality it was not. Kerry had to line out without Pat Spillane, who had a knee injury but as in 1980 when they had to play without 'Bomber' Liston, they improvised superbly.

Perhaps the first signs that Kerry were losing a little altitude came in the 1982 Munster final when they drew with Cork in Pairc Ui Chaoimh. Jimmy Deenihan and Pat Spillane were both out injured while Jack O'Shea had carried an ankle injury into the game. Behind the scenes, there was friction between the squad and the County Board over which gear the team should wear. Cork definitely had a chance to end Kerry's reign that day but the champions staggered into a replay where they re-discovered their touch *en route* to a twelve-point win. Armagh were seen off comfortably in the All-Ireland semi-final, setting up Kerry for a record-breaking bid against Offaly in the All-Ireland final.

The 1982 All-Ireland final has long since gone into football folklore. It is also the one game which Mick O'Dwyer and his team never could quite come to terms with. They were close, so very close, to taking their place in history as the only team ever to win five consecutive All-Ireland finals. Seamus Darby's late goal destroyed that ambition, leaving the whole of Kerry shell-shocked, heartbroken and totally bewildered.

Ten months later, Kerry re-lived the horror when Cork produced a similar late strike in the Munster final to grab a sensational victory, their first championship win over the Kingdom since 1974. That inevitably sparked off speculation that the end of the era would be completed by O'Dwyer's resignation. Deep down though, O'Dwyer felt that while Kerry had lost out in both 1983 and 1983, the circumstances of the defeats were so unusual that it would be easy to misinterpret them. Yes, Kerry needed to make adjustments but the nucleus of a great team was still there, as they showed when they won the 1984 League final, beating Galway in Limerick.

Asked about the championship afterwards, O'Dwyer embarked on one of his verbal solo-runs, trying to convince journalists that Kerry were re-building slowly and that it would take time before they were a serious championship force again. He sounded so convincing that if people didn't know better, they would have written Kerry off as a team who were still some way short of All-Ireland standard. Less than five months later, Kerry were back as All-Ireland champions, with no fewer than ten of the team which lost to Offaly in 1982. It would have been eleven if Mikey Sheehy hadn't been forced out of the team with an achilles tendon problem. What was that about building slowly for the future?

Once again, Dublin, who had won the 1983 title, were the victims in the All-Ireland final, just as they were in 1985. Ironically, Monaghan, brilliantly managed by Sean McCague, provided Kerry with their biggest problem in 1985, forcing the All-Ireland semi-final into a replay before losing out by 2–9 to 0–10. Dublin were blown aside in the first half of the final but recovered from a 1–8 to 0–2 deficit to come within a point of Kerry with eight minutes remaining. However, Kerry steadied themselves and added three points to clinch yet another two-in-a-row. They made it three-in-row a year later after hauling back a seven-point lead to beat Tyrone by 2–15 to 1–10.

The dream of a second four-in-a-row again beckoned so there was no way O'Dwyer could step down as manager. While there were still two All-Ireland titles to be won to earn a place in history, there was little firm evidence that Kerry's chief rivals were getting any better. Behind the scenes, though, something was stirring in Cork. Despite the 1983 success, Cork had been living in Kerry's shadow for ages. A certain pattern had emerged. New players would be introduced for the League and then thrown in against Kerry in the Munster final. They were being compared with people like John O' Keeffe, Paudie Ó Sè, Jack O'Shea, Mikey Sheehy, 'Bomber' Liston, the Spillanes etc., yet if they didn't produce top class performances they were squeezed out and replaced by a new bunch of hopefuls in the following season. The lack of stability resulted in quite a few good Cork players never getting a decent chance to mature at inter-county level for Cork.

In the Autumn of 1986, Billy Morgan, a man who knew more about Kerry than most, took over as Cork team manager. A few other interesting things were happening as well. Larry Tompkins had become totally disillusioned by the scene in his native Kildare and, after a spell in America, had returned to Ireland. More specifically, he returned to Cork, where he joined the Castlehaven club, thereby rendering him eligible to play for his adopted county. By a lucky coincidence, another Kildare star was also living in Cork and ready to make the break. Army-man, Shea Fahy joined Nemo Rangers and also declared for Cork for the 1987 season. In soccer terms it was the modern equivalent of getting ten million pounds of worth of talent for free. Cork could hardly believe their luck.

When Dublin beat Kerry in the 1987 National League final, Cork eyes flickered in hope. Could the great ones be slipping? Kerry tried to gloss over it but when things went poorly on a subsequent trip to the US, the doubts began to set in. Cork, meanwhile, were building rapidly, with Tompkins and Fahy blending in nicely with the squad. On Munster final day, the mix seemed right when Cork led by two points as the game entered its closing seconds. Then Mikey Sheehy, summoning one more miracle from his genius, somehow squeezed in along the endline to score an amazing goal. Directly from the kick-out, Cork worked the ball upfield and won a free which Tompkins converted to force a draw in Killarney on the following Sunday.

The general concensus was that Cork had blown it. That was far from the case. They rattled into Kerry with boundless enthusiasm and confidence in the replay. For once Kerry capitulated. They had Ger Power sent off and by half-time were on their way down from football's summit. Cork well and truly had their measure and won more convincingly that the 0–13 to 1–5 scoreline suggested. The end of an era!

Mick O'Dwyer stayed on as manager until after the 1989 Munster final, which was probably a mistake. Struggling between an innate and natural sense of loyalty to the players who had served him so well and the need to bring in fresh talent, Kerry lost to Cork in both 1988 and 1989. Only a point separated them in 1988 while Cork won by three a year later. The margins were not important — the real significance lay in the fact that Cork had won three Munster titles in a row. O'Dwyer stood down.

There are many who argue that O'Dwyer should have resigned after the 1986 All-Ireland final. After all, a moderate enough Tyrone team had pushed Kerry to the limit of their endurance before folding. Hindsight is a wonderful analyst. How could O'Dwyer have walked out on a team and a county which had just won three All-Ireland finals in a row? When the Kerry spell was finally broken in 1987, O'Dwyer felt that it would be wrong to quit on the basis of one defeat. In 1988, Kerry lost by a single point to Cork, tempting O'Dwyer to stay on once again. By 1989, he could take no more. However hard he tried to repair the punctures in the Kerry balloon, another appeared, bigger and more serious, allowing further air to hiss out.

O'Dwyer's subsequent stint with Kildare was far more damaging to his image as a great manager than the 1987–88–89 campaigns with Kerry. For while he brought a sense of excitement to Kildare and made some progress with the team, Kildare still failed to make the breakthrough. O'Dwyer's critics used this as ammunition to claim that he was extremely lucky in Kerry to have come across a special collection of players who had talent, determination and the mental endurance necessary to remain at the top for so long.

That assessment is partially true. Unquestionably, the Kerry squad(s) from 1975 to 1986 were unique. So too was O'Dwyer, who somehow managed to keep them motivated and organised for so long. The truth is that just as O'Dwyer was lucky to have such a great squad, they were fortunate to have a manager whose single-minded pursuit of success never once flinched in all those years.

The evolution of the Kerry squad in the 1975–86 era is extremely interesting. The team which won the 1975 final was: Paudie O'Mahony; Ger O'Keeffe, John O'Keeffe, Jimmy Deenihan; Paudie Ó Sé, Tim Kennelly, Ger Power; Paudie Lynch, Pat McCarthy; Brendan Lynch, Ogie Moran, Mickey O'Sullivan; Mikey Sheehy, Pat Spillane. Sub: Ger O'Driscoll for O'Sullivan.

John O'Keeffe had been a midfielder on the Kerry teams which played in the 1970 (beat Meath) and 1972 (lost to Offaly) All-Ireland finals. The defeats in 1976–77 brought some changes and when Kerry next won an All-Ireland in 1978, Charlie Nelligan had taken over in goal, Mick Spillane had come in at corner-back for Ger O'Keeffe, Jack O'Shea and Seanie Walsh were at midfield, with Paudie Lynch dropping back to wing-back and Ger Power switching to attack. Eoin Liston was in at full-forward. That was the general formation up to 1982, with minor adjustments here and there, mostly involving Tommy Doyle, who played both in defence and attack, depending on the team's overall requirements. Tom Spillane had come in at centre-forward in 1982.

When the team emerged for its 'second coming' in 1984, Seanie Walsh was at full-back and Tom Spillane was at centre-back. Kerry's policy of turning midfielders into full-backs worked a second time as Walsh enjoyed a fine innings at No.3. However, Kerry got somewhat carried away with the idea and some years later tried to convert Jack O'Shea into a full-back. It was a miserable failure and Jacko, in fact, finished his career as a full-forward, having had a most unproductive time at full-back.

By 1984, Ambrose O'Donovan had joined Jacko at midfield, John Kennedy was in the attack for the injured Mikey Sheehy while Ger Lynch was now at left half-back. Timmy O'Dowd replaced John Egan near the end of the game. It was to be Egan's last All-Ireland final. O'Dowd held onto his place for the 1985 final but lost out to Willie Maher in 1986.

The turnover of players was very gradual and was usually brought about by injury. It was inevitable that the injury toll would mount up on players who had been playing at the top level for so long. Pat Spillane, Mikey Sheehy and Jimmy Deenihan all suffered serious injuries while others picked up quite a lot of knocks too.

Given Kerry's supremacy, it was also inevitable that some opposition would try intimidatory tactics to knock them off their stride. It never worked because, despite their claims to the contrary, Kerry could be as physically imposing as the occasion demanded. The silky quality of so many of their moves and scores may have given the impression that the more rugged aspects of Gaelic football had no part to play in the Kerry success story. That was not the case — they could be as tough as they had to be.

Kerry's approach to the GAA in general was very professional. They pioneered sponsorship deals, much to the alarm of the GAA authorities, who took a fare less liberal view of corporate involvement back then. Kerry also took the holiday fund concept to new heights, raising massive amounts of money from a variety of activities. Inevitably, though, they will be remembered as the best team Gaelic football has seen. Not only that but they had so much to spare over most rivals that it is difficult to see their achievements ever being matched.

KERRY (All-Ireland final 1975): Paudie O'Mahony; Ger O'Keeffe, John O'Keeffe, Jimmy Deenihan; Paudie Ó Sé, Tim Kennelly, Ger Power; Paudie Lynch, Pat McCarthy; Brendan Lynch, Ogie Moran, Mickey O'Sullivan; John Egan, Mikey Sheehy, Pat Spillane. Sub: Ger O'Driscoll for O'Sullivan.

KERRY 1978: Charlie Nelligan; Jimmy Deenihan, John O'Keeffe. Mick Spillane; Paudie O'Shea, Tim Kennelly, Paudie Lynch; Jack O'Shea, Seanie Walsh; Ger Power, Ogie Moran, Pat Spillane; Mikey Sheehy, Eoin Liston, John Egan.

KERRY 1979: Same as 1978, except for Tommy Doyle at right half-forward in place of Ger Power.

KERRY 1980: Ger O'Keeffe replaced Mick Spillane; Ger Power returned at right half-forward, with Tommy Doyle slotting in for Eoin Liston at full-forward.

KERRY 1981: Mick Spillane was back in place of Ger O'Keeffe; Liston returned to full-forward with Tommy Doyle switching to left half-forward in place of Pat Spillane.

KERRY 1984: Charlie Nelligan; Paudie Ó Sé, Seanie Walsh, Mick Spillane; Tommy Doyle, Tom Spillane, Ger Lynch; Jack O'Shea, Ambrose O'Donovan; John Kennedy, Ogie Moran, Pat Spillane; Ger Power, Eoin Liston, John Egan.

KERRY 1985: Same as 1984, except that Timmy O'Dowd replaced Kennedy and Mikey Sheehy came in for Egan.

KERRY 1986: Willie Maher replaced O'Dowd.

DUBLIN 1974: Paddy Cullen; Gay O'Driscoll, Sean Doherty, Robbie Kelleher; Paddy Reilly, Alan Larkin, George Wilson; Brian Mullins, Steve Rooney; Bobby Doyle, Tony Hanahoe, David Hickey; John McCarthy, Jimmy Keaveney, Anton O'Toole.

DUBLIN 1976: Paddy Cullen; Gay O'Driscoll, Sean Doherty, Robbie Kelleher; Tommy Drumm, Kevin Moran, Pat O'Neill; Brian Mullins, Bernard Brogan; Anton O'Toole, Tony Hanahoe, David Hickey; Bobby Doyle, Jimmy Keaveney, Pat John McCarthy.

Subs: Fran Ryder for Hanahoe, Paddy Gogarty for Doyle.

DUBLIN 1977: Same starting line-up as 1976.

Meath 1987–88

(Royals On A Roll)

It was supposed to happen in 1984. After years of wandering aimlessly through the Leinster championship, never actually reaching the finishing line, Meath had finally made it to the final. Not only that, but they had built up such an impressive momentum that they were well fancied to dethrone All-Ireland champions, Dublin. The seeds of the revival had been planted in 1983 when they went the distance and beyond with Dublin before losing in extra time in a smashing first round game.

Their graph line had continued its upward trend with a win in the 1984 Centenary Cup, a special knock-out competition which was organised by the GAA to celebrate its 100th anniversary. Meath beat Monaghan in the final and were immediately installed as top contenders for the Leinster title. The pieces appeared to be fitting neatly into place. Sean Boylan, who was appointed manager in September 1982 at a time when hardly anybody wanted the job, had re-awakened the traditional passion of Meath football. Now the new model was facing its first big test against Dublin, who had sat gleefully on Meath's face for most of the previous decade.

Despite Meath's optimism, the suffocation continued in 1984. Meath's lack of inner confidence, plus their inability to think clearly and concisely when faced with their great rivals cost them the match. They missed a first-half penalty and failed miserably to make use of the extra man after John Caffrey had been sent off. The 2–10 to 1–9 defeat was the best they could have hoped for in the circumstances. A year later, things were considerably worse when Meath were wiped off the pitch by Laois in Tullamore, losing by 2–11 to 0–7. It was a terrible shock to Meath but, in the long run, it would prove to be the turning point.

Boylan and his co-selectors, Tony Brennan and Pat Reynolds were forced to make a choice — stay loyal to the team which had failed in 1985 or re-build. They chose the latter route and on 27 July 1986 Meath found themselves back in the Leinster final against a Dublin team whose confidence levels had been severely eroded by two successive defeats by Kerry in All-Ireland finals. Kevin Heffernan had checked out as manager earlier that year and was replaced by Brian Mullins, Sean Doherty and Robbie Kelleher. If ever Dublin were vulnerable, this had to be it. And yet, at half-time they led by 0–6 to 0–4. Nonetheless, Meath sensed that there was something ordinary about Dublin and that they could be jostled from the top spot with one big push. It happened in the second half as the rain came down. Meath expanded by the minute and, with Dublin scoring just one point in the second half, the Leinster title went back to Meath for the first time since 1970 on a 0–9 to 0–7 scoreline.

Although they may not even have recognised the psychological impact at the time, winning the Leinster final satisfied them for that year. They faced mighty Kerry in the All-Ireland semi-final and lost by 2–13 to 0–12. Now, as they look back on that game, they realise that had they pumped up their ambition after the Leinster final, they might well have beaten Kerry, who were then on the downward slide. Instead, Meath gifted Kerry a first-half goal, which began the decline. It didn't completely undermine them but it had acted like a slow puncture in their inner resolve and they were eventually beaten by seven points. Still, they had made an important statement in Leinster and had got invaluable All-Ireland semi-final experience.

Winning the All-Ireland final a year later seemed the most natural thing in the world. Kerry had finally succumbed to the ravages of time, losing to Cork in the Munster final replay. Meath looked obvious successors. They didn't always play like that in the summer of 1987. It was as if they were ultra-careful in everything they did. Conscious of their 1985 experience, they were very edgy against Laois in Portlaoise, eventually winning by three points but only after putting on a finishing sprint over the final ten minutes which shook off their gritty, but limited rivals. Brian Stafford's accuracy from frees saw Kildare off (0–15 to 0–9), setting up yet another Leinster final clash with Dublin.

Mattie McCabe scored an early goal but Meath still contrived to find themselves a point adrift at half-time. There was a time when Meath might have taken that as a signal that the gods were not with them but by 1987, they had begun to erect an inner wall of self-reliance which enabled them to recover from tricky situations. It was to be their hallmark for years to come. They improved in the second half and eventually won by three points.

The All-Ireland semi-final was a routine affair for Meath. At the time, Ulster's stock had local value only and Derry played to that role in the 1987 semi-final, losing by 0–15 to 0–8. Nothing could stop Meath now. Or could it? Cork had beaten Galway in the other semi-final (it went to a replay) but the general feeling was that Meath were at a more advanced state in terms of team development. Larry Tompkins and Shea Fahy had joined the Cork squad that year and had made a big difference, but somewhat like Meath in 1986, the team was still regarded as an unfinished article.

As events turned out, Cork '87 were a lot like Meath '86. They led by 0–7 to 0–2 after twenty-one minutes. The margin would have been greater had Jimmy Kerrigan not missed a glorious goal chance for Cork. In fairness, Mick Lyons had made a great block but the feeling in Cork — probably rightly so — was that if any other Cork forward had got the chance, he would have scored a goal. After all, Kerrigan was a converted defender and was never very comfortable staring at opposition goalkeepers.

Despite their big lead, Cork played like men who expected the worst. It was as if they were peering over their shoulders, waiting for Meath to pounce. It was a self-destructive policy, one which Meath ruthlessly exploited. Colm O'Rourke scored the game's only goal and Meath were very much back on line when they led by 1–6 to 0–8 at half-time. Mentally, Cork were shattered.

Liam Hayes, and Gerry McEntee took over at midfield causing Cork to lose further altitude. Liam Hayes was later to be selected as man-of-the-match. They missed frees, lost shape and eventually conceded the game. The last ten minutes was exhibition stuff as Meath savoured their return to the top. They had won their first All-Ireland final since 1967. Meath 1–14 Cork 0–11.

It's difficult to pinpoint at what stage Meath began to lose their public relations battle. They were popular winners in 1987 and seemed quite at ease with that. But, from a position of power, attitudes seemed to change. By the end of 1988, they were skulking deep in a paranoid bunker, convinced that the world and its mother, aunt and uncle were against them. The Sam Maguire trophy was there too, having survived a number of attempts by enemy forces to wrest it from them.

The 1988 season has gone down as one of the best in Meath history. They won the National League final, beating Dublin with fourteen men in a replay. Kevin Foley had been sent off in the 11th minute but typically it galvanised Meath into furious action. They gave a classic exhibition of fourteen-man play. Passing was crisp and accurate; possession was retained carefully and expertly and, above all, the mental resolve to survive took over.

Liam Hayes's brilliant solo goal early in the second half set Dublin an unattainable target and they were eventually beaten by 2–13 to 0–11. Meath were getting used to beating Dublin. What's more they were enjoying it. They did it again in the Leinster final, but only after surviving a late scare when Charlie Redmond had a chance to level the match from the penalty spot. However, he drilled the ball high over the bar, leaving Meath 2–5 to 0-9 winners. Meath beat Mayo by 0–16 to 2–5 in the All-Ireland semi-final in a game which was to give one of the first indications that the Royals had a problem maintaining an even rhythm throughout their games. They led by 0–12 to 0–2 ten minutes into the second half but instead of cruising easily into the final, they allowed Mayo to grab the initiative. Two Mayo goals (they had the ball in the net a third time but were whistled back for a square ball infringement) brought them right back into contention and while Meath finished stronger, that second-half lapse was worrying.

Predictably, Cork had also made it to the final, and while they looked marginally stronger than in 1987, there was no real evidence to suggest that they could make up the six-point gap which separated the teams a year earlier. Oh no? Cork's explosive start yielded a Teddy McCarthy goal and while Meath came back to lead by a point at half-time, Larry Tompkins inspired Cork in the second half. They were three points ahead with ten minutes to go and looked certain to avenge the '87 defeat. By now, Meath's recovery powers had been fine-tuned and, once more, they dug into their inner reserves to score three points and level the match. It was the first All-Ireland football final to finish level since Kerry–Offaly in 1972.

The Meath–Cork replay was the most controversial football final since Galway–Dublin in 1983. Meath, believing that they had allowed themselves to be pushed around in the drawn game, decided that they would stand up for themselves. The notion of that particular Meath team being pushed around was comical but that's how they felt. Their zeal to achieve physical dominance in the replay left them with fourteen players after just six minutes when Gerry McEntee was sent off for a foul on Niall Cahalane. Sixty-four minutes to go... and no McEntee! Surely Cork would win this time. They didn't. With McEntee gone, Meath shared out the added responsibility fourteen ways. It worked better than anticipated. Ignoring personal danger Meath bodies dived into tackles; backs covered each other like soldiers in the trenches, Hayes and Gillic worked well together as an emergency midfield while the five-man attack handled possession as carefully as if it were Waterford glass. Seven minutes left and Meath were four points clear. Subconsciously, they decided it was a target which Cork could not reach and set about defending their lead. Spotting the change in emphasis, Cork lunged forward and scored three points. One more minute and they would probably have forced the game into extra time but Meath managed to hold on — just. Meath 0–13 Cork 0–12.

The physical nature of the exchanges dominated most of the post-match discussion. Cork felt that Meath had used unfair tactics and were allowed to get away with them. Meath countered that Cork were nothing more than whiners who couldn't cope with being beaten by fourteen men. The subsequent refusal by two Meath players to accept their All-Ireland medals from the then GAA President, John Dowling, because they were unhappy with comments made by him at the post All-Ireland lunch added to the controversy.

Meath's relationship with the media took a turn for the worse around then. Meath contended that what they perceived as a Dublin-based (and by extension, pro-Dublin) media did not give them the credit they deserved. Meanwhile, some commentators depicted Meath as a sullen, paranoid lot, who didn't even seem comfortable with success. As in most matters, the truth rested somewhere in between. Meath had justifiable complaints against some media commentators who virtually accused them of being assassins who shot their way to glory. That was wildly unfair, of course, but it resulted in many of Meath's players becoming anti-media.

Those peripherals are not relevant in assessing Meath's status as All-Ireland champions. Love them, or hate them, the fact remains that Meath were an extremely good team. Privately, they believe that their All-Ireland haul (two wins from four final appearances) did not adequately reflect their talents. That is probably true but, on the other hand, Meath could consider themselves somewhat lucky to have won the 1988 title.

There is a tendency to categorise Meath as a dour, physical team who used more power than poise to wear opponents down. That is a rather superficial analysis. Yes, they were strong physically but they were also a very good footballing side. Mick Lyons, Gerry McEntee, Liam Hayes, Colm O'Rourke and Joe Cassells were the big anchor men who soldiered through some very bad days before reaching the promised land. While they provided the central thrust of Meath's game plan, players like Robbie O'Malley, Martin O'Connell, Brian Stafford, P.J. Gillic and Bernie Flynn were the expansion agents which enabled Meath to press on from the limited frontiers of the early 1980s. Ultimately the mix of old and new was to prove just right and brought Meath through the most exciting voyage of its football history.

MEATH (1987 All-Ireland final): Martin McQuillan; Robbie O'Malley, Mick Lyons, Terry Ferguson; Kevin Foley, Liam Harnan, Martin O'Connell; Liam Hayes, Gerry McEntee; David Beggy, Joe Cassells, P.J. Gillic; Colm O'Rourke, Brian Stafford, Bernie Flynn. Subs: Colm Coyle for Cassells, Padraig Lyons for O'Connell.

Changes for drawn final of 1988; Padraig Lyons started at left corner-back in place of Terry Ferguson; Mattie McCabe was at left half-forward with P.J. Gillic in the centre for Joe Cassells. For the replay, Colm Coyle replaced Kevin Foley, Cassells was in for McCabe and Ferguson replaced Padraig Lyons.

Cork 1989–90

(The Power of Perserverance)

The theory that a team has to to lose an All-Ireland final before it can learn how to win one has always been popular in Gaelic Games. Unlike so many other GAA maxims, it has a a fair content of accuracy. For while some teams get it right first time up in a final, others only hit their peak after experiencing defeat on the big day.

In football, Galway 1964, Meath 1967, Kerry 1969, Offaly 1971 and 1982 all lost finals before coming back to win them, while in hurling Kilkenny 1967, Cork 1970, Kilkenny 1972, Galway 1980, Offaly 1985, Tipperary 1989 and Kilkenny 1992 all lost the previous years' finals. There have been a few extreme cases where teams have lost two consecutive All-Ireland finals before getting it right. Cork hurlers lost two in a row before winning the 1984 title; Galway hurlers had similar heartbreak in 1985–86 before clinching a two-in-a-row while Cork footballers lost out in 1987–88, only to fight back and win the next two finals.

Losing two consecutive finals can really affect a team. There is a certain amount of public sympathy for first-time losers but when the second final is lost, nerves become frayed. Players begin to ask themselves the basic question — are we good enough? Team managements wonder whether or not the responsibility is theirs, while the supporters blame all concerned. Against that background, teams who lose two-in-a-row really have to dig deep to justify themselves.

At the end of 1988 Cork footballers found themselves in lonely street. They had played in three All-Ireland finals in a thirteen-month period (the

1988 final had ended level) and had still to win any of them. Away in the distance their great rivals, Meath, were celebrating, perhaps even gloating, at having kept Cork in submission. It was tough on Cork but deep inside they were convinced that they were good enough to ultimately land the big one.

Events in the 1988 final had convinced them of that. Yes, they eventually lost but only by a point. And while the winner takes it all, the reality was that Cork were so very, very close to Meath as to make the difference negligible. Cork were in Division Two of the National League at the time and although they lost their first game to Mayo in the 1988/89 season they re-shaped after that and went on to not only gain promotion but to actually win the title. Two of their victims were Kerry (semi-final) and Dublin (final), results which were to prove significant in the championship season later on.

Cork have always had a less than cosy relationship with the League, bouncing up and down between Divisions One and Two with yo-yo-like regularity. Early in 1989, they took a decision to press on and try to win the League. After successive All-Ireland final defeats they badly wanted to win a National title to re-establish momentum. Meath were out of the League race, having conducted a less than energetic campaign themselves. By now, the three-in-a-row was uppermost in Meath minds and their League performances suffered accordingly.

With their sights set on the League title, Cork trained harder than usual in the spring of 1989 and were rewarded with a comfortable win over Dublin in the League final. They retained the Munster title with a three-point win over Kerry and then watched from a distance as Dublin ended Meath's reign in Leinster. Cork's first reaction was one of disappointment as they would have liked a fourth shot at the Meathmen but, on reflection, they quite rightly adjudged that Dublin would be easier to beat in the All-Ireland semi-final. After all, this was Dublin's first semi-final appearance since 1985 so it was new to many of the team. This didn't seem to matter when they ran into a seven-point lead early on but Cork's vast experience, not to mention luck, intervened. Two goals from penalties by John Cleary steadied them and with Dublin down to fourteen men, following Keith Barr's dismissal, Cork went on to win by 2–10 to 1–9.

The GAA world viewed that game as the real All-Ireland final. Connacht and Ulster were the poor relations around then. Getting a team into the final when their semi-final paths crossed every three years seemed to be limit of either province's capabilities. In 1989, it was Connacht's turn when Mayo beat Tyrone to qualify for the final for the first time since 1951. The prospect of playing Mayo did not worry Cork, even if they had lost to them in the League in the previous October. All things being remotely equal, Cork's greater experience, not to mention their superior strength-in-depth, would prove crucial. It did, although in fairness to Mayo they offered a far more stern resistance than most people envisaged. Luck didn't smile very kindly on them either. They lost full-forward Jimmy Bourke through injury ten minutes before half-time, prompting them to bring in Anthony Finnerty, who had assumed a super-sub role that year. Finnerty was a certainty to be used at some stage but manager, John O'Mahoney had hoped to hold him in reserve until the second half. Bourke's injury forced him to change his plans. That apart, Bourke was a big loss as he had been playing extremely well.

Finnerty made up for their loss when he rifled in Mayo's goal early in the second half. When Mayo led by 1–11 to 0–13 nineteen minutes into the second half, a shock looked very much on. Minutes earlier Finnerty had come within inches of scoring a second goal for Mayo, something which might really have rattled Cork beyond the point of recovery. As it was, they steadied themselves and re-launched their efforts on all fronts. The impact was devastating. Mayo failed to score in the final sixteen minutes while Cork, who were in the lucky position of being able to call on subs of the calibre of John O'Driscoll, Mick McCarthy and Danny Culloty, added four points to win by 0–17 to 1–11.

The sense of relief in Cork was palpable. They might not have beaten Meath in the final but at least they had won a title. Mayo were subsequently accused of being naive and of not imposing themselves physically on Cork as Meath had done on 1988. The implication was obvious — Cork would not have won against a more aggressive team. Mayo's counter argument was that with a marksman of Larry Tompkins' calibre on the Cork team, it would have been utter folly to adopt an aggressive approach and risk giving away frees.

Sweet though it was, Cork felt strangely unfulfilled after winning the 1989 title. They badly wanted another shot at Meath in an All-Ireland final, just to prove that they could master their old rivals on a day when it really counted. They failed once again on a day that partially counted when they lost to Meath in a bad-tempered League semi-final in April '90. Meath seemed to have Cork locked in a psychological grip at the time, one which refused to be prised open, irrespective of how hard Billy Morgan's squad tried. And yet they longed for the opportunity to have one more winner-take-all duel with Meath in an All-Ireland final. The opportunity arose on 16 September 1990 when Cork v Meath (Mark 4) took place. All season, there had been an inevitability about it. Cork had absolutely no trouble in retaining the Munster title, beating Limerick by twenty-one points and Kerry by fifteen points. Roscommon were seen off with minimum fuss (0–17 to 0–10) in the All-Ireland semi-final.

Rejuvenated Meath regained the No.1 spot in Leinster with another final win over Dublin (having earlier easily beaten Longford and Laois), before finishing strongly to see off Donegal (3–9 to 1–7) in the All-Ireland semi-final. It would be wrong to classify the 1990 final as one of the great deciders of modern times. It was far too tense for that and a final scoreline of 0–11 to 0–9 in Cork's favour portrays exactly the dour nature of the struggle. The most amazing aspect of the game was the manner in which it formed an almost perfect mirror image of the 1988 final replay, only the roles were reversed. This time, it was Cork who had to cope with fourteen men for much of the game, after full-forward Colm O'Neill had been sent off for a foul on Mick Lyons three minutes before half-time.

It should have been easy for Meath from there on. Cork had yet to beat them on a day that really mattered; now here they were trying it with just fourteen men. It just wasn't on. Or was it? There is no explanation for the demons which drive fourteen-man teams. It's as if they become totally different entities, possessed by a form of motivation which nothing else can provide. Indeed, many Cork fans are convinced that O'Neill's dismissal was the kick start the team needed. It certainly was the last thing Meath wanted. They had always survived on the edge of desperation, requiring the odds to be stacked against them to really lock on to the task. Facing a fourteen-man Cork team became a mental chore, one which distracted them all day. One of the really surprising elements of the game was the manner in which Meath allowed Cork to break through so many tackles. It was alien to Meath's entire culture and is a perfect example of how their focus was so blurred in that final. A great save by John Kerins five minutes into the second half was also crucial to Cork as a goal at that stage might just have provided the lift Meath so badly needed.

Cork midfielder, Shea Fahy had a dream game, kicking four points from play while Larry Tompkins's four points from frees were also crucial on yet another day when the importance of the Kildaremen to the Cork team was underlined. At the other end of the field, Bernie Flynn and Colm O'Rourke, so often Meath's great opportunists, managed just one point between them. It was that sort of day for Meath. Cork's post-match elation was understandable. They had finally slid free of Meath's oppressive weight after three tough seasons. An interesting question which, for obvious reasons will always remain unanswered, is how would the Cork team of 1987–90 have fared against Kerry during their great days of the previous decade? More specifically, were some of the Cork teams of the 1970s as good as the 1987–90 team but they just never made the breakthrough because they had the bad luck to have been contemporaries of an outstanding Kerry team? Certainly, the Cork team of 1976 which took Kerry to extra time in the Munster final replay could well contend that they were on a par with the squad which won the two-in-a-row.

What's more, the 1976 crew was all home-grown, unlike the 1980s teams which had acquired the considerable skills of Larry Tompkins and Shea Fahy from Kildare. They made a massive difference to Cork. Fahy anchored their midfield for several seasons while Tompkins's influence extended far beyond his playing skills. Tompkins had come up the hard way, in football terms. Playing for a Kildare team which invariably promised more than it achieved was extremely frustrating for a man who invested his entire life in the pursuit of sporting success. A row over expenses for a flight home from the US to play for Kildare in the Leinster championship eventually led to him severing his links with his home county. When he first played in Cork, he was surprised by the attitude, not among the team management but among the players. He just couldn't understand how some players who had outstanding talents weren't as obsessed with the pursuit of success as he was.

Tompkins's single-minded attitude was a real tonic for Billy Morgan and his management team. Inside a very short space of time, Tompkins became the unofficial team leader, the man the rest looked up to because of his self-belief and commitment. Tompkins was well aware that his decision to leave Kildare would leave him open to criticism. In a way, that spurred him on. He reckoned that he owed Kildare nothing and that if all those concerned with the team — especially the County Board — had put in as much effort as he had, the Lilywhites would have done far better over the years.

Fahy's decision to quit Kildare did not provoke as much debate. He was based in Cork with the Army and switched from Sarsfields to Nemo

Rangers because of the amount of travelling involved in playing for the Newbridge club. Declaring for Cork was the next logical step in the process.

How would Cork have fared without Tompkins and Fahy? It's a question which many people in the GAA world have pondered. Frankly, the general concensus is that they would not have been anywhere nearly as effective in the 1987–90 period. In fact, it is unlikely that they would have won either of the 1989–90 All-Ireland finals without their Kildare 'imports'.

Ironically, both Tompkins and Fahy were to play a significant part in Mick O'Dwyer's coaching career. In Owen McCrohan's biography of O'Dwyer, Tompkins is described by O'Dwyer as being in 'a class of his own'. He includes Tompkins along with Kevin Moran, Brian Mullins, Jimmy Keaveney and Matt Connor in the players he would have liked to call into his Kerry squad at its peak in the 1978–79 period. How ironic then, that Tompkins should emerge in a Cork jersey to play a major part in Kerry's downfall in 1987 and in their decline over the coming years. Indeed, it was not until 1991 that Kerry finally managed to break Cork's dominance. Even then Tompkins's role was important — this time in a negative sense for Cork.

He had severed his cruciate ligament in the 1990 All-Ireland final against Meath and had fought a long, lonely battle through the winter and spring in an effort to be fit for the Munster semi-final against Kerry. He eventually made it but was way short of match practice, a factor which was critical in Cork's two-point defeat in Killarney. Without Tompkins and Fahy, Kerry's dominance over Cork would almost certainly have continued right up to the end of the 1980s. Indeed, they might well have taken another All-Ireland title around then. The Tompkins–Fahy factor would come back to haunt O'Dwyer a second time. When O'Dwyer took over in Kildare in the autumn of 1990, he greatly regretted that two of the county's finest were playing for Cork. Tompkins and Fahy would have been invaluable in the Kildare set-up in the O'Dwyer era. Fahy would have brought stability to midfield while Tompkins's leadership qualities, allied to his never-say-die attitude, would have added a whole new dimension to a Kildare attack which frequently lacked character on the big day.

The irony of the situation was not lost on the Kildare fans. While the County Board and the Supporters' Club showed great initiative in bringing in O'Dwyer, it was difficult for the ordinary fans to come to terms with the excitement being generated by O'Dywer's arrival while two of the county's best footballers were still wearing the red of Cork. Rumours circulated on several occasions during O'Dywer's reign that Tompkins was about to return to Kildare but it never materialised and O'Dwyer had to see out his term without success while pondering on how it might have been so very different. Kildare's and Kerry's losses were very definitely Cork's gain.

CORK (All-Ireland final 1989): John Kerins; Niall Cahalane, Stephen O'Brien, Jimmy Kerrigan; Michael Slocum, Conor Counihan, Tony Davis; Shea Fahy, Teddy McCarthy; Dave Barry, Larry Tompkins, Barry Coffey; Paul McGrath, Denis Allen, John Cleary.
    Subs: Michael McCarthy for Cleary, Danny Culloty for Fahy, John O'Driscoll for Coffey.

CORK (All-Ireland final 1990): John Kerins; Tony Nation, Niall Cahalane, Stephen O'Brien; Michael Slocum, Conor Counihan, Barry Coffey; Shea Fahy, Danny Culloty; Dave Barry, Larry Tompkins, Teddy McCarthy; Paul McGrath, Colm O'Neill, Michael McCarthy.
    Sub: John Cleary for McGrath.

Down 1991–94

(Just When You Thought They Were Down)

Fifteen minutes into the second half of the 1991 All-Ireland football final, Down led Meath by eleven points. They won by two. Fifteen minutes into the second half of the 1994 All-Ireland football final, Down led Dublin by six points. They won by two.

The similarities don't end there. In both 1991 and 1994, Down came from way off the early season pace to surge through the pack and place the black and red on top of the winning post. In between, Down had looked very ordinary, first relinquishing their title rather tamely to Derry in 1992 and then producing a positively wretched effort as they caved in to Derry in the first round of the 1993 Ulster championship.

The extraordinary feature of Down's double All-Ireland successes in 1991–94 was the background against which they were achieved. At the start of 1991 not even the most committed Down fans would have given their side a chance of winning the All-Ireland title. Down had come off two woeful championships in 1989–90, first losing to a fourteen-man Tyrone team and, a year later, showing a marked absence of determination or character when failing to Armagh in a replay. It was subsequently claimed that some of the players had arranged to travel to the US for the summer even before Down were eliminated. The 1990 championship shambles was followed by a dreadful League campaign where Down won just one of seven games in Division One to finish second last in the group. So as Down headed into the 1991 championship they were rank outsiders for the All-Ireland title and at suitably long odds to take the Ulster crown.

Although Down's odds were not as generous going into the 1994 championship, they were still third in line behind Derry and Donegal in Ulster. Nobody could argue with that since Down had to travel to Celtic Park in Derry to tackle the 1993 All-Ireland champions. Besides, there had been a great deal of unease in the Down camp after the 1993 championship defeat. Manager, Peter McGrath, was at the centre of the storm. He had been publicly critical of his team's performance against Derry, which did not go down well with the players. Efforts were made to force him out but he stood his ground, convinced that if the focus was re-adjusted back to the sharp, clear, single-minded picture of 1991, Down had as good a chance as any other side, including Derry.

The 1994 side had one distinct advantage over the 1991 squad. Most of them had been on the 1991 team and knew exactly what it took to win an All-Ireland title. It was all so very different in the spring of 1991 when McGrath had to contend with low morale, poor attendances at training and a general sense of apathy. McGrath decided it was ultimatum time, telling the squad to either back his strict regime or forget about the championship.

Most team managers will tell you that there are times in the development of a squad when something clicks into place which alters the whole perspective. In Down's case, the big change came in a challenge game against Kildare in Leixlip in May 1991. Kildare were flying high at the time, having just failed to Dublin in the League final in Mick O'Dwyer's first season in charge. A big crowd turned out for the challenge game, giving it a mini-championship atmosphere and Down responded in a way which really excited McGrath. He left Leixlip that night with a real sense of optimism. Maybe the season would not be such a flop after all.

It wasn't, even if it did start off with one of those typically dour games which were common in the Ulster championship around then. Down were at home to Armagh in Newry but didn't look at home with their football, scoring just one point in the first half to put alongside Mickey Linden's goal from a penalty. Down eventually won by 1–7 to 0–8. Suffice to say that few fans dashed out to the bookies the following morning to back Down for the Ulster title, not to mention the All-Ireland.

Their win over Derry in a semi-final replay was of much higher quality. Ross Carr's point from a long-range free earned Down a replay but once they got a second chance they improved dramatically and beat an improving Derry team by five points. They had eight points to spare over Donegal in the Ulster final and then saw off Kerry by seven points in the All-Ireland semi-final. Down's march to the final had been low-key by comparison with Meath, who had taken nine games to reach Croke Park on 15 September. That was, of course, the year of the four-match Dublin-Meath saga, followed by Meath's two-match quarter-final against Wicklow. Offaly were seen off in the semi-final before Meath recorded another Leinster final triumph, this time against Laois. While Meath struggled to beat Roscommon by a point in the All-Ireland semi-final, there was a feeling that somehow, somewhere, the gods had decided that Meath's name was on the Sam Maguire Cup that year. Even when Bobby O'Malley sustained a serious leg injury which ruled him out of the team, it was assumed that Meath's sheer hardness and spirit, not to mention their big-time experience, would overcome Down.

There was a limit, however, to how much punishment even that Meath team could take. As well as losing O'Malley, they also had to line out in the final without Colm O'Rourke, who had been ill during the previous week. Breaking point had been reached — Meath were suddenly very vulnerable. Down recovered from a shaky start to put together an unbelievably productive period between the 19th minute of the first half and the 14th minute of the second half. They out-scored Meath by 1–11 to 0–2 in those thirty minutes of magic to lead by 1–14 to 0–6 with twenty minutes remaining. Meath's recovery powers that season were legendary but an eleven-point deficit? Surely they couldn't wipe it out.

In the end they came desperately close to achieving the comeback of the century. Point by point, they clawed their way back and were totally ignited by a great goal from their captain, Liam Hayes. Thankfully for Down, they had given themselves the softest of cushions to rest on and although it hardened rapidly over the last quarter, they held on for a 1–16 to 1–14 win to become the first Ulster side to win the All-Ireland title since the Down team of 1968.

Having won the title, Down seemed set for a sustained spell at the top. Granted, there were question marks against the defence but with attacking players of such high quality as Mickey Linden, James McCartan, Greg Blaney and Ross Carr on board, Down looked to have more options than most of the their rivals, especially in Ulster. The fact is that they had. However, just as winning an All-Ireland can give a team a confidence which is invaluable, it also places question marks against them as individuals. Some respond to the challenge, seeing one title as merely a challenge to pursue a second. Others lose their ambition after tasting glory once. Down fell into both categories. It was important that the county was given time to rejoice. The climate of celebration was understandable in the pre-Christmas period but despite the best intentions of the management, it was very difficult to control as the 1992 season began to crank into life. A holiday in the Canaries was followed by a trip to the US. All very enjoyable but quite distracting in their own way. Meanwhile Derry were lying in wait....

Crunch time for Down came in the Ulster semi-final. They had coped comfortably enough with Armagh's disappointing challenge in the first round, but Derry, who had won the League title a few weeks earlier, were a different proposition. Derry were much hungrier, a factor which ultimately won them the game. Down had Peter Withnell sent off early in the second half and they eventually lost by 0–15 to 0–12. Down misread the lessons on offer that day. They reckoned that a loss of appetite, allied to injury problems, was the primary source of their difficulties. They were wrong, as events in 1993 showed when Derry hammered them by 3–11 to 0–9 in Newry. Many of Down's problems stemmed from the midfield and half-back areas. Anthony Tohill and Brian McGilligan overpowered Eamonn Burns and Barry Breen while the Derry half-forwards broke their markers' tackles with remarkable ease.

A year later, the Down set-up had changed dramatically. The autumn of discontent, punctuated by secret meetings of players who were keen to get rid of McGrath, had yielded nothing. The County Board backed McGrath and eventually the players had no option but to come back on side. That included Greg Blaney who had opted out of the panel completely. It must be said that the players were far from unanimous in their opposition to McGrath. Many felt that while he might have kept his critical remarks for the privacy of the dressing-room after the defeat by Derry, he had basically spoken the truth.

With his authority re-established and a visit to Celtic Park to plan for in May 1994, McGrath decided to work specifically for the Derry challenge. It was a bold gamble but he reckoned that dethroning the All-Ireland champions would (a) vindicate himself and (b) be just the catalyst required to re-launch Down on the glory trail. Tohill and McGilligan were his first targets on the Derry team. How would Down cope with them? McGrath opted for Gregory McCartan and Conor Deegan, who had been at full-back in the previous seasons, but who could play just as well — if not better — at midfield. Physically, he judged that Deegan and McCartan could stand up to the giant Derry pair. That left Eamonn Burns and Barry Breen free to slot into the half-back line, where they would add weight and height alongside team captain, D.J. Kane. Peter Withnell was no longer the dashing full-forward of 1991 and was replaced by Aidan Farrell. McGrath's tactics worked. Derry's midfield engine room was never allowed to operate at full throttle, while Burns and Breen, together with Kane, formed an imposing half-back line which broke up many of Derry's attacks.

It turned out to be not only one of the games of the year but of the decade. Derry, proud champions that they were, fought gallantly but a goal by Down sub, Ciaran McCabe, proved the tie-breaker in a 1–14 to 1–12 win. If McCabe was the super-sub, Mickey Linden was the super-starter, scoring six points in a personal blitz. With Derry gone, Down could throttle back a little for the semi-final against Monaghan who, despite a committed stand, were beaten as comprehensively as the 0–14 to 0–8 scoreline suggests. The same applied to Tyrone who went down 1–17 to 1–11 in the Ulster final.

Cork, who had lost the 1993 All-Ireland final to Derry, were quite confident of ending the Ulster dominance in the semi-final but conceded both halves (the first by 1–6 to 0–7, the second by 0–7 to 0–4) in a rather disappointing game. In fairness to Down, it was Cork's failure to raise their performance level which prevented the game living up to expectations. Indeed, Down played like a team which could have moved up another gear if the occasion demanded.

The All-Ireland final against Dublin was, in many ways, similar to the 1991 final, even if Down never got as far away from Dublin as they did from Meath. A great goal by James McCartan in the 17th minute set Down on their way and by the 50th minute Down were a full six points clear, 1–12 to 0–9. Down failed to score in the final twenty minutes as Dublin finally got to grips with the game. Point by point they whittled back Down's lead and when they won a penalty in the 62nd minute, a goal would have drawn them level. Not for the first time, Dublin's penalty kicking betrayed them as Charlie Redmond had his shot brilliantly saved by

Down keeper, Neil Collins. Even then, Dublin should have scored from the rebound but the ball was driven wide.

It was heartbreaking for Redmond who had also failed to goal from penalty kicks against Meath in the 1988 Leinster final and against Donegal in the 1992 All-Ireland final, two games which Dublin also lost. While the penalty miss was crucial, there was still time for Dublin to complete the recovery but some good possession was wasted and their only return from a final eight minutes of pressure was a Redmond point to leave it 1–12 to 0–13 in Down's favour at the finish. Probably never before in the history of Gaelic football has a team won two All-Ireland titles while scoring just two points in the final twenty minutes of both games but such were Down's experiences in 1991–94.

It's amazing how history repeated itself for Down who, as in 1991/92 had a disastrous League after the 1994 All-Ireland triumph, eventually being relegated alongside Dublin in the spring of 1995. In fairness to Down, they were badly hit by injury problems which left them heading into the 1995 championship with a proven team in terms of achievement but with grave doubts about their match fitness. These were well-founded as Down failed to clear the first hurdle, flattened by a Donegal team who had conducted a very vigorous League campaign, eventually losing the final to Derry.

Donegal's busy spring had tuned them perfectly for the Down challenge. Down, who had Gary Mason sent off in the 49th minute, were out of sorts all day and were completely over-run in the last quarter as Donegal stormed to a 1–12 to 0–9 win. As in 1992, Down's poor form during the winter/spring months had come back to haunt them in the championship. Again, retaining the Ulster title was beyond the capabilities of the defending champions.

DOWN (All-Ireland final 1991): Neil Collins; Brendan McKernan, Conor Deegan, Paul Higgins; John Kelly, Paddy O'Rourke, D.J. Kane; Barry Breen, Eamonn Burns; Ross Carr, Greg Blaney, Gary Mason; Mickey Linden, Peter Withnell, James McCartan. Subs: Liam Austin for Breen, Ambrose Rodgers for Withnell.

DOWN (1994): Neil Collins; Michael Magill, Brian Burns, Paul Higgins; Eamonn Burns, Barry Breen, D.J. Kane; Gregory McCartan, Conor Deegan; Ross Carr, Greg Blaney, James McCartan; Mickey Linden, Aidan Farrell, Gary Mason.
Subs: Ger Colgan for Deegan.

Chapter 7

❖ ❖ ❖

Hurling's Order Of Merit

(All-Ireland's Champions Parade 1971–96)

Sporting history is full of what might have been. The missed chance, the bad refereeing decision or an injury to a key player, take turns at dealing a mischievous hand just when everything seems to be going well. Throw in the sudden, unexpected loss of form and another confusing dimension is added to the list of obstacles which pop up in front of sports people.

The Kilkenny hurling team of 1972–73–74–75 have more reason than most to feel that they were poorly represented when the allocation of good luck was being handed out. Unquestionably, the injury crisis prior to the 1973 All-Ireland final against Limerick played a major part in preventing them from becoming the first Kilkenny team to win four All-Ireland titles in a row. Three years later, they were devastated by an inexplicable loss of form when they were beaten by Wexford in the Leinster final. It was nothing new for Kilkenny to be hit with a Wexford power surge; the difference in 1976 rested with Kilkenny's utter inertia as Wexford trod all over them in a 2–20 to 1–6 win. Despite the 1973–76 defeats and the fact that they didn't take their place as record breakers in their native county, there is still compelling evidence to place that particular Kilkenny team at the top of the rating list of modern All-Ireland winners.

Cork fans will contend that their 1976–77–78 three-in-a-row side deserves to be rated higher but the facts suggest otherwise. Kilkenny won their three All-Ireland finals by margins of seven points (1972 v Cork), twelve points (1974 v Limerick) and twelve points (1975 v Galway) respectively. Cork's triple success was achieved with margins of four points (1976 v Wexford), three points (1977 v Wexford) and four points (1978 v

Kilkenny). In itself that does not automatically make Kilkenny a better team. Nonetheless, their incredibly high strike rate in All-Ireland finals underlined their capacity to deliver fully on the really big days. They scored 3–24 against Cork, 3–19 against Limerick and 2–22 against Galway.

Interestingly, Wexford were Kilkenny's toughest rivals in that period. They drew the 1972 Leinster final before losing the replay, and lost the 1974 final by a single point.

The Cork team of 1976–77–78 would have been worthy opponents for Kilkenny 1972–74–75 but would almost certainly not have beaten them. Apart from anything else, Kilkenny had a greater capacity to score goals, as instanced by the fact that they scored eight in the three finals they won, whereas Cork only scored four. Kilkenny were physically stronger too and also possessed the ability to inject a burst of scoring pace at crucial times in games.

While the Cork team might have fallen a notch or two below that particular Kilkenny team, they would probably have beaten the 1979–82–83 Kilkenny side. That particular Kilkenny squad peaked in 1982–83 when as well as winning two All-Ireland titles in a row, they also won consecutive National League finals. At its best, it was a fine Kilkenny outfit but there is a suspicion that the standard of hurling generally had dipped a little in the early 1980s and that Cork's all-round skills in 1976–77–78 would have been a touch too refined for Kilkenny 1982–83.

In turn, it is unlikely that the Galway team of 1987-88 would have beaten Kilkenny 1982–83. For while that was an extremely rounded Galway side, it had one dangerous flaw in that it tended to fail to press home its advantages at critical junctures. Thus, Tipperary were allowed back into contention after being out-paced early in the 1987 All-Ireland semi-final while it also took a generous portion of luck to keep Tipperary at bay in the 1988 final. This, despite Galway's stretch of near total control for a period in the first half. Galway argue that they were unlucky not to have won at least one more All-Ireland final around that time, with 1989 standing out as the most obvious one. That is true, up to a point, but it must also be remembered that Galway were lucky to win two-in-a-row as both Kilkenny (1987) and Tipperary (1988) had chances to turn both games around. In the end, a two-in-a-row was probably a fair return on Galway's talents.

The Galway 1987–88 team deserve to be rated ahead of Cork 1984–86. Two successive All-Ireland defeats in 1982–83 (Galway were to suffer the same fate in 1985–86) placed a severe strain on Cork's resolve but they recovered in fine style in 1984 to take the Centenary All-Ireland title. Luck played a big part in their march to that title as Tipperary had them all but beaten in the Munster final, only to lose their nerve with the finish line in sight. Cork were fortunate that Tipperary lacked the conviction to win a game that was theirs for the taking. They were lucky too that Offaly went into the final in an over-confident mood. It defies belief that Offaly could be over-confident going in against Cork but after replacing Kilkenny as Leinster champions (even if it was Wexford who ended Kilkenny's three-in-a-row ambitions) they were convinced that they could add to Cork's All-Ireland-final misery. In 1986, Galway also made life relatively easy for Cork by using the same revolutionary tactics as in the semi-final when they wiped Kilkenny off the pitch. It was all so different against Cork and by the time Galway had reverted to a more orthodox line-up, Cork had grabbed the initiative and refused to concede it despite Galway's best efforts.

While luck definitely smiled on Cork in 1984–86, it would be unfair to undervalue their achievements. They were very skilful both in defence and attack and, like all formidable hurling teams, had a high goal rate. They deserve to be placed in the top five sides of modern times.

The Offaly team of 1981–85 are only just behind Cork. The 1981 side had the added pressure of being the first Offaly team to play in an All-Ireland final, a load they carried with impressive authority. If ever there was a team in the strictest sense of the word, it applied to Offaly 1981–85. Unlike so many other sides who look to a key nucleus for inspiration, Offaly tended to be more even all round. They were short perhaps on star individuals but long on uniformity, togetherness, and they had an incredible sense of determination.

The Tipperary team of 1989–91 might, in other circumstances, have won three or four All-Ireland titles in a row. Conversely, they might well have taken just one. Such is the confusing backdrop to a team which had the bad luck to emerge at a time when Galway had the best team in its history. Take Galway out of the equation and Tipperary would probably have won the 1987–88 finals too. Put a full Galway squad back into the equation and Tipperary probably would not have won the 1989 title. Deep down, Tipperary acknowledge that the 1989 success had a flawed pedigree, combining as it did wins over a weakened and grumbling Galway team and over an Antrim side which was clearly overwhelmed by the All-Ireland final occasion. For that reason, that Tipperary side badly needed another All-Ireland success to prove to themselves — and others —that they were the genuine articles. The 1991 win achieved that.

There was a time when the Kilkenny team of 1992–93 were being talked as likely history-makers. They had cut an impressive swathe through all contenders in those years and while luck had given them a hand up once or twice — notably against Offaly — they looked very much the form bet going into the 1994 championship. However, Offaly finally got their measure and repeated it with an even more impressive win in 1995. Any team which wins two-in-a-row has to be regarded as extremely good but, on the basis of the opposition, there is reason to believe that the Kilkenny team of 1992–93 might be just a little off the pace in a head to head contest with other double achievers.

Tipperary 1971 head the list of single All-Ireland winners. Their strike rate was phenomenal. They scored 4–16 against Limerick in the Munster final, 3–26 against Galway in the All-Ireland semi-final and 5–17 against Kilkenny in the final. Even allowing for the fact that the games were of 80 minutes duration, it was pretty impressive scoring.

Next in line comes the 1973 Limerick team. Their success was devalued somewhat in the public's estimation by Kilkenny's injury problems in the final but there can still be no disputing that Limerick had a fine side. As well as winning the 1973 All-Ireland title, they won two consecutive Munster titles (1973–74) and were unlucky not to have won the 1971 Munster crown.

Like Tipperary 1971, high scoring was very much the hallmark of Cork 1990. Their demolition of Tipperary in the Munster final, allied to their great comeback against Galway in the All-Ireland final, was based on their attacking flair against defences which had a miserly giveaway rate in previous years.

Galway 1980 come next in the ratings, marginally ahead of Clare 1995, Wexford 1996 and Offaly 1994. Galway 1980 have had that little bit more star quality than Clare, Wexford or Offaly, even if they weren't as relentless as the other three. It's probable that Clare 1995 would have just edged out Wexford 1996. It's a close one to call but Clare's attack might have been too mobile for the Wexford defence. All of which leaves the Offaly team of 1994 in 15th position in the 1971–96 ratings. They hurled superbly to win the Leinster final and when beating Galway in that year's All-Ireland semi-final. However, they were handed the 1994 final by a Limerick team which assumed the task was completed when they led by five points with five minutes to go. When Offaly retained the Leinster title in 1995 with a great win over Kilkenny, it looked as if their talents were still expanding but Clare's utter refusal to take no for an answer in the final located the weak spot in the Offaly set-up.

How The Hurling Champions Rate (1971–96)

1. Kilkenny 1972–74–75
2. Cork 1976–77–78
3. Kilkenny 1979–82–83
4. Galway 1987–88
5. Cork 1984–86
6. Offaly 1981–85
7. Tipperary 1989–91
8. Kilkenny 1992–93
9. Tipperary 1971
10. Limerick 1973
11. Cork 1990
12. Galway 1980
13. Clare 1995
14. Wexford 1996
15. Offaly 1994

Kilkenny 1972–74–75

(The Best Of Modern Times)

Only once in hurling history has any county won four consecutive All-Ireland hurling finals. That distinguished honour goes to Cork who kept the red flag at the summit in 1941–42–43–44. Not only did they win the four-in-a-row, they had extremely easy victories in each of the finals. In fact, the winning margin was never less that seven points. Clearly they were a team of great substance.

Since then, Cork have been the only county to win the three-in-a-row in 1976–77–78. So while Cork have been the most adept at putting consecutive wins together, there is a view that another team might, in luckier circumstances, have also accumulated the four-in-a-row. Kilkenny appeared in five consecutive finals in the early 1970s, winning three of them, including a two-in-a-row in 1974–75. They also won the 1972 final after an astonishing comeback against Cork. Sadly for Kilkenny, they were beaten by Limerick in the 1973 decider, thereby wrecking their four-in-a-row dream.

The launch of that particular Kilkenny team came in 1969 when, after being rather fortunate to beat Offaly by two points in the Leinster final, they beat Cork by six points in the All-Ireland final. A year later, they surrendered their Leinster title to Wexford and, in 1971, were beaten 5–17 to 5–14 by Tipperary in a pulsating All-Ireland final. The Leinster championship was very much a see-saw around then, mainly involving Kilkenny and Wexford. While the black-and-amber enjoyed longer spells on top, Wexford could always be relied upon to raise their game high enough every few years to take a Leinster title at least.

When they led Kilkenny by seven points well into the second half of the 1972 Leinster final, it looked as it would be another of those years when Wexford had hit the sweet spot against their great rivals. But, as has happened so often before and since, Kilkenny drilled deep into their sense of defiance and unleashed a powerful climax which earned them a draw. The final score was an amazing 6–13 each and although games were played over eighty minutes back then, it was still very high scoring. The rate dropped somewhat in the replay, especially for Wexford, who were eventually beaten by 3–16 to 1–14.

After spending a miserable decade locked in a losing mode in the Munster championship, Galway had reverted to taking their chances against the 'big boys' in the All-Ireland semi-finals but found Kilkenny bigger than most in 1972, losing by 5–28 to 3–7. Cork, who had earlier dethroned Tipperary in the Munster semi-final before beating Clare in the final, hammered London in the other semi-final to set up another All-Ireland final clash with Kilkenny. It would be the third final meeting between them in six years. There are many who claim that the 1972 final was one of the best in history. It was also was the first final to be played under the new rule which afforded the goalkeeper protection from marauding forwards who liked to show their macho tendencies by charging into goalies.

An early Cork goal by Ray Cummins set the trend and although Kilkenny's point-taking was impressive, a second Cork goal — scored this time by Mick Malone — gave them the edge at half-time, 2–8 to 0–12. Kilkenny equalised after the break but Cork regained the initiative through another goal by Malone. Then came the first real break for Kilkenny. Eddie Keher took a pass from Liam 'Chunky' O'Brien at pace and fired in a shot which Cork goalie, Pat Barry, would normally cope with quite easily. This time, the ball spun off his chest and into the net.

It was a sickening goal to give away but Cork recovered quickly to score two of their own, courtesy of Ray Cummins and Seanie O'Leary and when

Con Roche put Cork eight points clear with a magnificent score from 80 yards, the game looked to have been decided, even if there were twenty-three minutes left. Luckily for Kilkenny fans, their team had other ideas. The final quarter was as dramatic as hurling fans had ever witnessed. In a remarkable turnaround, Kilkenny not only clawed back the eight-point lead but by the end were seven points ahead, 3–24 to 5–11. Was it down to Cork complacency or sheer Kilkenny determination, liberally sprinkled with the class and craft which has always been the county's trademark? Whatever the explanation, the truth was that Kilkenny ran Cork off the pitch in the closing stages. Inspired by a great goal from a twenty-one–yard free by Eddie Keher, Kilkenny drove forward in relentless black-and-amber waves. Pat Delaney scored a fantastic point after bursting through the Cork defence, hopping the ball twice off the ground in an incredible exhibition of dexterity and then Frank Cummins blasted in Kilkenny's third goal from thirty yards to bring the sides level.

Shell-shocked Cork tried to fight back but Kilkenny were on a roll and would not be stopped. The points flowed from every angle and distance as Kilkenny ran riot. Eddie Keher, who had scored 2–11 and still ended up on the losing side in the previous year's final, scored 2–9 this time to bring his tally for the two finals to an astonishing 4–20. How Kilkenny would miss him in the 1973 final!

Arguments continue to this day as to how Limerick would have coped with a full-strength Kilkenny team in the 1973 final. As it was, Limerick won by 1–21 to 1–14. It was a comprehensive victory — well planned and executed but made considerably easier that it would otherwise have been by the absence of Keher (broken collar bone), Kieran Purcell (appendix operation), Jim Treacy (achilles tendon trouble) and Eamonn Morrissey (emigrated). Add in the fact that Pat Delaney had a severe dose of 'flu the week before the final and that Frank Cummins had to retire with a shoulder injury in the second half and you have a book of evidence to heavily support the theory that, for whatever reason, somebody very important did not like Kilkenny very much that year.

Not that anybody begrudged Limerick their success. They had held together bravely after the heartbreak of losing the 1971 Munster final by a point to Tipperary. In 1973, revenge was their pleasant reward when they beat Tipperary by a single point, 6–7 to 2–18, to win the Munster final for the first time since 1955. Kilkenny, meanwhile, had retained the Leinster final, beating Wexford by 4–27 to 3–15 in what Eddie Keher subsequently described as one of the best performances by that particular team. It was all so different in the final. Without so many star names, Kilkenny struggled all over the place and could never hope to cope with the sheer drive of a Limerick team which refused to take 'no' for an answer.

After the disappointment of 1973, Kilkenny's determination levels soared to new heights. They couldn't wait for the 1974 season simply to prove that injury problems had been at the heart of the 1973 defeat. Treacy, Purcell and Keher were back in place and providing the dimension which had been missing in 1973. It was badly needed as Wexford chose that season to make one of their truly gallant stands in the Leinster final. Not that many outside of the Wexford camp expected it to be so, judging by the fact that only 20,742 turned up in Croke Park. The general view was that Kilkenny couldn't be beaten.

Oh no? Clearly, Wexford didn't believe that, not even when they had Phil Wilson sent off just before half-time, or when they trailed by 5–10 to 1–15 in the second half. As if inspired by adversity, they trawled deep into their survival kit and came up with a rescue package which rocked Kilkenny. Wexford clawed their way back into contention with some magnificent scores and, when John Quigley put them ahead with ten minutes remaining, Wexford appeared poised for one of the most famous wins in Leinster final history. It was at this stage that Kilkenny's great survival qualities re-surfaced. Eddie Keher levelled it up with a pointed free before Tom Byrne gave Wexford the lead again. In a thrilling finale, Nicky Brennan equalised before Keher struck the winning point off a free in the closing seconds. Kilkenny 6–13 Wexford 2–24.

It was as if the gods, who had been so cruel to Kilkenny in 1973, had decided to back them again. Kilkenny beat Galway by 2–32 to 3–17 in the All-Ireland semi-final and then avenged the 1973 defeat by Limerick, beating them by 3–19 to 1–14 in the final. Kilkenny's comprehensive victory merely reinforced the view that had they been at full strength a year earlier they would have resisted Limerick's challenge.

Hurling's pecking order underwent the first major change of modern times in 1975 when Galway re-emerged as a force after years in the doldrums. With the fruits of the revival plan launched in the mid-1960s now becoming apparent, Galway won the National League title after completing a great treble over Cork, Kilkenny and Tipperary in the quarter-final, semi-final and final. Still, when they lined up against Cork in the All-Ireland semi-final, it was generally assumed that Cork would resume normal championship service and qualify for another final clash with Kilkenny. They didn't, or rather they weren't allowed to by a Galway team which built on the League final triumph. An early three-goal blitz set Galway on their way and although Cork came back in typical style, Galway held on for a famous win 4–15 to 2–19, thereby setting up a final date with Kilkenny. Suddenly the whole focus switched to Galway, who were appearing in their first All-Ireland final since 1958. That suited Kilkenny, who rode out Galway's early storm to eventually win easily by 2–22 to 2–10. It was an uneven contest in a number of ways but the prime difference between the teams was experience. Battle-hardened Kilkenny had been through the All-Ireland mill so often that it was all very routine. Galway found the whole occasion too much and didn't do themselves justice at all. At the start of 1976, hopes were very high in Kilkenny that they would win the three-in-a-row for the first time since 1911–12–13. There was no obvious blip on the Kilkenny screen. Certainly not until they ran into Wexford in the Leinster final. Suddenly, it all went blank for Kilkenny, who were beaten on an amazing scoreline of 2–20 to 1–6. Kilkenny's average score in the previous five Leinster finals had been 4–18; now they could only manage 1–6. Kilkenny were blown away right from the first whistle and were it not for some great saves by Noel Skehan they would have been humiliated in the first half. As it was, they trailed by 1–11 to 1–5 at half-time and Tony Doran's early second-half goal made the rest of the game a mere formality. It really was one of Wexford's greater days — the only pity was that they failed to follow-up with an All-Ireland success. The 1976 Leinster final defeat signalled the end of that particular Kilkenny team for while they regained the Leinster crown in 1978, they lost the All-Ireland final to Cork. Kilkenny won it back a year later but, by then, there were only seven survivors from the 1975 team.

The 1973 All-Ireland final defeat still hurts the Kilkenny team of that era. They are utterly convinced that their place in Kilkenny hurling history as the only side to win four-in-a-row was denied them by circumstances outside their control. Nevertheless, the fact remains that the Kilkenny teams of 1972–74–75 were outstanding. Noel Skehan's expertise in goal, after sitting so long on the bench waiting for the late Ollie Walsh to move on, was legendary. Not only did Skehan have the uncanny knack of making unbelievable saves, he also possessed an inspiring quality which so often lifted his colleagues while deflating the opposition. The defence, anchored with so much authority by Pat Henderson, was soundness personified; Frank Cummins and Liam 'Chunky' O'Brien were the perfect midfield combination; while up front, the spirit of enterprise and invention was limitless, with Eddie Keher the scoring maestro in virtually every game. A truly great team.

KILKENNY (1972 All-Ireland final): Noel Skehan; 'Fan' Larkin, Pa Dillon, Jim Treacy; Paddy Lalor, Pat Henderson, Eamonn Morrissey; Frank Cummins, Liam O'Brien; John Kinsella, Pat Delaney, Mick Crotty; Ned Byrne, Kieran Purcell, Eddie Keher. Subs: Mossie Murphy for Byrne, Martin Coogan for Larkin, Paddy Moran for Kinsella.

KILKENNY (1974 All-Ireland final): Noel Skehan; 'Fan' Larkin, Nicky Orr, Jim Treacy; Paddy Lalor, Pat Henderson, Tom McCormack; Liam O'Brien, Frank Cummins; Mick Crotty, Pat Delaney, Billy Fitzpatrick; Mick Brennan, Kieran Purcell, Eddie Keher.

In 1975, the only change on the team was Brian Cody for Jim Treacy at left full-back.

Cork 1976–77–78

(Leeside's Best Since the 1950s)

As the years pass, so too does the sense of loss, but it never disappears. Cork hurling fans still look back on the 1970s and reflect ruefully on what might have been. Yes, the county took four of the ten All-Ireland senior titles, including the three-in-a-row in 1976–77–78, but there is still an acute sense of disappointment that they didn't achieve the four-in-a-row.

The ultimate irony from a Cork viewpoint is that their great dream was broken not by eternal rivals Tipperary and Kilkenny but by Galway, a county which had emerged from the desert to take its place alongside the best. Indeed, Galway's victory over Cork in the 1975 All-Ireland semi-final, coming just two months after Galway had won the National League title, marked the official launch of a western surge which has continued to the present day.

It is impossible to quantify the degree to which over-confidence contributed to Cork's downfall in 1975. For while Galway had beaten them in the League quarter-final earlier in the year, Cork were convinced that it would be altogether different in the championship. Basically, Cork expected an early Galway storm, followed by a stabilisation period for Cork, prior to killing off the western challenge in the second half. The problem for Cork was that Galway's early blast wasn't just a storm but a howling tornado which had them 3–2 to 0–1 ahead after ten minutes. Cork won the remainder of the game by 2–18 to 1–13 but Galway's early blitz had left the Leesiders with too much to do.

Quite naturally, Cork were devastated. However, it probably safe to assume that even if they had beaten Galway, they would not have been good enough to match a great Kilkenny side which was then at the peak of its powers. Whatever the background to the defeat by Galway, Cork took it as an indication that it was time for adjustments; by the time they reached the 1976 All-Ireland final, they had a complete new half-back line and two different half-forwards. There were changes too at right corner-back and midfield. In fact, just eight of the 1975 side played in the 1976 final.

There are many who still believe that the 1976 Munster semi-final, between Cork and Tipperary, shaped the Munster, and possibly the All-Ireland, championships for the next few years. Given that the match was regarded as the unofficial Munster final, a rather disappointing crowd of 21,000 turned up in Limerick. Those who stayed away were the losers. It turned out to be a cracking contest, with the balance of power alternating from side to side on several occasions. Tipperary led by 1–8 to 1–5 at half-time, despite having played against the wind. It all went horribly wrong for them in the second half. First, they lost star defender, Tadhg O'Connor and then Cork goalkeeper, Martin Coleman, made two magnificent saves from Seamus Power and Tommy Butler. Cork gradually forced their way back into the game and a late point from Seanie O'Leary, who had done a lot of damage after O'Connor's retirement, won the game for Cork, 4–10 to 2–15.

Unquestionably luck played its part in Cork's victory when Tipperary had a second and final opportunity to win the game but Seamus Power's thundering drive crashed back off the upright. Cork did not have to call on anything special in the semi-final where they beat Limerick, 3–14 to 0–12 to qualify for yet another All-Ireland final. Their opponents were Wexford who, after hammering Kilkenny in the Leinster decider, took two attempts to beat Galway in the All-Ireland semi-final. For reasons best known to the GAA, the semi-final was fixed for Páirc Uí Chaoimh, a venue which could scarcely be described as convenient for either Galway or Wexford.

Both matches were of the highest quality. The first ended level 5–14 (Wexford) to 2–23 but Wexford won a rather controversial replay 3–14 to 2–14 to qualify for their first All-Ireland final since 1970, where coincidentally, Cork were also their opponents. Cork won that game by

6–21 to 5–10. Not that it was of much relevance going into the '76 final as Wexford had only six of the '70 team while Cork had just four.

The opening minutes of the 1976 final were as dramatic as anything produced by any All-Ireland final down the years. Directly from the throw-in Wexford attacked won a free which Mick Butler pointed. 0–1 to 0–0. Martin Coleman's puck-out was gathered by Ned Buggy, who made ground before firing the ball over the bar. 0–2 to 0–0. In the 5th minute, Tony Doran, a man of whom so much was expected, won possession, hooked the ball over his shoulder, where it was met by Martin Quigley, who whipped it to the net: 1–2 to 0–0. A minute later, the same pair combined and again Quigley lashed the ball to the Cork net. 2–2 to 0–2....and just six minutes gone!

Wexford had made an incredible start but obviously there was no way they could maintain that momentum. Cork dug deep and re-discovered their hurling instinct which enabled them to crawl back up from a deep hole. Gerald McCarthy and Pat Moylan asserted themselves at midfield and gradually the Cork attack began to find gaps through the Wexford defence. Cork scored six unanswered points as the pressure mounted on the Wexford defence and the comeback was completed by Ray Cummins who kicked Cork's first goal. Two more Cork points gave them the lead and while Wexford scored two points themselves before half-time, they were rather deflated to be merely level 2–8 to 1–11 at half-time.

The odds had now lengthened on Wexford. Losing a 2–2 lead was a dreadful psychological blow but, to their credit, they re-focused themselves at half-time and were back in front almost immediately on the re-start when Tony Doran shot their third goal. The initiative see-sawed over and back for most of the second half but, with ten minutes to go, Wexford were two points ahead. Then, Mick Butler mis-hit a free which would have put them three clear; the ball was cleared downfield and Pat Moylan pointed a free for Cork. Suddenly the gap was only one. It was as if Cork took that as a signal to strike for home and, as Wexford wilted, Jimmy Barry Murphy, who had moved to centre-forward, inspired a rebel surge which enabled them to go three points clear. In a last desperate effort to save the game, Tony Doran tried to break through the Cork defence for the equalising goal. Wexford fans howled for a penalty but the referee, presumably operating on the basis that Doran was both sinning and being sinned against, threw in the ball, much to Doran's disappointment. It looked a rather harsh decision from a Wexford viewpoint and with it went their chance of taking the title as Pat

Moylan stroked over the insurance point shortly afterwards, leaving Cork winners by 2–21 to 4–11.

A year later, the sides were back in Croke Park for another All-Ireland final clash having safely negotiated the Munster and Leinster championships, plus Galway's All-Ireland semi-final ambush. Clare, the newly-crowned League champions, were Cork's opponents in the Munster final and went down by 4–15 to 4–10 on a day when thieves helped themselves to £24,000 after a raid on the Semple Stadium counting room. The money was never recovered. Wexford had a much closer call against Kilkenny than in 1976 but held onto their title on a 3–17 to 3–14 scoreline. Cork weren't unduly troubled by Galway in the All-Ireland semi-final, winning by 3–14 to 1–15.

Cork won the final by 1–17 to 3–8 in a game which didn't live up to the 1976 standards. Not that it mattered to Cork who had now made it two-in-a-row. The talking point from the 1977 final was the stunning save made by Cork goalkeeper, Martin Coleman, from a Christy Keogh rocket a few minutes from the end at a time when his side was three points adrift. A year later, Cork completed the three-in-a-row with a 1–15 to 2–8 win over Kilkenny. Having lost to Kilkenny in the 1969 and 1972 finals, Cork were very determined to get the 1978 final right, which they duly did. It was level, 0–7 to 1–4 at half-time but Cork had gone three points clear twenty minutes into the second half. The decisive break came shortly afterwards when Jimmy Barry Murphy scored Cork's only goal. Billy Fitzpatrick countered with Kilkenny's second goal but Cork kept their shape to win by four points.

Prior to that, they had to dig very deep to resist the challenge of Clare, who had again won the National League title. Despite the fact that Cork were the defending champions, there were many who fancied Clare to finally end their championship drought in the Munster final. Clare had improved on the previous year while Cork had to play without Seanie O'Leary and Brian Murphy. Also, Clare were convinced that the 1977 final would have been a different affair had they not been reduced to fourteen men when full-back, Jim Power, was sent off just before half-time.

Cork had the wind behind them in the first half of the 1978 final but made little real use of it and were just two points ahead at half-time, fuelling Clare's optimism to an even higher degree. Cork's second-half performance was a fantastic example of how an experienced, well organised side can instinctively improvise. Clare huffed and puffed but couldn't blow Cork's defensive house down and were eventually beaten by 0–13 to 0–11. It was heartbreaking for Clare. They had conceded just thirteen points and still somehow managed to lose the game.

At the end of 1978, God was very much in his hurling heaven as far as Cork were concerned. Not only had they captured their third consecutive senior title, their minors had also won the All-Ireland final. The future looked extremely bright. That was very much the position by the end of July 1979 too. Earlier, Tipperary had emerged as a new threat in Munster after winning the National League title and were oozing confidence when they travelled to Pairc Ui Chaoimh for a Munster semi-final clash with Cork. They came desperately close to ending Cork's four-in-a-row dream, just as Tipperary had done in 1945, but in the end, the champions held on for a one-point win, 1–14 to 2–10. Cork easily beat Limerick in the Munster final and looked sound value to complete the All-Ireland four-in-a-row. Kilkenny had made it to the final again and while Cork were conscious that Galway would offer them a stern test in the All-Ireland semi-final, there was nothing to suggest that it would be any more than that. After all, Galway had been hammered by Tipperary in the League final some months earlier and seemed to have run out of steam after the exciting days of 1975–76. Deep down, Cork felt that Galway could not possibly beat them. They warned each other about complacency but, like a rust which is eating away below the surface, the damage was being done with each passing day bringing more references to a Cork–Kilkenny final. Galway, who had brought in 'Babs' Keating as coach, plotted and planned down in Athenry. Privately, they were peeved by the general assumption that they would be no more than a warm-up act for Cork as they moved inexorably towards the four-in-a-row.

The extent to which Cork were fancied was underlined by the fact that only 12,000 turned up for the All-Ireland semi-final. Cork should have been warned by memories of 1975 but clearly they weren't. Once again, Galway exploded from the starting blocks and put their imprint on the game by establishing a six-point lead after twenty-five minutes. Cork rallied but were off tune and eventually lost by 2–14 to 1–13. The four-in-a-row dream had died. Cork were disgusted by their performance, not least when Kilkenny went on to beat Galway by seven points in the All-Ireland final.

Cork still deeply regret events of 1979 as they believe that it was their own questionable attitude rather than any big improvement by opposition forces, which prevented them from emulating the Cork four-in-a-row side of the 1940s. There is plenty evidence to support that viewpoint.

CORK (1976 All-Ireland final): Martin Coleman; Brian Murphy, Pat McDonnell, Martin O'Doherty; Pat Barry, John Crowley, Denis Coughlan; Gerald McCarthy, Pat Moylan; Mick Malone, Brendan Cummins, Jimmy Barry Murphy; Charlie McCarthy, Ray Cummins, Seanie O'Leary.
   Subs: Eamonn O'Donoghue for O'Leary, John Horgan for Barry.

CORK (1977 All-Ireland final): Martin Coleman; Brian Murphy, Martin O'Doherty, John Horgan; Dermot MacCurtain, John Crowley, Denis Coughlan; Tom Cashman, Tim Crowley; Mick Malone, Gerald McCarthy, Jimmy Barry Murphy; Charlie McCarthy, Ray Cummins, Seanie O'Leary.
   Subs: Pat Moylan for Malone; Tadhg Murphy for G.McCarthy.
   In 1978, the only change in personnel was Pat Moylan for Mick Malone. There were several positional switches. Eamonn O'Donoghue (for O'Leary) and John Allen (for Cashman) came on as subs.

Galway 1987–88

(Farrell's History Makers)

On the Sunday before the 1987 All-Ireland final, Galway manager Cyril Farrell took the unusual step of declaring that if they were beaten in the final, he would close the dressing-room door behind him for the last time.
   Farrell made his shock announcement in *The Sunday Press* and had told nobody in advance. He did it quite deliberately, deciding that a public declaration of his intention to resign would provide a sharp focus for the team to dwell on in the days leading up to the final.
   He had been manager since the Autumn of 1984 and, after losing All-Ireland finals to Offaly and Cork in 1985 and 1986, he felt that he would have no option but to quit had Galway made it a losing hat-trick. Farrell knew that many would interpret his pre-final announcement as a defeatist attitude. It was, in fact, designed to generate the opposite effect on the players who, as far as he was concerned were the only people who mattered.

> I wanted to use it as a rallying point. If we lost, I would have been
> replaced as manager anyway. The players knew the implications.
> What new coach would have wanted three-time losers? I reckoned

that my announcement would encourage every player to take that little extra responsibility, on the basis that if Galway lost, they would be finished as a team.

In a sense, it was a desperate throw of the dice by Farrell. But then he had always been a gambler when it came to preparing teams. This was just one more little ploy which may, or may not, have worked. Either way, there wasn't a whole lot to lose. By that stage, desperation had settled over Galway hurling like a November fog. The somewhat lucky win over Clare in the 1987 League final had provided only a temporary respite from the cynics. The perception was that when it came to coping with the searing heat of an All-Ireland final, Galway's resolve melted far too easily.

Yes, they had dazzled defending All-Ireland champions, Cork, in the 1985 All-Ireland semi-final to win by 4–12 to 5–5, but in the final against Offaly they were edgy and unsure *en route* to a 2–11 to 1–12 defeat.

They had climbed back to reach the 1986 League final but were beaten by Kilkenny more convincingly than the 2–10 to 2–6 scoreline suggested.

Three months later they produced one of the great performances of their era when they hammered Kilkenny by 4–12 to 0–13 in the All-Ireland semi-final. It was the closest that Galway team came to perfection. Farrell's bizarre, but brilliant, attacking strategy mesmerised Kilkenny while the darting enterprise of Joe Cooney, Anthony Cunningham and Martin Naughton, allied to the calm maturity of Noel Lane and Brendan Lynskey produced a forward strike-force of unstoppable dimensions. The tactical adjustments which left Galway with three midfielders and two full-forwards looked brilliant. The element of surprise had stunned Kilkenny who were over-confident anyway after tying Galway up so easily in the League final. It was one of those days when everything worked to plan for Galway.

How could they be curbed in the final? Very easily as it happened. Their new game-plan never worked against Cork. The players who had been in brilliant form in the semi-final were now listless and edgy. Cork craftily exploited Galway's naivete and got full value for their 4–13 to 2–15 win.

The All-Ireland final defeats of 1985–86 made serious inroads on Galway's confidence reserves. The 'Dream Team', which had come together so quickly after Farrell, Phelim Murphy and Bernie O'Connor took over in October 1984 was fast becoming a nightmare. It had been based on the survivors from the 1984 All-Ireland semi-final wreckage and the emerging talents of the successful 1983 minor and U-21 teams but while it appeared to have all the right ingredients, it had difficulty coping with real heat.

There are many who contend that if Galway had lost the 1987 League final to Clare (and they came mighty close to doing so), the team would have sunk without trace. Even those close to the squad acknowledge that the League final success was the catalyst which lit the winning fuse. It gave them the confidence to resist Tipperary in the All-Ireland semi-final, after falling behind in the second half. By now, Eanna Ryan, one of the game's great natural poachers, had slotted neatly into attack while further back, the Pete Finnerty–Tony Keady–Gerry McInerney trio were maturing into a half-back line of great substance. Behind them, Sylvie Linnane, Conor Hayes and Ollie Kilkenny formed a cute, experienced full-back line.

The improving mix finally got it right in the 1987 All-Ireland final when they beat Kilkenny by 1–12 to 0–9 in one of those finals which will never be recalled for its quality. It was more a battle of wills than skills between two teams who knew each other very well. Unquestionably, luck threw its comforting arms around Galway. Ger Fennelly, normally the deadliest of free-takers, missed some good scoring opportunities for Kilkenny while his brother, Liam, then the most lethal goal-grabber in the business, failed to beat John Commins in a one-to-one situation at a time when the game was see-sawing precariously in the second half. Noel Lane, hurt and shocked at being left off the team in the first place, harnessed his disappointment into a positive force to score a super-sub goal which swung the title Galway's way.

While accepting that most of the good fortune landed on Galway's side of the fence, few would argue that they deserved it. 'After all, we didn't get much luck in either 1985 or 1986 so we were entitled to something,' said Cyril Farrell. The most significant feature of Galway's 1987 success was that it established them as a team which could adapt to different circumstances, a capacity which eluded them in previous seasons. They had beaten Tipperary by 3–20 to 2–17 in a high-speed, free-flowing semi-final on a beautiful day. A month later, they were able to cope with a dour, low-scoring struggle on a wet afternoon. Times had changed. Previously, Galway almost always lost low-scoring games.

The extent of the change is underlined by the fact that Galway remained unbeaten in League and Championship for sixteen months between November 1986 and March 1988. Offaly eventually ended their run with a win in the League quarter-final but they picked up again and won the 1988 All-Ireland final, followed by the 1989 League title.

The 1998 championship campaign provided a whole new challenge to Galway. Tipperary, now much more seasoned, always looked likely to be their main rivals and so it proved. Offaly won the Leinster title but were comprehensively beaten by Galway, 3–18 to 3–11, in the All-Ireland semi-final. In truth, the final score flattered Offaly who were beaten by half-time, when they trailed by seven points. Two late goals by Pat Delaney, who had lined out at centre-forward, took the grim look off the scoreline for Offaly but there was no denying Galway's massive superiority.

Few finals in modern times generated as much interest as the Galway–Tipperary decider of 1988. Tipperary, hoisted high on a storm of hype after ending the Munster championship famine in 1987, were well fancied to dethrone Galway. So great was the buzz in Tipperary that the team actually trained behind closed doors to keep them away from the hordes of fans. When news of that filtered into Galway, it was greeted with delight. 'My view was that if they had problems dealing with big crowds in training, what chance had they of coping with 64,000 screaming spectators in Croke Park on All-Ireland final day,' said Cyril Farrell.

The 1988 final became the tale of two captains. Galway's Conor Hayes, in his second year at the helm, was under massive pressure after a poor semi-final. Meanwhile, Nicholas English, promoted to the captaincy after Pat O'Neill failed to hold his place, was seen as the Tipperary match-winner. It was widely thought that he would destroy Hayes. He didn't. Hayes played superbly, repeatedly denying English space in front of goal. Further out, Galway's new midfielder, Michael Coleman, plucked from obscurity for the final, was doing well, while the Galway half-back line, anchored splendidly by Tony Keady, was as solid as ever.

Galway led by 0–10 to 0–6, after playing with the wind in the first half, a scoreline which sent contrasting signals to either camp. Tipperary assumed that the wind would create a natural momentum in the second half which would enable them to overtake Galway. Galway reckoned that playing against the wind could, in fact, be an advantage with their hand-passing, keep-ball game plan.

Galway were proved right. Tipperary edged close in the second half but could never draw level and as the game ticked into its critical closing minutes, Galway were defending a two-point lead. The decisive break came when Noel Lane, who had been left off for the final after scoring 1–4 in the semi-final, once again performed his super-sub act to score the game's only goal. It had all gone horribly wrong for Tipperary who could only earn a point off a late penalty which Nicholas English drove the ball over the bar. Galway 1–15 Tipperary 0–14! They had won the two-in-a-row.

As in 1987, Galway had ridden their luck in the final. Their goal had a few narrow escapes in the second half as Tipperary strove desperately to level. Tipperary remain convinced that had they equalised they would have got a rapid injection of confidence which would have enabled them to press on and win. Cyril Farrell disputes this, claiming that there was a control about Galway at that time which kept them going during times of crisis.

> The squad had been together for nearly four years and had come to rely on each other. There was nothing hurried or panicky in anything they did. I suppose that really it comes down to the confidence you gain when you win an All-Ireland final.

Galway remained unbeaten right through the 1988/89 League, beating Tipperary in a great final by 2–16 to 4–8. It was a significant win as it maintained Galway's psychological grip on Tipperary at a time when 'Babs' Keating's forces were reaching maturity. The three-in-a-row now seemed a very distinct possibility but there was a dramatic change of emphasis during the summer of '89. First, Tony Keady was suspended for playing in New York, then Martin Naughton sustained a bad knee injury two weeks before the semi-final while Noel Lane and Steve Mahon were also out with long term injuries. Suddenly, all had changed in Galway, which even threatened to withdraw from the semi-final in protest at the Keady suspension. Galway went into the 1989 semi-final, convinced that God, the GAA authorities and the dogs in the street were involved in a conspiracy to prevent them winning the three-in-a-row.

Whether or not their state of mind played a part in their defeat is a matter of opinion. Cyril Farrell claims that it didn't but others allege that the Keady affair had built a paranoid wall around Galway which restricted their natural flow. Certainly, they had good reasons to feel aggrieved over the Keady suspension.

Quite how Galway came to be within three points of Tipperary at the end of the 1989 semi-final remains a mystery. They produced a dreadful first half, rescued only by two opportunist goals by Eanna Ryan. They were well off the pace and, Ryan apart, no outfield player could feel happy with the first half performance. Still, Galway were only two points behind at half-time, 0–11 to 2–3. Galway's problems really mounted in the second half. Sylvie Linnane was sent off and, later on, as the match temperature soared in line with frustration levels, 'Hopper' McGrath was also dismissed.

Even with two extra men, Tipperary couldn't put Galway away. Galway's dominance of the previous two seasons had left a residue of respect, which caused Tipperary to keep looking over their shoulders, although they were being pursued by just thirteen men. It was as if they feared the worst. In the end though, they held on to win by 1–17 to 2–11 and easily won the final against Antrim, who had shocked Offaly in the other semi-final.

Tipperary's easy win over Antrim added to Galway's frustration. The three-in-a-row would have been a formality for Galway, had they beaten Tipperary in the semi-final. To this day, they believe they were 'cheated' out of the 1989 championship by the GAA's sudden zeal to clamp down on players travelling to New York on weekend playing junkets.

Nonetheless, they had created history by bringing the All-Ireland title to Galway in consecutive seasons. Not only that but they had also won League titles in 1987 and 1989, the Oireachtas title in 1988, and, as Connacht's representatives, the Railway Cup in 1986, 1987 and 1989.

GALWAY 1987: John Commins; Sylvie Linnane, Conor Hayes, Ollie Kilkenny; Pete Finnerty, Tony Keady, Gerry McInerney; Steve Mahon, Pat Malone; 'Hopper' McGrath, Joe Cooney, Martin Naughton; Eanna Ryan, Brendan Lynskey, Anthony Cunningham.

Subs: P.J. Molloy for Cunningham, Noel Lane for Naughton, Tony Kilkenny for McGrath.

In 1988, the only change in personnel was Michael Coleman for Steve Mahon at midfield. Lane, Kilkenny and Gerry Burke came on as subs.

Kilkenny 1982-83

(A Large Double Over Cork)

In the spring of 1982, Kilkenny hurling was frisking like a young lamb. Although the county had been overshadowed by Offaly in 1980 and Wexford in 1981, the traditional black-and-amber roots were as deep as ever...and sprouting new growth.

The nucleus of the 1979 All-Ireland winning side was still very much in tune with the demands of a new decade while young talent had emerged which would later dovetail brilliantly with the seasoned campaigners. Former star defender, Pat Henderson was in charge of the team and while they had wintered in Division Two of the National Hurling League in 1981/82, it was regarded as no more than a pit-stop *en route* back to the fast lane.

Kilkenny duly made it out of Division Two and had their first test of life on the Formula One circuit against Galway in the League quarter-final. They coped extremely well, winning by 1–11 to 1–6. Next up were Waterford who drew with Kilkenny in the semi-final before losing the replay. By now, things were really taking shape in Kilkenny, who went on to beat Wexford in the final by 2–14 to 1–11. In many counties, winning a League title would crown the season but not in Kilkenny where each year is judged almost solely in championship terms.

The 1982 Leinster draw virtually handed Kilkenny a place in the final. They were drawn on the same side as Dublin and Westmeath, a duo which lacked the necessary cutting edge to challenge Kilkenny. Westmeath beat Dublin by a point in the quarter-final but were then hammered (7–31 to 0–13) by Kilkenny in the semi-final. Meanwhile, Offaly had discovered that winning the 1981 All-Ireland title was no insulation against the growing ambition of teams such as Wexford and Laois. Wexford ran Offaly to a point (2–16 to 3–12) in the opening round and then Laois forced the champions to a replay (3–13 each) before winning by nine points (2–17 to 0–14) to set up the eagerly awaited final with Kilkenny.

The 1982 Leinster final has gone down in history, not for the quality of the hurling, but for the controversial incident which ended Offaly's reign. They were leading by three points with eight minutes to go when Offaly goalkeeper, Damien Martin, attempted to shepherd a long ball wide. However, Liam Fennelly kept going and flicked the ball across an open Offaly goal where Matt Ruth was ideally positioned to whip it into the net. That goal turned the game. Kilkenny suddenly found a new gear and finished strongly to win by 1–11 to 0–12. Offaly players protested afterwards that the ball had gone wide prior to Fennelly's cross but in the minds of the umpires and referee that was not the case so the goal stood.

Inevitably, Martin was blamed for not clearing the ball rather than waiting for it to trickle out over the endline. That was an understandable viewpoint but given that Martin was convinced the ball had gone wide prior to Fennelly making his cross, it was difficult not to have sympathy for one of the great goalkeepers of modern hurling.

As the arguments raged about the goal's legality, Kilkenny simply got on with preparing for the All-Ireland semi-final against a Galway team which was now breaking up after three seasons at, or near, the top. The extent to which the Galway team had slipped was underlined in the first half of the semi-final when Kilkenny tore them apart, building up a 2–11 to 1–3 lead in the process. Kilkenny eventually won by 2–20 to 2–10 to set up an All-Ireland final clash with Cork, who had fairly scorched through Munster. Inspired by teenage sensation, Tony O'Sullivan, Cork beat Tipperary by 1–19 to 2–8, Clare by 3–19 to 2–6 and Waterford by 5–31 to 3–6. O'Sullivan had contributed twenty-six points of that total while Seanie O'Leary's poaching skills had yielded five goals. Cork's amazing strike rate hoisted them into the favourite's position for the final, something which suited Kilkenny perfectly.

While all the focus was on the high-scoring feats of O'Sullivan, O'Leary and Co., Kilkenny had their own ace in the form of the Glenmore giant, Christy Heffernan. Largely unknown going into the 1982 final, Heffernan emerged as the Kilkenny hero, scoring 2–3 in a personal *tour de force* which left Cork full-back, Martin O'Doherty mesmerised. O'Doherty had returned from the US some weeks earlier and clearly lacked the match sharpness required at the highest level, especially against a man like Heffernan whose two goals just before half-time destroyed Cork, who trailed by ten points at the break. Kilkenny's grip on proceedings was so tight that the outcome was never in doubt from there on. Tony O'Sullivan managed just two points — one from a free — for Cork and was eventually replaced. In fairness to O'Sullivan the pre-match hype surrounding him was ridiculously disproportionate to what he had achieved up to then. Not that he was the only Corkman to perform way below par. All through the field, they were out-hurled by a fiercely determined Kilkenny outfit.

Having won the title in such pleasant circumstances, Kilkenny might have been expected to coast through the League but no, they kept going at full throttle right through the subsequent winter/spring campaign. Clare beat them by a point in the opening League game and Offaly drew with them but, those apart, it was victories all the way as Wexford, Tipperary, Galway, Waterford, Cork, Laois and Limerick all felt the awesome power of an ultra-confident Kilkenny squad. Their closest call was in the League final where Limerick ran them to two points, 2–14 to 2–12.

While the championship was very much Kilkenny's priority for 1993, winning the League maintained their momentum in a manner which left nobody in any doubt about their intentions. They headed into the championship with a fantastic record behind them. Since the beginning of the 1981/82 League, they had played twenty-four competitive games, winning twenty-two, drawing one and losing one. By the end of the 1983 championship, that record had improved to twenty-five wins, one draw and one defeat from twenty-seven games. Their defence of the Leinster championship began with another win over rivals, Wexford (5–13 to 3–15) in the semi-final while Offaly were seen off, 1–17 to 0–13 in the final.

Cork, chastened by their 1982 experience, had re-grouped and had again negotiated their way through the Munster campaign. This time, though, it was tougher, with Limerick providing them with the sternest of tests in the semi-final. The sides drew in Limerick and while Cork were hot favourites to win the replay in their beloved Pairc Ui Chaoimh, Limerick pushed them all the way before eventually going down by 1–14 to 1–12. With Tipperary still in a deep depression, Waterford made it back to another final but, as in 1982, they found Cork on a different level, and were beaten by 3–22 to 0–12. Cork's improving graph line took them way above Galway too, who were beaten by 5–14 to 1–16 in the All-Ireland semi-final.

High winds swept across Croke Park for the final, making the Railway end very much the scoring goal. In fact, of the 4–26 total, 3–15 was scored into that goal. Significantly though, the one goal which was scored against the wind came to Kilkenny. Ultimately, it was to prove vital. Kilkenny had first call on the elements and while they hurled quite well, their interval lead of 1–10 (Liam Fennelly had scored the goal) to 0–7 looked somewhat insecure. A six-point target looked very much within Cork's range as the teams lined up for the start of the second half but the lead quickly increased to 10. Cork were stunned within seconds of the re-start when Richie Power got through for Kilkenny's second goal, a score which probably turned out to be the match-winner. Earlier, Billy Fitzpatrick's deadly accuracy from frees and play had been central to Kilkenny's dominance.

Having set out their stall, Kilkenny set about defending it. Ger Cunningham's puck-outs were dropping on the Kilkenny twenty-one-yard line but the defence held out magnificently, anchored superbly by centre-back, Ger Henderson. It was possibly his finest game for Kilkenny. Revelling in the challenge, his courage, energy and utter determination was an inspiration to his colleagues while also breaking Cork hearts. Flanked by Joe Hennessy and Paddy Prendergast, Henderson broke up several Cork attacks while further out Frank Cummins was working tirelessly to lift some of the pressure off his over-worked backs. Despite their heroics, Kilkenny had to yield ground to the non-stop barrage and the gap had been cut to just three points with two minutes to go. Then came a lucky break. Kevin Hennessy's shot whizzed by the post when a goal seemed certain. Kilkenny goalie, Noel

Skehan, who gave another excellent performance, insisted that he had the shot covered. Whether or not that was the case nobody will ever know.

Eventually time ran out for Cork, who were beaten by 2–14 to 2–12 — the exact same scoreline as in the Kilkenny–Limerick League final some months earlier. It was extremely disappointing for Cork captain, Jimmy Barry Murphy, who for the second year in a row, had failed to make any impression on the final. It was all very frustrating for him for while the ball was dropping into the Kilkenny goal area almost repeatedly during the second half, neither he, nor his fellow-forwards, got any room. Cork were criticised afterwards — and probably justifiably so — for not varying their tactics when it became apparent that their route one, down the middle approach was not working.

It was a special day for Noel Skehan, who won a record-breaking ninth All-Ireland medal. Three of them had been won as a sub (1963–67–69) to the late Ollie Walsh while Skehan was actually in goal for the 1972–74–75–79–82–83 finals. Not that the details mattered — the fact was that he had won nine medals in a glittering career. Having achieved the double League and All-Ireland success, Kilkenny were very much the No.1 force in the land going into 1984 which was, of course, Centenary Year in the GAA. The talk in Kilkenny was of the three-in-a-row, an honour which had eluded the county since 1911–12–13. But, as in 1976, when Wexford intervened to short-circuit their ambitions, they did again in 1984, beating Kilkenny in the Leinster semi-final. Wexford led by six points at one stage in the second half but, in a typical Kilkenny comeback, they battled back and actually took the lead, only for Tony Doran to score the match-winning goal two minutes from the end. Kilkenny's three-in-a-row dream was over but that in no way detracts from the fine achievement of achieving the county's fifth two-in-a-row.

KILKENNY (1982 All-Ireland final): Noel Skehan; John Henderson, Brian Cody, Dick O'Hara; Nicky Brennan, Ger Henderson, Paddy Prendergast; Joe Hennessy, Frank Cummins; Richie Power, Ger Fennelly, Kieran Brennan; Billy Fitzpatrick, Christy Heffernan, Liam Fennelly.

In 1983, Harry Ryan for Nicky Brennan was the only change in personnel. There were some positional switches: Joe Hennessy moved from midfield to right half-back, Ger Fennelly moved from centre-forward to midfield, Kieran Brennan switched from left half-forward to centre, Liam Fennelly moved from No.15 to No.12, with Ryan coming at left corner-forward.

Index

A

Ahearne, Mick 97
Allen, Denis 179
Allen, John 199
Allen, Terry 49, 51
Armstrong, Donal 79
Austin, Liam 184

B

Baker, Ollie 11, 13, 16
Baker, Pat 97
Barr, Ciaran 78–79
Barr, Keith 57, 60
Barry Murphy, Jimmy 13, 63, 196–197, 199, 208
Barry, Dave 179
Barry, John 87–88
Barry, Pat 190, 199
Barton, Damien 27
Bealin, Paul 60
Beggy, David 58, 60, 173
Bermingham, Brendan 33, 36–37
Blaney, Greg 182, 184
Bonner, Colm 65
Bonner, Conal 65
Bonner, Cormac 63–65
Bonner, Declan 32, 89, 93
Boylan, Sean 119, 123, 129, 134–135, 152, 168
Boyle, Manus 30–32, 89, 91, 93
Boyle, Tony 30, 32, 91, 93
Bradley, Simon 55
Brady, Brendan 51
Brady, Philip 89

Breen, Barry 29, 141, 182–184
Breen, Brian 21
Breen, Eamonn 84
Brennan, Barry 121
Brennan, Kieran 208
Brennan, Michael 121
Brennan, Mick 194
Brennan, Nicky 192, 208
Brennan, Tony 168
Brennan, Willie 96–97
Brewster, Paul 55
Brogan, Bernard 72
Brogan, Jim 137
Brogan, Padraig 30
Brolly, Joe 27
Brophy, Pat 97
Brown, Gerry 97
Browne, Colm 97
Browne, Richard 64–65
Buckley, Carthage 96
Buckley, Niall 49, 51
Buckley, P.J. 121
Buckley, Pat 63, 65
Buggy, Ned 196
Burke, Frank 35, 41, 108
Burke, Gerry 204
Burke, Sean 84
Burns, Brian 184
Burns, Eamonn 24, 27, 141, 182–184
Burns, Jarlath 55
Butler, Mick 196
Butler, Tommy 195
Byrne, Billy 5, 8–9, 139, 146
Byrne, Damien 88
Byrne, Ned 194
Byrne, Pat 97

M